GOLDONI'S COMEDIES

A Hyperion Reprint Edition

HYPERION PRESS, INC.
Westport, Connecticut

THE COMEDIES OF CARLO GOLDONI

EDITED WITH INTRODUCTION BY
HELEN ZIMMERN

HYPERION PRESS, INC.
Westport, Connecticut

Published in 1892 by A.C. McClurg & Co., Chicago
Hyperion reprint edition 1978
Library of Congress Catalog Number 76-48424
ISBN 0-88355-544-1 (cloth ed.)
Printed in the United States of America

Library of Congress Cataloging in Publication Data
Goldoni, Carlo, 1707-1793.
    The comedies of Carlo Goldoni.
    Reprint of the 1892 ed. published by A.C. M'Clurg, Chicago, in series: Masterpieces of foreign authors.
    CONTENTS: A curious mishap. — The beneficent bear. — The fan. — The spendthrift miser.
    I. Title. II. Series. III. Series: Masterpieces of foreign authors.
PQ4695.E5   1977   852'.6   77-5358
ISBN 0-88355-544-1

CONTENTS.

	PAGE
INTRODUCTION,	7
A CURIOUS MISHAP,	33
THE BENEFICENT BEAR,	95
THE FAN,	147
THE SPENDTHRIFT MISER,	229

Goldoni,—good, gay, sunniest of souls,—
Glassing half Venice in that verse of thine,—
What though it just reflect the shade and shine
Of common life, nor render, as it rolls,
Grandeur and gloom? Sufficient for thy shoals
Was Carnival: Parini's depths enshrine
Secrets unsuited to that opaline
Surface of things which laughs along thy scrolls.
There throng the People: how they come and go,
Lisp the soft language, flaunt the bright garb,—see,—
On piazza, calle, under portico,
And over bridge! Dear King of Comedy,
Be honoured! Thou that didst love Venice so,
Venice, and we who love her, all love thee!

        Robert Browning.

INTRODUCTION.

"PAINTER and son of nature," wrote Voltaire, at that time the arbitrator and the dispenser of fame in cultured Europe, to Carlo Goldoni, then a rising dramatist, "I would entitle your comedies, 'Italy liberated from the Goths.'" The sage of Ferney's quick critical faculty had once again hit its sure mark, for it is Goldoni's supreme merit, and one of his chief titles to fame and glory, that he released the Italian theatre from the bondage of the artificial and pantomime performances that until then had passed for plays, and that, together with Molière, he laid the foundations of the drama as it is understood in our days. Indeed, Voltaire, in his admiration for the Venetian playwright, also called him "the Italian Molière," a comparison that is more accurate than such comparisons between authors of different countries are apt to be, though, like all such judgments, somewhat rough and ready. It is interesting in this respect to confront the two most popular dramas of the two dramatists, Molière's "Le Misanthrope" and Goldoni's "Il Burbero Benefico." Goldoni, while superior in imagination, in spontaneity, deals more with the superficial aspects of humanity. Molière, on the contrary, probes deep into the human soul, and has greater elegance of form. In return, Goldoni is more genial and kindly in his judgments, and, while lacking none of

Molière's keenness of observation, is devoid of his bitter satire. Both have the same movement and life, the same intuitive perception of what will please the public, the same sense of dramatic proportion. Goldoni was, however, less happy than Molière as regards the times in which his lines were cast. The French dramatist, like Shakespeare, was born at an age in which his fatherland was traversing a glorious epoch of national story. The Italian lived instead in the darkest period of that political degradation which was the lot of the fairest of European countries, until quite recently, when she emancipated herself, threw off the chains of foreign bondage, and proclaimed herself mistress of her own lands and fortunes. And manners and customs were no less in decadence in private as well as in public,—a sad epoch, truly, though to outsiders it looked light-hearted and merry enough. Goldoni's lot was cast in the final decades of the decrepitude of Venice, the last of the Italian proud Republics, which survived only to the end of the eighteenth century, indeed dissolved just four years after her great dramatist's demise. His long life comprised almost the whole of that century, from the wars of the Spanish Succession, which open the history of that era, to the Peace of Aix-la-Chapelle and the French Revolution.

Historical events had, however, merely an outward and accidental influence on this great artist-nature, entirely absorbed in his work, and indifferent, even unconscious, to all that surged around him in this respect. To be assured that this is so, we need merely peruse Goldoni's own Memoirs, composed by him in his old age, and which, according to Gibbon's verdict, are even more amusing to read than his very comedies.

"The immortal Goldoni," as his countrymen love to call him, was born in Venice in 1707. His family were of Modenese origin. The grandfather, who held a lucrative and honourable post in the Venetian Chamber of Commerce, married as his first wife a lady from his native town, who died, leaving him a son. He then espoused a widow with two daughters, the elder of whom, in due course, he gave in marriage to this son. The couple became the parents of the playwright.

This grandfather had a considerable influence over Goldoni's youth, and also modified his later life. A good-natured, not ill-intentioned man, he was nevertheless hopelessly extravagant, and inordinately addicted to material pleasures,—at that time, it must ever in justice be remembered, the only outlet possible to male energies and ambitions. For a pleasure-lover, the Venice of that day was an earthly paradise, and the result in this case was that the elder Goldoni put no restraint upon himself whatever. It so happened that he had the entire control not only of his wife's comfortable fortune, but of that of her two daughters. With this he hired a large villa, six leagues from Venice, where he lived in so free and open-handed a manner as to rouse the jealousy of the neighbouring proprietors. A fanatic for the stage and all that pertained to it, he caused comedies and operas to be performed under his roof; the best singers and actors were hired to minister to his amusement; reckless expenditure and joyous living were the watchwords of the house. It was in this atmosphere that the child Carlo was reared, no wonder it affected his character. It may be said that he imbibed a love for the play with his first breath. Unfortunately, ere he was a man, the pleasure-loving and open-handed grandfather caught cold and died, to be followed soon after by his wife. At a blow all was changed for the Goldoni family. Carlo's father, having lacked proper training, was unable to maintain himself in his father's position, which was offered him; the property had to be sold, and when all debts were paid there remained only the mother's dowry for the maintenance of the whole family. However, there was clearly good stuff in Goldoni's father. Already a man of some years, he resolved nevertheless to study medicine in order to earn an honest livelihood, and, wonderful to tell, he became a very popular and successful physician, practising first at Perugia. It was there that, only eight years old, Carlino, as he was then called, wrote a comedy, which so vastly pleased his father that in consequence he resolved to give him the best education within his reach. To this end he placed him in the local Jesuit school. At first the boy, shy and repressed, cut a bad figure, but by the end of the first term he came out at the head of his class, to the immense delight of his father. To reward him for this success, his parents instigated for his benefit what we should now call private theatricals. As women were forbidden to appear on the stage within the Papal States, to which Perugia then belonged, Carlino took the part of the prima donna, and was further called upon to write a prologue, which, according to the taste of the day, was absurdly affected and hyperbolical. Goldoni gives in his Memoirs the opening sentence of this literary effort, and it may serve as a measure of the extent to which he became a reformer of Italian style:—

"Most benignant Heaven, behold us, like butterflies, spreading in the rays of your most splendid sun, the wings of our feeble inventions, which bear our flight towards a light so fair."

To compare this bombast with the crystal clearness and simplicity of the language of Goldoni's comedies, is to gain a fair estimate of what he had to overcome and what he achieved.

A while after, the family removed to Chioggia, the climate of Perugia not being suited to Goldoni's mother. He himself was sent to Rimini to study philosophy in the Dominican school, a study which in those days was considered indispensable for the medical career to which he was destined. But philosophy as taught at Rimini did not attract our hero, and instead of poring over the long passages dictated to him by his professor, he read Plautus, Terence, Aristophanes, and the fragments of Menander. Nor did the philosophic debates amuse him half as much as a company of actors with whom he contrived to knock up an acquaintance. Hearing that these people, to his immense regret, were leaving Rimini, and that of all places in the world they were proceeding to Chioggia, it occurred to the youthful scamp that nothing could be more easy and delightful than to go with them in the big barge they had hired for their transit. The rogue knew full well that his mother at least would forgive him his escapade in the pleasure of having him back again. So he went, and there was an end of his philosophy. As he foresaw, his mother pardoned him, and his father happened to be absent on business. From Pavia, where he was staying with a relative, at that time governor of the city, Dr. Goldoni wrote that his Marchese had promised to be kind to his eldest son. "So," went on the letter, "if Carlo behaves well, he will provide for him." This sentence filled Carlo the disobedient with alarm. Nevertheless, when his father returned, he forgave him almost as readily as his mother had done. They were not strict disciplinarians, these Goldoni, but easy-going folk, who liked to live and let live.

The father now resolved to keep his son at home at Chioggia, that he might begin to study medicine under his guidance. Very desultory study it was, both father and son thinking more of the theatre and of actors than of the pharmacopœia. So medicine, too, had to be abandoned. Goldoni's mother then bethought her of the law, and Carlo was sent to Venice to study under the care of an uncle. At Venice he found no less than seven theatres in full swing, and all of them he frequented in turn, enjoying especially the operas of Metastasio, which were the latest novelty,—that author who may be said to have done for Italian opera what Goldoni did for Italian comedy, though unfortunately the music to which his graceful verses have been set has not, like them, proved immortal. After some months of alternate gaiety and study of jurisprudence, Carlo was moved to Pavia to complete his studies, a vacancy having been found for him there in the Papal College. Various preliminaries were needful to obtain admission, among them the tonsure. During the delay caused by these formalities, Carlo devoted himself to the study of dramatic literature in the library of one of the professors. Here he found, beside his old friends, the classical dramatists, the English, Spanish, and French playwrights. But the Italian, where were they? he asked himself, and at once the resolve awoke in him that he would do his very utmost towards reviving the drama of his native land and tongue. What he would do should be to imitate the style and precision of the great authors of antiquity, but to give to his plays more movement, happier terminations, and characters better formulated. "We owe," he says, "respect to the great writers who have smoothed the way for us in science and in art, but every age has its dominant genius and every climate its national taste. The Greek and Roman writers knew human nature and copied it closely, but without illusion and without skill. To this is owing that want of moderation and decency which has led to the proscription of the drama by the Church."

At Pavia, Goldoni spent his time over everything else but study, nor was his sojourn there long, for a satire composed and published, taken together with other pranks, led to his expulsion from the College. His parents as usual forgave him, and he was allowed to accompany his father on one of his business journeys, during the course of which Goldoni tells that he obtained much knowledge of men and things. At Modena, it happened that the pair fell in with some very devout people, and saw the "admonition" of an abbé of their acquaintance, who was punished in public after a severe and impressive fashion. Carlo, who was at the time suffering from a juvenile attack of disgust with the world, felt this spectacle arouse in him the desire to become a Capuchin monk. His wise father did not contradict him, and took him to Venice, ostensibly to present him to the Director of the Capuchins. But he plunged him also into a round of gaieties, dinners, suppers, theatres; and Carlo discovered that, to avoid the perils of this world, it was not needful to renounce it altogether. He had now arrived at man's estate, it was requisite he should have an occupation. Through the kindness of friends he obtained a position in the service of the government, not lucrative but yet remunerative, which he contrived to make useful to his dramatic training, the one idea to which he ever remained faithful. This position, Chancellor to the Podestà, required almost continual change of place, and although Goldoni himself liked it very well, his mother disapproved of it highly, calling it a gipsy's post.

In 1731, Goldoni lost his father, an irreparable sorrow to him. He now found himself, at twenty-four, the head of his family. His mother consequently insisted he should give up his wanderings and assume the lawyer's toga. He therefore went to Padua to finish his studies, and this time he studied really, passing a brilliant examination, though the whole night previously he had spent at the gaming-table, whence the University beadle had to fetch him to come before his examiners.

Behold him now a full-fledged lawyer, but with few clients and causes to defend. His fruitless leisure was employed in scribbling almanacs in terza rima, in which he sought to insert such prophecies as were likely to fulfil themselves. In hopes of further bettering his fortunes, he also wrote a tragedy called "Amalasunta." He had hoped this would bring him in one hundred zecchini. Unfortunately, however, he had at the same time let himself in for a love affair, from which there was no other exit but that which his father had taught him to adopt in similar cases, namely, flight from the scene of action. So, putting the MSS. of "Amalasunta" under his arm, he bolted from his native town. This was to be the beginning of his artistic career. Milan was his destination, where he arrived in the full swing of the Carnival. Here he was brought in contact with Count Prata, Director of the Opera. At a reception at the house of the prima ballerina, Goldoni undertook to read his "Amalasunta." The leading actor took exception to it from the outset, and by the time the reading was ended none of the audience were left in the room except Count Prata. The play ended, the Count told the author that his opera was composed with due regard to the rules of Aristotle and Horace, but was not framed according to the rules laid down for Italian opera in their day.

"In France," he continued, "you can try to please the public, but here in Italy, it is the actors and actresses whom you must consult, as well as the composer of the music and the stage decorators. Everything must be done according to a certain form, which I will explain to you. Each of the three principal personages of the opera must sing five airs, two in the first act, two in the second, and one in the third. The second actress and the second soprano can only have three, and the lower rank of artists must be contented with one, or at most two. The author must submit his words to the musician, and must take care that two pathetic airs do not follow each other. The same rule must be observed with regard to the airs of bravura, of action, of secondary action, as also with regard to the minuet and rondeau. And above all things remember that on no account must moving or showy airs be given to the performers of the second rank. These poor people must take what they can get, and make no attempt to shine."

The Count would have said more, but the author had heard enough. He thanked his kind critic, took leave of his hostess, went back to the inn, ordered a fire, and reduced "Amalasunta" to ashes. This performance completed, not without natural regret, he ordered a good supper, which he consumed with relish, after which he went to bed and slept tranquilly all night. On the morrow, dining with the Venetian Ambassador, he recounted to him his adventures. The Ambassador, compassionating his destitute condition, and finding pleasure in his company, found a post for him in his household as a sort of chamberlain. This position, by no means arduous, left Goldoni plenty of time for himself. He now made the acquaintance of a quack doctor, a certain Buonafede, who went by the name of the Anonimo, and was a very prince of charlatans. This man, among other devices to attract customers, carried about with him a company of actors, who, after assisting him in distributing the objects which he sold and collecting the money for them, gave a representation in his small theatre erected in the public square. It so happened that the company of comedians which had been engaged for that Easter season at Milan unexpectedly failed to keep their engagement, so that the Milanese were left without players. The Anonimo proposed his company, Goldoni through the Venetian Minister helped him to attain his end, and wrote for the first performance an intermezzo, "The Venetian Gondolier," which was set to music by the composer attached to the company, and had, as Goldoni himself says, all the success so slight an effort deserved. This little play was the first of his works performed and afterwards published.

At this time in Italy, the so-called *Commedie dell' arte* or *a soggetto* held the boards; extremely artificial, stilted forms of dramatic composition, which, it is true, testified to the quick and ready wit of the Italians, but also to a puerile taste, far removed from artistic finish. These plays were all performed by actors in masks, after the manner of the classical drama, and in the greater number of cases the players were supplied merely with the plot and the situations of the play, the dialogue having to be supplied by the invention of the actors themselves; the outline was often of the roughest nature, much after the manner of modern drawing-room charades, but there were certain stock characters, such as an old man who is the butt of the tricks and deceptions of the others, an extravagant son, scampish servants, and corrupt or saucy chambermaids. These characters and their established costumes were derived from different cities of Italy, and were traditional from the earliest appearance of the *Commedie dell' arte*. Thus, the father, Pantaloon, a Venetian merchant, the doctor, a lawyer or professor from learned Bologna, and

Brighella and Harlequin, Bergamasque servants as stupid as the corrupt or saucy maid-servants and lovers from Rome and Tuscany were sharp. Lance and Speed in "Two Gentlemen of Verona" are good specimens of these characters. The merchant and the doctor, called in Italian "the two old men," always wore a mantle. Pantaloon, or Pantaleone, is a corruption of the cry, *Plantare il Leone*, (Plant the Lion), to the sound of which, and under shadow of their banner, the Lion of their patron St. Mark, the Venetians had conquered their territories and wealth. Pantaloon was the impersonation, however, not of fighting but of trading Venice, and wore the merchant costume still in use, with but slight modification, in Goldoni's day. The dress of the doctor was that of the lawyers of the great university, and the strange mask which was worn by this character imitated a wine-mark which disfigured the countenance of a certain well-known legal luminary, according to a tradition extant among the players in Goldoni's time. Finally, "Brighella and Arlecchino," called in Italy Zanni,* were taken from Bergamo as the extremes of sharpness or stupidity, the supposed two characteristics of the inhabitants of that city. Brighella represented a meddlesome, waggish, and artful servant, who wore a sort of livery with a dark mask, copied after the tanned skin of the men of that sub-Alpine region. Some actors in this part were called Finocchio, Scappino (Molière's Scapin), but it was always the same character, and always a Bergamasque. Arlecchino, or Harlequin, too, had often different names, but he never changed his birthplace, was always the same fool, and wore the same dress, a coat of different-coloured patches, cobbled

---

* Jacks; Zanni being a nickname for Giovanni, John.

together anyhow (hence the patchwork dress of the modern pantomime). The hare's tail which adorned his hat formed in Goldoni's time part of the ordinary costume of the Bergamasque peasants. Pantaloon's disguise was completed by a beard of ridiculous cut, and he always wore slippers. It is in allusion to this that Shakespeare calls the sixth age of man, "the lean and slippered pantaloon."

When Goldoni began to write, the drama had fallen into a sadly burlesque condition. Shortly after the first performance of his "Venetian Gondolier," a play called "Belisario" was represented, in which the blinded hero was led on to the stage by Harlequin, and beaten with a stick to show him the way. This indignity of presentation awoke in Goldoni a desire to write a play on the same theme. Asking the principal actor in this farce what he thought of it, the man replied, "It is a joke, a making fun of the public, but this sort of thing will go on till the stage is reformed." And he encouraged Goldoni to put his purpose into action. He did indeed begin a play on this theme, but wars and sieges hindered its performance; for the War of the Polish Succession broke out, that war called the war of Don Carlos, regarding which Carlyle is so sarcastic in his Life of Frederick the Great; and Milan was occupied by the King of Sardinia, to the great astonishment of Goldoni, who, although he lived in the house of an ambassador, and should have been well informed of current events, knew no more about them than an infant. He now accompanied his chief to Crema, Modena, and Parma, in which latter city, he the man of peace *par excellence*, assisted at the great battle of June 1734. The impressions then gained, he afterwards utilised in his comedy, "L'Amante Militare." Indeed, skilful workman that he was, he always

INTRODUCTION.

turned to account whatever befell him, whatever he saw or heard, and his wandering and adventurous life furnished him many opportunities for studying men and manners.

It would lead us too far to follow Goldoni through all the incidents of his varied history. It must suffice to indicate the salient points. In 1736, having freed himself from service to the Ambassador, and having again now consorted with actors, now exercised his legal profession, he married the woman who proved his good angel, Nicoletta Conio, who accompanied him all his life, modest, affectionate, indulgent, long-suffering, light-hearted even in the midst of adverse fortune, enamoured of him and of his fame, his truest friend, comforter, inspirer, and stay : in a word, an ideal woman, whose character has been exquisitely sketched by the modern Italian playwright, Paolo Ferrari, in his graceful comedy, "Goldoni e le sue sedici Commedie." Shortly after this marriage, and in large part thanks to his wife's encouragement and faith in him, Goldoni issued finally from out the tortuous labyrinth of conventional tragedies, *intermezzi cantabili*, and serious and comic operas in which hitherto his talents had been imprisoned, and found his true road, that of character comedy. His first attempt at a reforming novelty was the abolition of the mask, to which he had a just objection, considering it, with perfect reasonableness, as fatal to the development of the drama of character.

But he was not to go on his road unhindered. War, so frequent in those days of petty States, once more crossed his plans, and this conjoined to his native love for roaming, inherited from his restless father, caused him to sojourn in many cities, and encounter many adventures gay and grave, all recounted by him with unfailing good temper in his Memoirs, in which he never says an unkind word, even of his worst enemies; for Goldoni's was an essentially amicable character. He writes of himself:—

"My mental nature is perfectly analogous to my physical; I fear neither cold nor heat, neither do I let myself be carried away by anger, nor be intoxicated by success. . . . My great aim in writing my Comedies has been not to spoil nature, and the sole scope of my Memoirs is to tell the truth. . . . I was born pacific, and have always kept my equanimity."

These words sum up the man and the author. In Goldoni the perfect equilibrium of the faculties of the man correspond to the perfectly just and accurate sense of truth and naturalness which is revealed in the writer.

After five years spent in Pisa, practising, and not unsuccessfully, as a lawyer, and hoping he had sown his theatrical wild oats, and had now settled down as a quiet burgher, Goldoni was roused from this day-dream (which after all did not reflect his deepest sentiments, but only an acquired worldly wisdom) by an offer from Medebac, the leader of a group of comedians, to join his fortune to theirs as dramatic author to the company. After some hesitation, his old love for the stage gained the upper hand, and Goldoni assented, binding himself to Medebac for a certain number of years. From that time forward he remained true to his real passion, the theatre.

The company proceeded to Venice, at that time in the last days of its glory, but dying gaily, merrily. The Venice of those days, an author of the time said, was as immersed in pleasure as in water. And above all did its inhabitants love the play. To this city, among this people, Goldoni returned, one of its own children, endowed with its nature, apt to understand its wishes and inclinations. And here, among his compatriots, he resolved not to follow the bad theatrical taste in vogue in favour of spectacular plays and scurrilous *Commedie dell' arte*, but to take up for Italy the task accomplished by Molière for France, and to re-conduct comedy into the right road, from which it had wandered so far.

"I had no rivals to combat," he writes, "I had only prejudices to surmount."

The first play written for unmasked actors proved unsuccessful. Goldoni was not daunted. He wrote a second. It was applauded to the echo, and he saw himself well launched upon his career as a reformer. The great obstacle to his entire success lay in the difficulty of finding actors, as the masked parts could be taken by greatly inferior players; and also by the circumstance, already pointed out to him by his critic of "Amalasunta," that an Italian playwright had to think more of pleasing his actors than his public. What Goldoni had to endure from this *gens irritabilis*, from their rancour, vapours, caprices, stolid and open opposition to his reform, is told with much good nature and sense of fun in his Memoirs. It can have been far from easy to endure, and no doubt often exasperated the author, though in his old age he can speak of it so calmly and dispassionately. But Goldoni, even as a young man, was wise, and proceeded slowly, first making himself and his name known and popular on the old lines, and only risking his new ideas under favourable conditions. Thus he respected the antique unities of time and action, which, after all, save in the hands of great genius, are most conducive to dramatic success, and he only infringed the unity of place to a certain extent, always confining the action of the comedies within the walls of the same town. He says, with a sagacity not common in his profession, that he should not have met with so much opposition, had it not been for the indiscreet zeal of his admirers, who exalted his merits to so excessive a degree, that wise and cultivated people were roused to contradict such fanaticism. As to the ill feeling roused by the ridicule freely showered by Goldoni upon the corrupt customs of his time, he takes no heed of it, save to redouble his efforts in the same direction. Like Molière, he had the courage to put upon the boards the defects and absurdities of his own age, not merely those of a bygone time. And his satire, though keen, is never bitter. His laugh is an honest one. As Thackeray says of Fielding, "it clears the air." His dramatic censure is considered to have been instrumental in putting down the State-protected gambling which was the plague-spot of Venice in those days, and further in giving the first death-blows to that debased survival from the time of chivalry, the *Cavaliere Serrente*, or *Cicisbeo*.

Goldoni's diligence was as great and untiring as his invention was fertile. Thus once, provoked by an unjust *fiasco*, he publicly promised that he would write and produce sixteen new comedies in the course of the next year, and he kept his pledge, though at the time of making it he had not one of these plays even planned. And among this sixteen are some of his masterpieces, such as "Pamela" and the "Bottega del Caffè." The theme of Pamela was not exactly his choice. He had been teased to compose a play after the novel of Richardson, then all the fashion in Italy. At first he believed it an impossible task, owing to the great difference in the social rules of the two countries. In England a noble may marry whom he likes ; his wife becomes his equal, his children in no wise suffer. Not so in the Venice of that time. The oligarchical rule was so severe, that a patrician marrying a woman of the lower class forfeited his right to participate in the government, and deprived his offspring of the patriciate. "Comedy, which is or should be," says Goldoni, "the school of society, should never expose the weakness of humanity save to correct it, wherefore it is not right to recompense virtue at the expense of posterity." However, the necessity of finding themes, conjoined to this insistence on the part of his friends, induced Goldoni to try his hand with Pamela. He changed the *dénouement*, however, in compliance with Venetian social prejudices, making Pamela turn out to be the daughter of a Scotch peer under attainder, whose pardon Bonfil obtains.

It must not be supposed, however, that Goldoni, although he had now reached the apex of success and fame, was to find his course one of plain sailing. Enmities, rivalries, assailed him on all sides; and these, in the Italy of that date, took a peculiarly venomous character, men's ambitions and energies having no such legitimate outlets as are furnished to-day by politics and interests in the general welfare. Everything was petty, everything was personal. Goldoni's chief rival, and consequently enemy, was Carlo Gozzi, the writer of fantastic dramas, and stilted, hyperbolical dramatic fables, entirely forgotten now, which found a certain favour among the public of that day, one having indeed survived in European literature in the shape of Schiller's "Turandot." A fierce skirmish of libellous fly-sheets and derisive comedies was carried on by the respective combatants and partisans, filling now one theatre, now another, according as the taste of the public was swayed or tickled.

Annoyances with the actors, graspingness on the part

of Medebac, made Goldoni abandon his company and pass over to that conducted by Vendramin, an old Venetian noble,—for in those days men of birth thought it no dishonour to conduct a theatre. He was then forty-six years of age, and had written more than ninety theatrical works. For his new patron and theatre he laboured with various interruptions, caused by political events and by his own restless temperament, until 1761, in which space of time he produced some sixty more comedies, besides three comic operas and plays written for a private theatre. And all this labour in less than ten years, and among them some of his best works, such as the trilogy of the Villeggiatura, *Il Curioso Accidente*, *I Rusteghi*, *Le Barufe Chiozote*, and many others, removed from changes of fashion, schools, methods, to which no public has ever been or can be indifferent, eternally fresh and sunny, filled with the spirit of perpetual youth. Notwithstanding, however, the excellence of Goldoni's dramas, the current literary rivalries made themselves felt, and there was a moment when Gozzi's Fables left Goldoni's theatre empty.

It then happened that at this juncture there came to him an offer from Paris to go thither as playwright to the Italian Comedy Company, established there under royal patronage. Was it fatigue, a desire for new laurels, a love of change, the hope of larger gains, that induced him to accept the offer? Perhaps a little of all these. In any case, he assented, binding himself for two years. He was never again to leave France. Paris fascinated him, though he regretted his lovely Venice, and a certain nostalgia peeps forth from his letters now and again. Still his social and pecuniary position was good in the French capital, he was honoured and esteemed, his nephew and adopted son had found lucrative employment there, and, added to all this, even Goldoni was growing old. His eyesight began to fail; he was often indisposed, and no longer inclined to move about and pitch his tent in various cities. A post as Italian teacher at the court brought him much in contact with the royal family. It strikes the readers of the Memoirs with some amazement to see how Goldoni could live in that society, could hear the talk of intellectual Paris, and not be aware upon the brink of how frightful a precipice all French society then hovered. He actually held the king to be adored by his subjects, and these subjects as happy as it was possible for a people to be, well ruled, kindly governed. The narrative of his life ends at the age of eighty, six years before his death, two before the outbreak of the Revolution. We have not, therefore, his impression of the storm when it broke. We only know, alas! that this light-hearted, gay old child—for a child he remained to the end—died in misery, involved in the general ruin and wreck that overwhelmed all France within that brief space of time. It was, in fact, his nephew who stood between him and starvation; for with the king's deposition had vanished the pension allowed to the aged Italian dramatist. A day after his death a decree of the National Convention restored it to him for the term of his days. The proposed gift came too late, but it honours those who voted it and him who pleaded for it, no less a person than Joseph-Marie Chénier, the poet. When the orator learned that the benevolence he invoked could no longer help its object, he again pleaded for the octogenarian, or rather that the pension should be passed on to the faithful wife in whose arms Goldoni had passed away. "She is old," said Chénier, "she is seventy-six, and he has left her no heritage save his illustrious name, his virtues, and his poverty." It is pleasant to learn that this request was conceded to by the Convention. The French, to their honour be it said, are ever ready to pay tribute to genius.

So sad, so dark, so gloomy, was the end of that gay, bright spirit, Italy's greatest and most prolific comic author. To sum up his merits in a few words is no easy task. It is doubtful whether we should rank him among the geniuses of the world. On the plea of intelligence he certainly cannot claim this rank; his intellectual perceptions might even be called mediocre, as his Memoirs amply prove, but he had a gift, a certain knack of catching the exterior qualities of character and reproducing them in a skilful and amusing mode upon the boards. His art is not of the closet kind. What he put down he had seen, not elaborated from out his brain, and his own genial temperament gave it all an amiable impress. The turning-point of his comedies is always the characters of his personages. His plays are founded on that rather than on the artifice of a plot, which, as compared to the former, was held by him as of secondary importance. He distinguished between the comedy of plot and the comedy of character, and imposed the latter on the former, which he held the easier of the two. His mode was in direct contrast to that of the Spanish dramatists, then held in great vogue, who were masters at spinning plots, but whose characters were usually mere conventional types. In Goldoni, action results in most part as a consequence of the individuality of the personages depicted, and his intrigue is directed and led with the purpose that this may develop itself, more especially in the protagonist. Herein consists his great claim to being a theatrical reformer. What is to-day a commonplace was then a novelty. We moderns study character almost to exaggeration. In earlier drama it was ignored, and complicated plot absorbed its place.

It was on this that Goldoni prided himself, and justly. It was he who first invented the Commedia del Carattere. Yet another of Goldoni's merits was his rare skill in handling many personages at the same time, without sacrificing their individuality or hindering the clear and rapid progress of the scene. This gift is specially manifest in "The Fan."

Roughly speaking, we may perhaps divide Goldoni's plays into three classes: Those that deal with Italian personages, and which are written in pure Italian, among which may be comprised those written in Martellian verse; those, including the largest number, which are written partly in Italian and partly in dialect; and finally, those written entirely in Venetian dialect, which are the fewest, eleven in all. From this it will be seen how unjust is the criticism of those who would look on Goldoni as merely a writer of comedies in a local dialect. It is this admixture of dialect, however,—and a racy, good-humoured, and amiable dialect it is, that Venetian,—which renders Goldoni's works so difficult, indeed impossible, to translate, especially into English, where dialects such as the Italian, which form quite distinct languages, are unknown. Happily, for we are thus saved much confusion of tongues, and we hence know no such schism between written and spoken language such as exists in Italy. Even in translation, however, much as Goldoni's plays suffer, their life and movement, their excellent dramatic action, and their marvellous play of character, are not lost. To understand, however, how eminently they are fitted for the boards, it is needful to see them acted. Those who have witnessed either Ristori, or her younger and more modern rival, Eleonora Duse, in "Pamela" or "La Locandiera," will not easily forget the dramatic treat. Goethe in his Italian journey, while at Venice relates how he witnessed a performance of "Le Barufe Chiozote," and how immensely he was struck with the stage knowledge possessed by Goldoni, and with his marvellous truth to the life that surged around him. "This author," writes Goethe, "merits great praise, who out of nothing at all has constructed an agreeable pastime." It has been objected by foreign critics that Goldoni's dialogue is sometimes a little dull and tame. Charles Lever, for example, could never be brought to find Goldoni amusing. It is, however, more than probable that a very accurate acquaintance with Italian is required to appreciate to the full the manner in which the plays are written, the way in which each person's conversation is made to fit his or her character. "La Donna di Garbo" (the title may be rendered as "A Woman of Tact") is a case in point. This young person seizes on the peculiar hobby or weakness of the people around her, and plays on it in her talk. Desirous, for weighty reasons, of becoming the wife of the young son of a great family, this "woman of tact" gets herself hired as a chambermaid in the household, and so pleases every member of it that all are in the end glad to assist her in gaining her cause. The extreme simplicity of Goldoni's plots is truly astonishing. None but a true adept in human nature and stage artifice could hold audiences, as he does, spell-bound with interest over such everyday occurrences as he selects. His comedies recall one of Louis Chardon's articles in Balzac's "Grand Homme de Province à Paris," beginning, "*On entre, on sort, on se promène.*" People go and come, talk and laugh, get up and sit down, and the story grows meanwhile so intensely interesting, that for the moment there seems nothing else in the world worthy of attention. And the secret of this? It lies in one word: Sympathy. Goldoni himself felt with his personages, and therefore his hearers must do the same.

Goldoni in his Memoirs gives no account of the production of "The Fan." It was written and first brought out in Paris, and soon became universally popular, especially in Venice. "The Curious Mishap" was founded on an episode of real life which happened in Holland, and was communicated to Goldoni as a good subject for a play. The *dénouement* is the same as in the real story, the details only are slightly altered. The intrigue is amusing, plausible, and happily conceived. The scene in which Monsieur Philibert endeavours to overcome the scruples of De la Cotterie and gives him his purse, is inimitable. Indeed, it is worthy of Molière; for if it has not his drollery and peculiar turn of expression, neither has it his exaggeration. There is no farce, nothing beyond what the situation of the parties renders natural. "The Beneficent Bear" was first written in French, and brought out at the time of the *fêtes* in honour of the marriage of Marie Antoinette and the Dauphin, afterwards Louis XVI. Played first in the city, and then before the court at Fontainebleau, it was immensely successful in both cases. For this play the writer received one hundred and fifty louis d'or. The published edition also brought him much money.

It was certainly a rare honour for a foreigner to have a play represented with such success in the fastidious French capital and in the language of Molière. He followed it with "L'Avaro Fastoso" ("The Ostentatious Miser"), also written in French. The fate of this drama was less happy, owing, however, to a mere accident, for which Goldoni was in no wise responsible. Nevertheless, he would not allow it to be represented a second time. He seems to have been discontented with it as

a dramatic work, though it has qualities which bring it
nearer to the modern French *comédie de société* than
perhaps any other play he has left behind him. "It
was born under an evil constellation," writes Goldoni,
"and every one knows how fatal a sentence that is,
especially in theatrical affairs." "The Father of the
Family" is, according to Goldoni's own opinion, one of
his best comedies; but, as he considers himself obliged
to abide by the decision of the public, he can, he says,
only place it in the second rank. It is intended to
show the superiority of a domestic training for girls
over a conventual one. "The aunt, to whom one of
the daughters is consigned, figures allegorically as the
convent," says the author, "that word being forbidden
to be pronounced on the Italian stage." "Action and
reaction are equal," says the axiom; and much, if not
all, of the present irreverent attitude of Italians towards
religious matters must be attributed to the excessive
rigour, petty and despicable detail, of the regulations
in vogue under their former priestly and priest-ridden
rulers in these respects.

Goldoni, during his residence in Paris, had an amusing colloquy with Diderot, who was furious at an
accusation made that he had plagiarised from Goldoni
in his own play, "Le Père de Famille,"—an absurd idea,
as there is no resemblance, save in name, between the
two. It was from the *Lamoyant* plays of Diderot and
his school, which reflected the false sentimental tone of
the day both in France and Germany, that Goldoni had
liberated his countrymen, quite as much as from the
pseudo-classical plays to which their own land had
given birth. Diderot did not perceive this, and in his
fury wrote a slashing criticism of all the Italian's plays,
stigmatising them as 'Farces in three Acts." Goldoni,
who, with all his sweetness of temper, was perfectly

fearless, simply called on Diderot, and asked him what cause for spite he had against him and his works. Diderot replied that some of his compositions had done him much harm. Duni, an Italian musician, who had introduced them to each other, at this point interposed, saying that they should follow the advice of Tasso, —

"Ogni trista memoria ormai si taccia
E pognansi in oblio le andate cose,"

which may be freely rendered as "Let bygones be bygones." Diderot, who understood Italian well, accepted the suggestion, and the two parted friends. It is an anecdote creditable to all parties, and not least to the two Italians.

It is a pity that Goldoni's Memoirs, from which the above sketch of his life is derived, were written in French instead of Italian, and with regard to a French rather than an Italian public. Had he written in his own language and for his own people, he might have produced a work worthy to rank beside the wondrous tale of Cellini, though of course of a very opposite character. As it is, the narrative is little known, though it has been translated into Italian and issued in cheap form.

Such, briefly, the Italian dramatist, whose best works in substance are the continuation of the ancient plays of Menander and Terence, imitated by the Italians in the sixteenth century, but allowed to degenerate, and then again renovated and carried to perfection by Molière in France and by himself in Italy.

A CURIOUS MISHAP

(*UN CURIOSO ACCIDENTE*)

A COMEDY IN THREE ACTS

DRAMATIS PERSONÆ

PHILIBERT, *a rich Dutch merchant.*
GIANNINA, *his daughter.*
RICCARDO, *a broker.*
COSTANZA, *his daughter.*
DE LA COTTERIE, *a French lieutenant.*
MARIANNA, *Mademoiselle Giannina's servant.*
GASCOIGNE, *De la Cotterie's servant.*

The Scene is at the Hague, in the house of PHILIBERT.

A CURIOUS MISHAP.

ACT I.

SCENE I.—Gascoigne, *packing his master's trunk.*

Enter Marianna.

Mar. May I wish good-morning to Monsieur Gascoigne?

Gas. Yes, my sweet Marianna, I thank you for your good-morning, but good-night would be more agreeable to me from your lips.

Mar. From what I see, I should rather wish you a pleasant journey.

Gas. Oh, my precious jewel, such a melancholy departure must be followed by a most doleful journey!

Mar. Then you are sorry to go?

Gas. How can you doubt it? After having enjoyed your delightful society for six months, can I leave you without the deepest sorrow?

Mar. And who forces you to do what is so disagreeable?

Gas. Do you not know? My master.

Mar. Masters are not wanting at the Hague, and you can easily find one who will give you better wages than a poor French officer, a prisoner of war, and a man in every way roughly used by fortune.

Gas. Pardon me, such language does not become so

good a girl as you are. I have for many years had the
honour of serving my excellent master; his father, I
may say, recommended me to him; I have attended
him in the war, and have not shunned danger to show
my fidelity. He is poor, but never man had a better
heart. Were he promoted, I am sure I should share
his good fortune. Would you desire me to abandon
him, and let him return to France without me?

Mar. You speak like the worthy fellow you are; but
I cannot conceal my affection for you.

Gas. Dear Marianna, I am as much distressed as you
are, but I hope to see you again, and then to be able to
say, Here I am, I can support you, and, if you wish it, I
am yours.

Mar. Heaven grant it! But why is the Lieutenant
in such haste to depart? My master is fond of his
company, and I think the daughter not less so than the
father.

Gas. Too true; and that is his reason for going.

Mar. What! does he dislike people to be fond of him?

Gas. Ah, my Marianna, my poor master is desperately
in love with your young mistress; he leads the most
wretched life in the world; he knows their love for
each other is increasing every day, and, as they can no
longer hide it, he fears for himself, and for Mademoiselle
Giannina. Your master is rich, and mine is poor.
Monsieur Philibert has this only daughter, and will
not give her to a younger son, a soldier; one, in short,
who would have to live on her means. The Lieutenant,
though poor, is a man of honour; he respects the obligations of hospitality, of friendship, of good faith; he
fears he may be overcome and seduced by love, and
that he in turn may seduce his mistress from her duty.
This being the case, he does violence to his feelings,
sacrifices love to principle, and is resolved to go.

Mar. I admire his heroic conduct, but could not imitate it.

Gas. We must exert self-control.

Mar. You can do so more easily than I.

Gas. Indeed, a man's resolution is stronger than a woman's.

Mar. Say rather his affections are weaker.

Gas. So far as regards me, you are wrong.

Mar. I look at acts, not words.

Gas. What can I do to convince you of my love?

Mar. Monsieur Gascoigne does not need me for a teacher.

Gas. Do you wish me to marry you before I go?

Mar. That would, indeed, remove all doubt.

Gas. But then I should have to leave you.

Mar. And could you have the heart to abandon me?

Gas. Oh, you might go with me!

Mar. That would be much better.

Gas. To encounter so many hardships?

Mar. In truth, that would not suit me so well.

Gas. Should I remain here with you, would that satisfy you?

Mar. Perfectly.

Gas. For how long?

Mar. A year at least.

Gas. And after a year, would you let me go?

Mar. Yes, a year after our marriage, if you found it easy to do so.

Gas. I daresay you would let me go after a month.

Mar. I know better.

Gas. I am sure of it.

Mar. Let us try.

Gas. My master is coming; another time we will talk it over.

Mar. Ah, Monsieur Gascoigne, this conversation has

unnerved me; do what you please, I trust to you.— [*Aside.*] Indeed, I know not what I say. [*Exit.*

Gas. If I had not more sense than she, the folly would have been committed before now.

Enter De la Cotterie.

De la Cot. [*To himself.*] Oh, Heaven! how wretched I am! how unfortunate!

Gas. The trunk, sir, is packed.

De la Cot. Ah, Gascoigne! I am in despair.

Gas. Alas! what misfortune has happened?

De la Cot. The worst that could befall me.

Gas. Our troubles seldom come alone.

De la Cot. Mine is alone, but so great that I cannot support it.

Gas. I suppose you allude to your love?

De la Cot. Yes; but it has increased to such a degree that I have no longer firmness enough to resist it.

Gas. What if the lady is unconcerned at your departure, and does not love you as you imagine she does?

De la Cot. On the contrary, she is more affectionate, and more devoted to me than ever. Oh, God! what will my despair drive me to? I saw her weep.

Gas. Well, this is bad enough, but I thought it was something much worse.

De la Cot. Inhuman! unfeeling! vile plebeian soul! can you imagine anything worse in the world than the tears of a tender-hearted, distressed lady, who accuses me of cruelty, who makes my resolution waver, and puts to a severe trial my honour, my reputation, and my friendship?

Gas. I am not conscious of deserving so harsh a reproof; this is a just recompense for ten years' service.

De la Cot. Ah! put yourself in my place, and then,

if you can, condemn my transports. My wounds, my blood, my being a prisoner of war, which prevents my promotion, the narrowness of my fortune, all appear nothing in comparison with the love which inflames my soul. The excellent principles of the young lady prevented her from assuring me that I possessed her heart, and in consequence I resolved to leave her. Ah! at the moment of taking leave, tears and sobs prevented her from speaking, and they proved her love was equal to mine. My wretchedness is extreme; my resolution seems barbarous; and now, frantic with love, reason appears to desert me.

Gas. Take time, sir; remain here. Monsieur Philibert is the best man in the world; in Holland they pride themselves on their hospitality, and our host takes the greatest interest in you, and in your health. You are not perfectly cured, and this is a good reason for not going.

De la Cot. I will think over what you say; very little would change my determination.

Gas. With your leave I will at once unpack the trunk. [*Unpacking.*]

De la Cot. [*Apart.*] What will they say if I remain after having taken my leave?

Gas. [*Apart.*] Marianna will not be sorry for this.

De la Cot. [*Apart.*] If I allege I am unwell, my sadness will make it appear so.

Gas. [*Apart.*] Nor indeed am I.

De la Cot. But the longer I remain, the more my love increases; and what remedy can there be for it? what hope is there for my desperate passion?

Gas. Time accomplishes wonders. [*Still unpacking.*]

De la Cot. How much better to meet death at once than to live in such torture!

Gas. My master will be obliged to me

De la Cot. What shall I do?

Gas. The trunk is unpacked, sir.

De la Cot. Who told you to unpack it?

Gas. I said I was going to do it, and you did not forbid me.

De la Cot. Blockhead! put up the clothes. I shall go.

Gas. Well, whatever happens, let them remain now.

De la Cot. Do not make me angry.

Gas. I will put them up this evening.

De la Cot. Do it at once, and order the post-horses at twelve o'clock.

Gas. And the tears of Mademoiselle?

De la Cot. Wretch! have you the heart to torment me?

Gas. My poor master!

De la Cot. Indeed, I am an object of compassion.

Gas. Let us stay.

De la Cot. No.

Gas. Shall I pack up the things, then?

De la Cot. Yes.

Gas. How I pity him! [*Putting the clothes in the trunk.*]

De la Cot. Can I leave this house without seeing her again?

Gas. While he continues in this state of mind, we shall never be done.

De la Cot. By leaving her, I fear my love will not leave me.

Gas. Alas, poor master! [*Looking out.*] What do I see?

De la Cot. What is the matter? Why do you stop?

Gas. I am going on, sir.

De la Cot. You are confused?

Gas. A little.

De la Cot. What are you looking at?

Gas. Nothing.

De la Cot. Oh, Heaven! Mademoiselle Giannina! What an encounter! What do you advise me to do?

Gas. I do not know; any course is dangerous.

De la Cot. Do not leave me.

Gas. I will not.

De la Cot. I will go away.

Gas. As you please.

De la Cot. I cannot.

Gas. I pity you.

De la Cot. Why does she stop? Why does she not come in?

Gas. She is afraid of disturbing you.

De la Cot. No; it is because you are here.

Gas. Then I will go. [*Going.*]

De la Cot. Stay.

Gas. I will remain, then.

De la Cot. Have you the snuff-box? bring it.

Gas. I will go for it. [*Exit.*

De la Cot. Hear me! where are you going? Poor me! Gascoigne! [*Calls.*]

Enter Giannina.

Gian. Are you in want of anything?

De la Cot. Excuse me, I want my servant.

Gian. If yours is not here, there are others. Do you want any one?

De la Cot. No, I thank you; my trunk must be packed up.

Gian. And are you disturbed in this manner about so trifling an affair? do you fear there will not be time? Perhaps you are already expecting horses? If the air of this country is not favourable to your health, or rather if you are tired of us, I will myself hasten forward your departure.

De la Cot. Mademoiselle, have compassion on me; do not add to my suffering.

Gian. If I knew the cause of your suffering, instead of increasing, I would endeavour to diminish it.

De la Cot. Seek the cause in youself; there is no need for me to tell you.

Gian. Then you go away on my account?

De la Cot. Yes, it is on your account that I am compelled to hasten my departure.

Gian. Have I become so odious in your sight?

De la Cot. Oh, Heaven! you never appeared to me so lovely; your eyes never beamed with so much tenderness.

Gian. Ah, were this true, you would not be so anxious to go.

De la Cot. If I loved only the beauty of your person, I should yield to the strength of my attachment, which bids me stay with you; but I love you for your virtues; I see your peace of mind is in danger, and in return for the kindness you have shown me, I mean to sacrifice the dearest hopes of my life.

Gian. I do not believe you have so little resolution as not to be able to control your passion, and you do me injustice if you think I cannot resist the inclinations of my heart. I own my love for you without a blush: this virtuous love, I feel, will never leave me, and I cannot persuade myself a man is less able than I am to sustain with glory the conflict of his passions. I can love you without danger; it is happiness enough for me to see you. You, on the contrary, by determining to depart, go in quest of more easy enjoyment, and show that your obstinacy prevails over your love. It is said hope always comforts the lover. He who will not use the means proves he cares but little for the end, and, if you go, you will still suffer the tortures of disappointed desire; you will act either with culpable weakness, or unfeeling indifference. Whatever cause hurries you away, go, proud of your resolution, but be at least ashamed of your cruelty.

De la Cot. Ah, no, Mademoiselle! do not tax me with ingratitude, do not accuse me of cruelty. I thought, by my departure, to do you an act of kindness. If I am wrong, pardon me. If you command it, I will remain.

Gian. No; my commands shall never control your inclination; follow the dictates of your own heart.

De la Cot. My heart tells me to remain.

Gian. Then obey it without fear, and, if your courage does not fail, rely on my constancy.

De la Cot. What will your father say to my change of mind?

Gian. He is almost as much grieved at your departure as I am; he is not satisfied about your recovery; and whether it is the consequence of your wound, or of mental affliction, the surgeons do not believe your health is re-established, and my father thinks it too soon for you to undertake the journey. He loves and esteems you, and would be much pleased at your remaining.

De la Cot. Has he any suspicion of my love for you? and that it is mutual?

Gian. Our conduct has given him no cause for suspicion.

De la Cot. Can it be possible it has never passed through his mind that I, an open, frank man, and a soldier, might be captivated by the beauty and merit of his daughter?

Gian. A man like my father is not inclined to suspicion; the cordiality with which he received you as a guest in his family, assures him he may rely on the correct conduct of an officer of honour; and his knowledge of my disposition makes him perfectly easy : he does not deceive himself in regard to either of us. A tender passion has arisen in our hearts, but we will neither depart from the laws of virtue, nor violate his confidence.

De la Cot. Is there no hope his goodness may make him agree to our marriage?

Gian. My hope is that in time it will; the obstacles do not arise from motives of interest, but from the customs of our nation. Were you a merchant of Holland, poor, with only moderate expectations, you would immediately obtain my hand, and a hundred thousand florins for an establishment; but an officer, who is a younger son, is considered among us as a wretched match, and were my father inclined to give his consent, he would incur the severe censure of his relations, his friends, and indeed of the public.

De la Cot. But I cannot flatter myself with the prospect of being in a better condition.

Gian. In the course of time circumstances may occur that may prove favourable to our union.

De la Cot. Do you reckon among these the death of your father?

Gian. Heaven grant that the day may be distant! but then I should be my own mistress.

De la Cot. And do you wish me to remain in your house as long as he lives?

Gian. No, Lieutenant; stay here as long as your convenience permits, but do not appear so anxious to go while there are good reasons for your remaining. Our hopes do not depend on the death of my father, but I have reasons to flatter myself our attachment in the end may be rewarded. Our love we must not relinquish, but avail ourselves of every advantage that occasion may offer.

De la Cot. Adorable Giannina, how much am I

indebted to your kindness! Dispose of me as you please; I am entirely yours; I will not go unless you order me to do so. Persuade your father to bear with my presence, and be certain that no place on earth is so agreeable to me as this.

Gian. I have only one request to make.

De la Cot. May you not command?

Gian. Have regard for one defect which is common to lovers;—do not, I entreat you, give me any cause for jealousy.

De la Cot. Am I capable of doing so?

Gian. I will tell you. Mademoiselle Costanza, in the last few days, has visited our house more frequently than usual; her eyes look tenderly on you, and she manifests rather too much sympathy for your misfortunes. You are of a gentle disposition, and, to own the truth, I sometimes feel uneasy.

De la Cot. Henceforth I will use the greatest caution, that she may indulge no hopes, and that you may be at ease.

Gian. But so conduct yourself, that neither my jealousy nor your love for me shall be remarked.

De la Cot. Ah, would to Heaven, Mademoiselle, our troubles were at an end!

Gian. We must bear them, to deserve good fortune.

De la Cot. Yes, dearest, I bear all with this delightful hope. Permit me now to inquire for my servant, to get him to countermand the horses.

Gian. Were they ordered?

De la Cot. Yes, indeed.

Gian. Unkind one!

De la Cot. Pardon me.

Gian. Let the order be countermanded before my father knows it.

De la Cot. My hope and my comfort! may Heaven be

propitious to our wishes, and reward true love and virtuous constancy. [*Exit.*

Gian. I never could have believed it possible for me to be brought to such a step; that I should, of my own accord, use language and contrive means to detain him. But unless I had done so, in a moment he would have been gone, and I should have died immediately afterwards. But here comes my father; I am sorry he finds me in our visitor's room. Thank Heaven, the Lieutenant is gone out! All appearance of sorrow must vanish from my face.

Enter Philibert.

Phil. My daughter, what are you doing in this room?

Gian. Curiosity, sir, brought me here.

Phil. And what excites your curiosity?

Gian. To see a master who understands nothing of such things, and an awkward servant endeavouring to pack up a trunk.

Phil. Do you know when he goes away?

Gian. He intended going this morning, but, in walking across the room, his legs trembled so, that I fear he will not stand the journey.

Phil. I think his present disease has deeper roots than his wound.

Gian. Yet only one hurt has been discovered by the surgeons.

Phil. Oh, there are wounds which they know nothing of.

Gian. Every wound, however slight, makes its mark.

Phil. Eh! there are weapons that give an inward wound.

Gian. Without breaking the skin?

Phil. Certainly.

Gian. How do these wounds enter?

Phil. By the eyes, the ears, the touch.

Gian. You must mean by the percussion of the air.

Phil. Air! no, I mean flame.

Gian. Indeed, sir, I do not comprehend you.

Phil. You do not choose to comprehend me.

Gian. Do you think I have any mischievous design in my head?

Phil. No; I think you a good girl, wise, prudent, who knows what the officer suffers from, and who, from a sense of propriety, appears not to know it.

Gian. [*Aside.*] Poor me! his manner of talking alarms me.

Phil. Giannina, you seem to me to blush.

Gian. What you say, sir, of necessity makes me blush. I now begin to understand something of the mysterious wound of which you speak; but, be it as it may, I know neither his disease nor the remedy.

Phil. My daughter, let us speak plainly. Monsieur de la Cotterie was perfectly cured a month after he arrived here; he was apparently in health, ate heartily, and began to recover his strength; he had a good complexion, and was the delight of our table and our circle. By degrees he grew sad, lost his appetite, became thin, and his gaiety was changed to sighs. I am something of a philosopher, and suspect his disease is more of the mind than of the body, and, to speak still more plainly, I believe he is in love.

Gian. It may be as you say; but I think, were he in love, he would not be leaving.

Phil. Here again my philosophy explains everything. Suppose, by chance, the young lady of whom he is enamoured were rich, dependent on her father, and could not encourage his hopes; would it be strange if despair counselled him to leave her?

Gian. [*Aside.*] He seems to know all.

Phil. And this tremor of the limbs, occurring just as he is to set out, must, I should say, viewed philosophically, arise from the conflict of two opposing passions.

Gian. [*Aside.*] I could imprecate his philosophy!

Phil. In short, the benevolence of my character, hospitality, to which my heart is much inclined, humanity itself, which causes me to desire the good of my neighbours, all cause me to interest myself in him; but I would not wish my daughter to have any share in this disease.

Gian. Ah, you make me laugh! Do I look thin and pale? am I melancholy? What says your philosophy to the external signs of my countenance and of my cheerfulness.

Phil. I am suspended between two opinions: you have either the power of self-control, or are practising deception.

Gian. Have you ever found me capable of deception?

Phil. Never, and for that reason I cannot believe it now.

Gian. You have determined in your own mind that the officer is in love, which is very likely; but I am not the only person he may be suspected of loving.

Phil. As the Lieutenant leaves our house so seldom, it is fair to infer his disease had its origin here.

Gian. There are many handsome young ladies who visit us, and one of them may be his choice.

Phil. Very true; and, as you are with them, and do not want wit and observation, you ought to know exactly how it is, and to relieve me from all suspicion.

Gian. But if I have promised not to speak of it?

Phil. A father should be excepted from such a promise.

Gian. Yes, certainly, especially if silence can cause him any pain.

Phil. Come, then, my good girl, let us hear.—[*Aside.*] I am sorry I suspected her.

Gian. [*Aside.*] I find myself obliged to deceive him.—Do you know, sir, that poor Monsieur de la Cotterie loves to madness Mademoiselle Costanza?

Phil. What! the daughter of Monsieur Riccardo?

Gian. The same.

Phil. And does the girl return his affection?

Gian. With the greatest possible ardour.

Phil. And what obstacle prevents the accomplishment of their wishes?

Gian. Why, the father of the girl will hardly consent to give her to an officer who is not in a condition to maintain her reputably.

Phil. A curious obstacle, truly. And who is this Monsieur Riccardo, that he has such rigorous maxims? He is nothing but a broker, sprung from the mud, grown rich amid the execrations of the people. Does he think to rank himself among the merchants of Holland? A marriage with an officer would be an honour to his daughter, and he could not better dispose of his ill-got wealth.

Gian. It seems, then, if you were a broker, you would not refuse him your daughter?

Phil. Assuredly not.

Gian. But, being a Dutch merchant, the match does not suit you?

Phil. No, certainly not; not at all—you know it very well.

Gian. So I thought.

Phil. I must interest myself in behalf of Monsieur de la Cotterie.

Gian. In what manner, sir?

Phil. By persuading Monsieur Riccardo to give him his daughter.

Gian. I would not advise you to meddle in the affair.
Phil. Let us hear what the Lieutenant will say.
Gian. Yes, you should hear him first.—[*Aside.*] I must give him warning beforehand.
Phil. Do you think he will set out on his journey immediately?
Gian. I know he has already ordered his horses.
Phil. I will send directly to see.
Gian. I will go myself, sir.—[*Aside.*] I must take care not to make matters worse.   [*Exit.*
Phil. [*Alone.*] I feel I have done injustice to my daughter in distrusting her; it is a happiness to me to be again certain of her sincerity. There may be some concealed deception in her words, but I will not believe her so artful; she is the daughter of a man who loves truth, and never departs from it, even in jest. Everything she tells me is quite reasonable: the officer may be in love with Mademoiselle Costanza; the absurd pride of the father considers the match as far below what his daughter is entitled to. I will, if possible, bring about the marriage by my mediation. On the one hand, we have nobility reduced in circumstances; on the other, a little accidental wealth; these fairly balance one another, and each party will find the alliance advantageous.

Enter Marianna.

Mar. Isn't my mistress here, sir?
Phil. She is just gone.
Mar. By your leave.   [*Going.*]
Phil. Why are you in such haste?
Mar. I am going to find my mistress.
Phil. Have you anything of consequence to say to her?
Mar. A lady has asked for her.
Phil. Who is she?

Mar. Mademoiselle Costanza.

Phil. Oh! is Mademoiselle Costanza here?

Mar. Yes; and I suspect, by her coming at this unusual hour, that it is something extraordinary that brings her here.

Phil. I know what this extraordinary something is. [*Smiling.*] Say to Mademoiselle Costanza, that, before going to my daughter's room, I will thank her to let me see her here.

Mar. You shall be obeyed, sir.

Phil. Is the officer in?

Mar. No, sir, he is gone out.

Phil. As soon as he returns, ask him to come to me in this room.

Mar. Yes, sir. Do you think he will go away to-day?

Phil. I am sure he will not.

Mar. Indeed, his health is so bad, that it would be dangerous for him to proceed on his journey.

Phil. He shall remain with us, and he shall get well.

Mar. My dear master, you alone have the power of restoring him to health.

Phil. I? How! do you know what is the Lieutenant's disease?

Mar. I know it; but do you, sir?

Phil. I know everything.

Mar. Who told you?

Phil. My daughter.

Mar. Indeed! [*With an expression of surprise.*]

Phil. Why are you surprised? Would not my daughter be wrong to conceal the truth from her father?

Mar. Certainly; she has acted most wisely.

Phil. Now we can find the remedy.

Mar. In truth, it is an honourable love.

Phil. Most honourable.

Mar. The Lieutenant is an excellent young man.

Phil. Most excellent.

Mar. It is his only misfortune that he is not rich.

Phil. A handsome fortune with his wife would indeed make his situation more comfortable.

Mar. If the father is satisfied, no one has a right to complain.

Phil. A father with an only child, when he finds an opportunity of marrying her respectably, ought to be pleased to avail himself of it.

Mar. May God bless you! these are sentiments worthy of so good a man. I am delighted both for the officer and the young lady.—[*Aside.*] And not less so for myself, as my beloved Gascoigne may now remain with me. [*Exit.*

Enter Mademoiselle Costanza.

Phil. [*To himself.*] Good actions deserve praise, and every person of sense will approve of what I am doing.

Cost. Here I am, sir, at your commands.

Phil. Ah, Mademoiselle Costanza! it gives me great pleasure to see you.

Cost. You are very kind.

Phil. I am gratified at your friendship for my daughter.

Cost. She deserves it, and I love her with all my heart.

Phil. Ah, do not say with all your heart!

Cost. Why not? are you not convinced I love her sincerely?

Phil. Sincerely, I believe, but not with all your heart.

Cost. Why should you doubt it?

Phil. Because, if you loved my daughter with all your heart, there would be none of it left for any one else.

A CURIOUS MISHAP.

Cost. You make me laugh; and who should have a part of it?

Phil. Ah, Mademoiselle, we understand!

Cost. Indeed, I do not understand.

Phil. Now let us dismiss Lady Modesty, and introduce Lady Sincerity.

Cost. [*Aside.*] I cannot discover what he is aiming at.

Phil. Tell me, have you come on purpose to visit my daughter?

Cost. Yes, sir.

Phil. No, Mademoiselle.

Cost. For what, then?

Phil. Know I am an astrologer. I am visited by a certain spirit that tells me everything, and hence I have learnt this: Mademoiselle Costanza has come not to visit those who stay, but those who go away.

Cost. [*Aside.*] I suspect there is some truth in what the spirit says.

Phil. What! are you puzzled how to answer?

Cost. I will answer you frankly: if I have come to show civility to your guest, I do not perceive I deserve reproof.

Phil. Reproof! on the contrary, praise; acts of civility ought not to be omitted — especially when dictated by a more tender feeling.

Cost. You seem to be in a humour for jesting this morning.

Phil. And you seem to be out of spirits; but I lay a wager I can cheer you up.

Cost. Indeed?

Phil. Without fail.

Cost. And how?

Phil. With two words.

Cost. And what are those fine words?

Phil. You shall hear them. Come this way—a little nearer. The Lieutenant is not going away. Does not your heart leap at this unexpected news?

Cost. For mercy's sake! Monsieur Philibert, do you believe me in love?

Phil. Say no, if you can.

Cost. No; I can say it.

Phil. Swear to it.

Cost. Oh, I will not swear for such a trifle.

Phil. You wish to hide the truth from me, as if I had not the power of serving you, or was unwilling to do so, and of serving the poor young man too, who is so unhappy.

Cost. Unhappy, for what?

Phil. On account of you.

Cost. On account of me?

Phil. Yes, you; we are in the dark, so that his love for you is in a manner hidden, and every one does not know that his despair sends him away.

Cost. Despair for what?

Phil. Because your father, from pride and avarice, will not consent to give you to him: this, my girl, is the whole affair.

Cost. It appears that you know more of it than I do.

Phil. You know, and do not choose to know. I make allowance for your modesty; but when a gentleman speaks to you, when a man of my character exerts himself in your behalf, you ought to lay aside modesty and open your heart freely.

Cost. You take me so by surprise, I am embarrassed what answer to make.

Phil. Let us end this conversation. Tell me, like an honest girl as you are, do you not love Monsieur de la Cotterie?

Cost. You force me to own it.

Phil. [*Aside.*] Thank Heaven! so my daughter spoke the truth.—And he loves you with an equal affection.

Cost. Of that, sir, I know nothing.

Phil. If you do not know it, I tell you so; he loves you to perdition.

Cost. [*Aside.*] Can it be possible? and he has never declared it to me!

Phil. And I have undertaken to persuade your father.

Cost. But does my father know I am in love with the officer?

Phil. He certainly ought to know.

Cost. He has never mentioned it to me.

Phil. Oh, your father will soon come and talk with you on the subject.

Cost. He has never objected to my coming here, where I meet the officer.

Phil. He knows that you are visiting in an honourable house; no greater liberty would be allowed you here than is proper for a modest young lady. In a word, are you willing that I should manage the affair?

Cost. Entirely willing.

Phil. Bravo! this is enough; and what would it avail you to deny with your lips what your looks proclaim? the flame that burns in your heart sparkles in your eyes.

Cost. You have a most penetrating glance.

Phil Ah, here comes the officer.

Cost. By your leave, sir.

Phil. Where are you going?

Cost. To Mademoiselle Giannina.

Phil. Remain here, if you will.

Cost. Oh no, sir, excuse me—your servant.—[*Aside.*] I am overjoyed! I know not in what world I am!

[*Exit.*

Philibert, *alone.*

Phil. How amusing these girls are! Boldness and modesty are mingled in so strange a manner, that it is a pleasure to observe them. Here is an instance of love to devotion, and if it succeeds it will be owing to my daughter's intervention.

Enter De la Cotterie.

De la Cot. They told me, sir, that you asked for me.

Phil. Have you seen Mademoiselle Giannina?

De la Cot. No, sir, I have not seen her.

Phil. I am sorry that you appear so melancholy.

De la Cot. One whose health is bad cannot be expected to look cheerful.

Phil. Do you not know I am a physician, and have the skill to cure you?

De la Cot. I did not know that you were skilled in the medical art.

Phil. Well, my friend, capacities often exist where they are not suspected.

De la Cot. Why, then, have you not prescribed for me before now?

Phil. Because I did not sooner know the nature of your disease.

De la Cot. Do you think you know it now?

Phil. Yes, certainly—indubitably.

De la Cot. If you are learned in the medical art, sir, you know much better than I do how fallacious and how little to be relied on are all the symptoms that seem to indicate the causes of disease.

Phil. The indications of your disease are so infallible, that I am confident there is no mistake, and on condition that you trust to my friendship, you shall soon have reason to be content.

De la Cot. And by what process do you propose to cure me?

Phil. My first prescription shall be for you to abandon all intention of going away, and to take the benefit of this air, which will speedily restore you to health.

De la Cot. On the contrary, I fear this air is most injurious to me.

Phil. Do you not know that even from hemlock a most salutary medicine is extracted?

De la Cot. I am not ignorant of the late discoveries, but your allusion covers some mystery.

Phil. No, my friend; so far as mystery is concerned, each of us is now acting his part; but let us speak without metaphor. Your disease arises from love, and you think to find a remedy by going away, whereas it is an act of mere desperation. You carry the arrow in your heart, and hope to be relieved; but the same hand which placed it there must draw it out.

De la Cot. Your discourse, sir, is altogether new to me.

Phil. Why pretend not to understand me! Speak to me as a friend who loves you, and takes the same interest in you as if you were his son. Consider: by dissembling you may destroy your happiness for ever. My attachment to you arises from a knowledge of your merit, and from your having spent several months with me; besides, I should be mortified for you to have contracted in my house an unhappy passion; and therefore I most zealously interfere in your favour, and am anxious to find a remedy for you.

De la Cot. My dear friend, how have you discovered the origin of my unhappiness?

Phil. Shall I say the truth?—my daughter revealed it to me.

De la Cot. Heavens! had she the courage to disclose it?

Phil. Yes, after a little persuasion she told me everything.

De la Cot. Oh, by the friendship you possess for me, have pity on my love!

Phil. I have pity on you; I know what human frailty is at your age, and the violence of passion.

De la Cot. I confess I ought not to have encouraged my affection, and concealed it from such a friend.

Phil. This is the only complaint I have to make. You have not treated me with that unreserved confidence which I think I was entitled to.

De la Cot. I had not the courage.

Phil. Well, Heaven be praised! There is yet time. I know the girl loves you, for she told me so herself.

De la Cot. And what do you say to it, sir?

Phil. I approve of the marriage.

De la Cot. You overwhelm me with joy.

Phil. You see I am the good physician who understands the disease and knows the remedy.

De la Cot. I can hardly feel assured of this great happiness.

Phil. Why not?

De la Cot. I thought the narrowness of my fortune an insuperable obstacle.

Phil. Family and merit on your side are equal to a rich dower on the other.

De la Cot. Your kindness to me is unequalled.

Phil. But my kindness has yet done nothing; now it shall be my endeavour to provide for your happiness.

De la Cot. This will depend entirely on your own good heart.

Phil. We must exert ourselves to overcome the difficulties.

De la Cot. And what are the difficulties?

Phil. The consent of the father of the girl.

De la Cot. My friend, it seems you are making game of me; from the way you spoke just now, I thought all obstacles were removed.

Phil. But I have not mentioned it to him yet.

De la Cot. To whom have you not mentioned it?

Phil. To the father of the girl.

De la Cot. Oh, Heavens! and who is the father of the girl?

Phil. Good! You do not know him? you do not know the father of Mademoiselle Costanza, that horrid savage, Monsieur Riccardo, who has grown rich by usury, and has no idol but his money?

De la Cot. [*Aside.*] I shall go mad! Thus end all my hopes.

Phil. Riccardo does not visit at my house, you never go out, so it is not surprising you do not know him.

De la Cot. [*Aside.*] Ah! I am obliged to dissemble, not to disclose my love at a moment so unpropitious.

Phil. But how did you know the father would not give you his daughter if you did not know him?

De la Cot. I had reasons for thinking so, and for my despair there is no remedy.

Phil. Am I not your physician?

De la Cot. All your attention will be unavailing.

Phil. Leave it to me; I will go immediately to find Monsieur Riccardo, and I flatter myself—

De la Cot. No, sir, do not.

Phil. It seems the prospect of success turns your head; just now you were all joy. Whence arises this sudden change?

De la Cot. I am certain it will end unfortunately.

Phil. Such despondency is unworthy of you, and unjust to me.

De la Cot. Do not add to my unhappiness by your interference.

Phil. Are you afraid the father will be obstinate? let me try.

De la Cot. By no means; I am altogether opposed to it.

Phil. And I am altogether for it, and will speak to him.

De la Cot. I shall leave the Hague; I shall go in a few minutes.

Phil. You will not treat me with so much incivility.

Enter Giannina.

Gian. What, sirs, is the cause of this altercation?

Phil. Monsieur de la Cotterie acts towards me with a degree of ingratitude that is anything but agreeable.

Gian. Is it possible he can be capable of this?

De la Cot. Ah, Mademoiselle, I am a most unfortunate man!

Phil. I may say he does not know his own mind. He confessed his passion, and, when I offered to assist him, fell into transports; and then, when I promised to obtain the hand of Mademoiselle Costanza for him, he got furious, and threatened to go away.

Gian. I am surprised the Lieutenant should still speak of leaving us.

De la Cot. Would you have me stay and entertain such hopes? [*Ironically.*]

Gian. I would have you stay, and entertain a mistress who loves you. With my father's permission, you shall hear what Mademoiselle Costanza has just said of you.

Phil. May I not hear it?

Gian. Impossible; my friend directed me to tell it to him alone.

Phil. [*Aside.*] I shall hear all from my daughter when we are by ourselves.

Gian. [*Apart to* De la Cotterie.] I have contrived to make my father believe you were in love with Mademoiselle Costanza. As you love me, say it is so, and talk no more of going away.

De la Cot. [*Aside.*] Oh, the stratagems of love!

Phil. Will you still persist in your obstinacy?

De la Cot. Ah, no, sir; I rely on your kindness.

Phil. Do you desire me to speak to Monsieur Riccardo?

De la Cot. Do what you please.

Phil. Are you still anxious to go?

De la Cot. I promise you to remain here.

Phil. [*Aside.*] What magic words have wrought this change? I am curious to hear them.

De la Cot. Pardon, I pray you, my strange conduct.

Phil. Willingly; the actions of lovers are often extravagant. Tell me, Giannina, is Mademoiselle Costanza gone?

Gian. No, sir; she is waiting in my room.

Phil. Go, Lieutenant, and keep her company for a little while.

De la Cot. I would rather not, sir.

Gian. Go, go. — [*Aside to* De la Cotterie.] Listen! Wait for me in the antechamber; I will be there presently.

De la Cot. I shall obey you, sir.   [*Exit.*

Phil. [*Aside.*] The power of words! — Well, what did you say to him?

Gian. I told him to go to his mistress; that she expected him.

Phil. But the first time you spoke to him?

Gian. I said that Mademoiselle Costanza had hope she could persuade her father.

Phil. Why did you not tell him so openly, before me?

Gian. Things said in private often make the greatest impression.

Phil. Perhaps so.

Gian. By your leave. [*Going.*]

Phil. Where are you going?

Gian. To encourage this timid gentleman.

Phil. Yes, by all means; I recommend him to you.

Gian. Doubt not I shall take good care of him. [*Exit.*

Phil. My girl has a good heart, and mine is like hers.

END OF THE FIRST ACT.

ACT II.

Scene I.—*The chamber of* Mademoiselle Giannina.

Mademoiselle Costanza, *alone, seated.*

Cost. Who would ever have thought Monsieur de la Cotterie had such a liking for me? It is true he has always treated me with politeness, and been ready to converse with me; but I cannot say I have observed any great signs of love. Now I have always loved him, but have not had courage enough to show it. I flatter myself he too loves me, and for the same reason conceals it; in truth a modest officer is a strange animal, and it is hard to believe in its existence. Monsieur Philibert must have reasons for what he says, and I am well pleased to think him not mistaken, especially as I have no evidence that he is so. Here comes my handsome soldier—but Mademoiselle Giannina is with him; she never permits us to be alone together for a moment. I have some suspicion she is my rival.

Enter Mademoiselle Giannina *and* De la Cotterie.

Gian. Keep your seat, Mademoiselle; excuse me for having left you alone for a little while. I know you will be kind enough to forgive me, and I bring some one with me, who, I am sure, will secure your pardon.

Cost. Though surely in your own house and with a real friend such ceremony is needless, your company is always agreeable. I desire you will put yourself to no inconvenience.

Gian. Do you hear, Lieutenant? You see we Dutch are not without wit.

De la Cot. This is not the first time I have observed it.

Cost. Monsieur de la Cotterie is in a house that does honour to our country, and if he admires ladies of wit, he need not go out of it.

Gian. You are too polite, Mademoiselle.

Cost. I simply do justice to merit.

Gian. Let us not dispute about our merits, but rather leave it to the Lieutenant to decide.

De la Cot. If you wish a decision, you must choose a better judge.

Gian. A partial one, indeed, cannot be a good judge.

Cost. And to say nothing of partiality, he feels under obligations to you as the mistress of the house.

Gian. Oh, in France, the preference is always given to the guest: is it not so, Lieutenant?

De la Cot. It is no less the custom in Holland, than in my own country.

Cost. That is to say, the greater the merit, the greater the distinction with which they are treated.

Gian. On that principle you would be treated with the most distinction.

De la Cot. [*Aside.*] I shall get into trouble if this conversation continues.

Cost. By your leave, Mademoiselle.

Gian. Why do you leave us so soon?

Cost. I am engaged to my aunt; I promised to dine with her to-day, and it is not amiss to go early.

Gian. Oh, it is too early; your aunt is old, and you will perhaps still find her in bed.

De la Cot. [*Aside.*] Do not prevent her from going.

Gian. He begs me to detain you.

Cost. I am overpowered by your politeness. [*Curtsying.*]—[*Aside.*] Her amusement is to torment me.

Gian. [*To* Costanza.] What say you, my friend, have I not a good heart?

Cost. I must praise your kindness to me.

Gian. [*To* De la Cotterie.] And do you, too, own you are under obligations to me?

De la Cot. Yes, certainly, I have reason to be grateful to you; you, who know my feelings, must be conscious of the great favour you do me. [*Ironically.*]

Gian. [*To* Costanza.] You hear him? he is delighted.

Cost. My dear friend, as you have such a regard for me, and take so much interest in him, allow me to speak freely to you. Your worthy father has told me a piece of news that overwhelms me with joy and surprise. If all he has told me be true, I pray you, Monsieur De la Cotterie, to confirm it.

Gian. This is just what I anticipated; but as your conversation cannot be brief, and your aunt expects you, had you not better defer it to another opportunity?

De la Cot. [*Aside.*] Heaven grant I may not be still more involved!

Cost. A few words are all I ask.

Gian. Come, Lieutenant, take courage, and say all in a few words.

De la Cot. Indeed, I have not the courage.

Gian. No, my dear, it is impossible to express in a few words the infinite things he has to say to you.

Cost. It will be enough if he says but one word.

Gian. And what is that?

Cost. That he really loves me.

Gian. Pardon me; the Lieutenant is too polite to speak of love to one young lady in the presence of another; but I can, by going away, give you an opportunity of conversing together, and so remove all obstacles to an explanation. [*Going.*]

De la Cot. Stay, Mademoiselle!

Cost. Yes, and mortify me no more. Be assured I should never have spoken with the boldness I have done, had you not led me to do so. I do not comprehend your meaning; there is an inconsistency in your conduct; but, be it as it may, time will bring the truth to light. And now permit me to take leave.

Gian. My dear friend, pardon my inattention to you on first coming. You are mistress to go or remain as you please.

Enter Philibert.

Phil. What delightful company! But why are you on your feet? why do you not sit down?

Gian. Costanza is just going.

Phil. [*To* Costanza.] Why so soon?

Gian. Her aunt expects her.

Phil. No, my dear young lady, do me the favour to remain; we may want you, and in affairs of this kind moments are often precious. I have sent to your father, to say I desire to have a conversation with him; I am certain he will come. We will have a private interview, and, however little he may be inclined to give his consent, I shall press him so as not to leave him time to repent; if we agree, I will call you both immediately into my room.

De la Cot. [*Aside.*] Our situation is becoming more critical every moment.

Phil. [*To* De la Cotterie.] You seem to me to be agitated.

Gian. It is the excess of joy.

Phil. [*To Costanza.*] And what effect has hope on you?

Cost. I have more fear than hope.

Phil. Rely on me. For the present, be content to remain here; and, as we do not know exactly when your father will come, stay to dinner with us.

Gian. She cannot stay, sir.

Phil. Why not?

Gian. Because she promised her aunt to dine with her to-day.

Cost. [*Aside.*] I see she does not wish me to remain.

Phil. The aunt who expects you is your father's sister?

Cost. Yes, sir.

Phil. I know her; she is my particular friend. Leave it to me. I will get you released from the engagement, and, as soon as Monsieur Riccardo comes here, I will send word to her where you are, and she will be satisfied.

Cost. I am grateful, Monsieur Philibert, for your great kindness; permit me for a moment to see my aunt, who is not well. I will soon return, and avail myself of your politeness.

Phil. Very well; come back quickly.

Cost. Good morning to you; you will soon see me again.

Gian. Good-bye.—[*Aside.*] If she does not come back I shall not break my heart.

Phil. Adieu, my dear.—One moment. Lieutenant, for a man who has been in the wars, you do not seem quite as much at your ease as you should be.

Cost. Why do you say so, sir?

Phil. Because you are letting Mademoiselle go away without taking notice of her—without one word of civility.

Cost. Indeed, he has said but few.

De la Cot. [*To* Philibert.] I ought not to abuse the privilege you have given me.

Phil. [*Aside.*] I understand.—Giannina, a word with you.

Gian. Yes, sir?

Phil. [*Aside to* Giannina.] It is not right for a young lady to thrust herself between two lovers in this manner; on account of you, they cannot speak two words to each other.

Gian. [*To* Philibert.] They spoke in whispers together.

Phil. [*To* De la Cotterie.] Well, if you have anything to say to her—

De la Cot. There will be time enough, sir.

Phil. [*To* Giannina.] Attend to me.

Cost. [*Aside to* De la Cotterie.] At least assure me of your affection.

De la Cot. [*Aside to* Costanza.] Excuse me, Mademoiselle. [Giannina *coughs aloud.*] [*Aside.*] I am exceedingly embarrassed.

Cost. [*Loud enough for all to hear.*] Is it possible you will not say once that you love me?

Gian. [*To* Costanza, *with asperity.*] How many times do you want him to tell you so? Did he not say so before me?

Phil. [*To* Giannina, *with asperity.*] No meddling, I tell you.

Cost. Do not disturb yourself, Mademoiselle; to see clearly here is not easy. I wish you all a good morning. Adieu, Lieutenant.—[*Aside.*] He is worried by this troublesome girl. [*Exit.*

Phil. [*To* Giannina.] I am not pleased with your ways.

Gian. My dear father, let me amuse myself a little. I, who am so free from love, like sometimes to vex these lovers. As it was I who discovered their passion for each other, they are under obligations to me for their approaching happiness; hence they may pardon my jokes.

Phil. You girls are the devil! but the time will come, my daughter, when you will know how trying to lovers are these little teasing ways. You are now old enough, and the first good offer that presents itself, be prepared to accept it. What says Monsieur de la Cotterie! Am I not right?

De la Cot. Quite right.

Gian. Monsieur Quite Right, that is for me to decide, not for you.

Phil. Are you averse to being married?

Gian. If I could find a husband to my taste—

Phil. I shall be pleased if he is to your taste—to mine he certainly must be; the fortune I intend for you will make you equal to the best match in Holland.

Gian. The father of Mademoiselle Costanza says the same.

Phil. Do you compare Monsieur Riccardo with me? or do you compare yourself to the daughter of a broker? You vex me when you talk so. I will hear no more.

Gian. But I do not say—

Phil. I'll hear no more. [*Exit.*

De la Cot. Ah, my Giannina, our affairs are worse than ever. How much better not to have taken such a step!

Gian. Who could have foreseen my father would involve himself as he has done?

De la Cot. I see no remedy but my immediate departure.

Gian. Such weakness I did not expect.

De la Cot. Then I may be forced to marry Mademoiselle Costanza.

Gian. Do so, if you have the heart.

De la Cot. Or shall the whole mystery be explained?

Gian. It would be a most unhandsome act, to expose me to the shame of having contrived such a deception.

De la Cot. Then do you suggest some plan.

Gian. All I can say is this: think no more of going away. As to marrying Mademoiselle Costanza, it is absurd; to discover our plot preposterous. Resolve, then, on some plan to secure at the same time our love, our reputation, and our happiness. [*Exit.*

De la Cot. Excellent advice! but among so many things not to be done, where shall we find what is to be done? Alas! nothing remains but absolute despair. [*Exit.*

SCENE II.—*Enter* Monsieur Philibert, *alone.*

Phil. I can never believe Monsieur Riccardo refuses to come here; he knows who I am, and that it is to his interest not to offend one who can do him either good or harm. He must remember I lent him ten thousand florins when he commenced business, but there are persons who easily forget benefits, and regard neither friends nor relations, when they can no longer make use of them.

Enter Marianna.

Mar. If I do not interrupt you, Monsieur Philibert, I would say something to you.

Phil. I am now at leisure.

Mar. I would speak to you of an affair of my own.

Phil. Well, be quick, for I am expecting company.

Mar. I will tell you in two words: with your permission, I would get married.

Phil. Get married, then! much good may it do you!

Mar. But this is not all, sir. I am a poor girl, and

have now lived ten years in your family; with what attention and fidelity I have served you, you know. I ask you, not for the value of the thing, but as a mark of your favour, to make me a small present.

Phil. Well, I will do something for you as a recompense for your faithful services. Have you found a husband?

Mar. Yes, sir.

Phil. Bravo! I am glad of it. And you tell me of it after it is all arranged?

Mar. Pardon me, sir; I should not do so now, but accident has led me to an engagement with a young man of small means, which makes me come to you.

Phil. I will lay a wager it is the servant of the officer whom you are in love.

Mar. You are right, sir.

Phil. And are you willing to travel all over the world with him?

Mar. I am in hopes he will live here, if his master marries, as they say—

Phil. Yes, it is likely he will get married.

Mar. No one should know better than you, sir.

Phil. I am most anxious to see him happy.

Mar. As that is the case, sir, I consider it as though it were already done.

Phil. There may be difficulties in the way, but I hope to overcome them.

Mar. There are none, I think, on the part of the young lady.

Phil. No; she is much in love with him.

Mar. That is evident.

Phil. And when do you propose to be married?

Mar. If it please you, sir, at the same time my young lady is married.

Phil. What young lady?

Mar. My mistress, your daughter.

Phil. If you wait till then, you will have time enough.

Mar. Do you think her marriage will be long delayed?

Phil. Good! Before talking of her marriage, the husband must be found.

Mar. Why, is there not a husband?

Phil. A husband! not that I know of.

Mar. You do not know?

Phil. Poor me! I know nothing of it. Tell me what you know, and do not hide the truth.

Mar. You astonish me! Is she not to marry Monsieur de la Cotterie? Did you not tell me so yourself, and that you were pleased at it?

Phil. Blockhead! Did you suppose I would give my daughter to a soldier—the younger son of a poor family? to one who has not the means of supporting her in the way she has been accustomed to from her birth?

Mar. Did you not say just now that Monsieur de la Cotterie was about to be married, and that you were most anxious for his happiness?

Phil. To be sure I did.

Mar. And, pray, who is he to marry, if not Mademoiselle Giannina?

Phil. Blockhead! Are there no girls at the Hague but her?

Mar. He visits at no other house.

Phil. And does nobody come here?

Mar. I do not perceive that he pays attention to any one but my young mistress.

Phil. Blockhead! Don't you know Mademoiselle Costanza?

Mar. A blockhead cannot know everything.

Phil. Has my daughter made you her confidant?

Mar. She always speaks of the officer with the greatest esteem, and expresses much pity for him.

Phil. And did you believe her pity proceeded from love?

Mar. I did.

Phil. Blockhead!

Mar. I know, too, he wanted to go away, because he was in despair—

Phil. Well?

Mar. Fearing her father would not give his consent.

Phil. Excellent!

Mar. And are you not that father?

Phil. Are there no other fathers?

Mar. You gave me to understand they were to be married.

Phil. How absurd is your obstinacy!

Mar. I will venture my head I am right.

Phil. You should understand your mistress better, and respect her more than to think so.

Mar. Indeed, it is an honourable love.

Phil. Begone directly!

Mar. I see no great harm in it.

Phil. Here comes some one—Monsieur Riccardo. Go quickly.

Mar. You are too rough, sir.

Phil. Blockhead!

Mar. We shall see who is the blockhead, I or—

Phil. You or I the blockhead?

Mar. I—or that man passing along the street. [*Exit.*

Phil. Impertinent! whether she gets married or not, she shall stay no longer in my house. To have such an opinion of my daughter! Giannina is not capable of it; no, not capable.

Enter Monsieur Riccardo.

Ric. Your servant, Monsieur Philibert.

Phil. Good day to you, Monsieur Riccardo. Excuse me if I have put you to any inconvenience.

Ric. Have you any commands for me?

Phil. I wish to have some conversation with you. Pray be seated.

Ric. I can spare but a few moments.

Phil. Are you much engaged just now?

Ric. Yes, indeed; among other things, I am harassed by a number of people about the case of the smugglers who have been arrested.

Phil. I have heard of it. Are these poor people still in prison?

Ric. Yes; and I wish they may remain there until their house is utterly ruined.

Phil. And have you the heart to bear the tears of their children?

Ric. Had they not the heart to violate the laws of the customs—to defraud the revenue? I wish I could catch them oftener; do you not know that smugglers on conviction pay all costs?

Phil. [*Aside.*] Oh! his vile employment.

Ric. Well, what have you to say to me?

Phil. Monsieur Riccardo, you have a daughter to marry.

Ric. Yes, and a plague to me she is.

Phil. Does her being in your house put you to any inconvenience?

Ric. No; but the thought of providing for her when she marries does.

Phil. [*Aside.*] How contemptible!—If she wishes to marry, you must provide for her.

Ric. I shall do so; I shall be obliged to do so; but

on one of two conditions: without a fortune, if she marries to please herself,—with one, if to please me.

Phil. I have a proposal to make to you.

Ric. Let me hear it, but be quick.

Phil. Do you know a certain French officer who is a guest in my house?

Ric. Do you propose him for my daughter?

Phil. Say I did, would you have any objection?

Ric. An officer, and a Frenchman! He shall have my daughter neither with nor without a fortune.

Phil. Are you, then, opposed to the French and the military?

Ric. Yes, to both equally; much more so if they are united in the same person. I hate the French, because they are not friends to commerce and industry, as we are; they care for nothing but suppers, the theatre, and amusement. With soldiers I have no reason to be pleased; I know how much I lose by them. They contend we contractors are obliged to maintain their infantry—their horse; and when they are in quarters, they waste a whole arsenal full of money.

Phil. The French officer of whom I speak is an honourable man; he has no vice, and is moreover of a noble family.

Ric. Is he rich?

Phil. He is a younger son.

Ric. If he is not rich, I value but little his nobility, and still less his profession.

Phil. My dear friend, let us speak confidentially. A man like you, blessed with a large fortune, can never better employ fifty or sixty thousand florins, than by bestowing them on his daughter, when she marries so worthy a man.

Ric. On this occasion, I would not give ten livres.

Phil. And to whom will you give your daughter?

Ric. If I am to dispose of so large a sum of money, I wish to place it in one of the best houses in Holland.

Phil. You will never do so.

Ric. I shall never do so?

Phil. No, never.

Ric. Why not?

Phil. Because the respectable houses in Holland have no occasion to enrich themselves in this manner.

Ric. You esteem this French officer highly?

Phil. Most highly.

Ric. Why not then give him your own daughter?

Phil. Why not? Because—because I do not choose.

Ric. And I do not choose to give him mine.

Phil. There is some difference between you and me.

Ric. I do not perceive in what it consists.

Phil. We know very well how you began.

Ric. But we do not know how you will end.

Phil. Your language is too arrogant.

Ric. Were we not in your house, it should be stronger.

Phil. I will let you know who I am.

Ric. I am not afraid of you.

Phil. Go; we will speak of this again.

Ric. Yes, again.—[*Aside.*] If he ever falls into my hands—if I catch him in the least evasion of the revenue laws—I swear I will destroy him. [*Exit.*

Phil. A rascal! a brute without civility! an impertinent fellow!

Enter De la Cotterie.

De la Cot. [*Aside.*] Their conference, ending in an altercation, makes me hope he has refused his daughter.

Phil. [*Aside.*] I am not I, if I do not let him see—

De la Cot. Monsieur—

Phil. An ill-tempered, worthless—

De la Cot. Are these compliments intended for me, sir?

Phil. Pardon me; I am carried away by my anger.

De la Cot. Who has offended you?

Phil. That insolent fellow, Monsieur Riccardo.

De la Cot. And has he refused his consent to the marriage?

Phil. [*Aside.*] I am sorry I must bring this new trouble on the poor Lieutenant.

De la Cot. [*Aside.*] Heaven be praised! fortune at last aids me.

Phil. My friend, never give way to resentment—to impatience of temper.

De la Cot. Tell me the truth; does he refuse his daughter?

Phil. A man in this world ought to be prepared for any event.

De la Cot. I am impatient to hear the truth.

Phil. [*Aside.*] Ah! if I tell him, he will drop down dead.

De la Cot. [*Aside.*] This suspense is intolerable.

Phil. [*Aside.*] Yet he must know.

De la Cot. By your leave, sir. [*Going.*]

Phil. Stay a moment.—[*Aside.*] If he goes, there is danger he will destroy himself from despair.

De la Cot. Why not tell me at once what he said to you?

Phil. Control yourself. Do not give way to despair, because an avaricious, presumptuous, ignorant father refuses to marry his daughter respectably. There is a way to manage it in spite of him.

De la Cot. No, sir; when the father refuses, it is not proper for me to persist.

Phil. Well, what do you mean to do?

De la Cot. To go far away, and to sacrifice my love to honour, duty, and universal quiet.

A CURIOUS MISHAP.

Phil. And have you the heart to abandon a girl who loves you?—to leave her a prey to despair?—soon to receive the sad intelligence of her illness, perhaps of her death!

De la Cot. Ah, Monsieur Philibert, your words will kill me! if you knew their force, you would be cautious how you used them.

Phil. My words will conduct you to joy, to peace, to happiness.

De la Cot. Ah, no! rather to sorrow and destruction.

Phil. It is strange that a man of spirit like you should be so easily discouraged.

De la Cot. If you knew my case, you would not talk so.

Phil. I know it perfectly, but do not consider it desperate. The girl loves you—you love her passionately. This will not be the first marriage between young persons that has taken place without the consent of parents.

De la Cot. Do you approve of my marrying the daughter without the consent of the father?

Phil. Yes—in your case—considering the circumstances, I do approve of it. If the father is rich, you are of a noble family. You do him honour by the connection; he provides for your interest by a good dowry.

De la Cot. But, sir, how can I hope for any dowry when I marry his daughter in this manner? The father, offended, will refuse her the least support.

Phil. When it is done, it is done. He has but this only child; his anger may last a few days, and then he must do what so many others have done: he will receive you as his son-in-law, and perhaps make you master of his house.

De la Cot. And may I hope for this?

Phil. Yes, if you have courage.

De la Cot. I do not want courage; the difficulty lies in the means.

Phil. There is no difficulty in the means. Hear my suggestions. Mademoiselle Costanza must now be at her aunt's. Do what I tell you. Give up your dinner to-day, as I shall do mine on your account. Go and find her. If she loves you in earnest, persuade her to show her love by her actions. If the aunt is favourable to your designs, ask her protection, and then, if the girl consents, marry her.

De la Cot. And if the injured father should threaten to send me to prison?

Phil. Carry her with you into France.

De la Cot. With what means? With what money?

Phil. Wait a moment. [*Goes and opens a bureau.*]

De la Cot. [*Aside.*] Oh, Heavens! how unconscious is he that he is encouraging me to an enterprise, of which the injury may fall on his own head!

Phil. Take this. Here are a hundred guineas in gold, and four hundred more in notes: these five hundred guineas will serve you for some time; accept them from my friendship. I think I can make the father of the girl return them to me.

De la Cot. Sir, I am full of confusion—

Phil. What confuses you? I am astonished at you! you want spirit; you want courage. Go quickly, and do not lose a moment. In the meantime, I will observe the movements of Monsieur Riccardo, and if there is any danger of his surprising you, I will find persons to keep him away. Let me know what happens, either in person or by note. My dear friend, you seem already to have recovered your spirits. I rejoice for your sake. May fortune be propitious to you!—[*Aside.*] I am anxious to see Monsieur Riccardo in a rage—in despair. [*Closes the bureau.*]

De la Cot. [*Aside.*] He gives me counsel; and money to carry it into effect. What shall I resolve on? what plan shall I follow? Take fortune on the tide; and he can blame no one but himself, who, contriving a stratagem against another, falls into his own snare.

[*Exit.*

Monsieur Philibert, *alone.*

Phil. In truth, I feel some remorse of conscience for the advice and aid I have given. I remember, too, that I have a daughter, and I would not have such an injury done to me. Nature tells us, and the law commands, not to do to others what we should not wish done to us. But I am carried along by several reasons; a certain gentleness of disposition inclining me to hospitality, to friendship, makes me love the Lieutenant, and take almost the same interest in him as if he were my son. The marriage appears to me to be a suitable one, the opposition of Monsieur Riccardo unjust, and his severity to his daughter tyranny. Add to all this the uncivil treatment I have received from him, the desire to be revenged, and the pleasure of seeing his pride humbled. Yes, if I lose the five hundred guineas, I shall have the satisfaction of seeing my friend made happy, and Monsieur Riccardo mortified.

Enter Mademoiselle Costanza.

Cost. Here I am, sir.
Phil. [*Disturbed.*] What brings you here?
Cost. Did you not send for me?
Phil. [*As before.*] Have you seen Monsieur de la Cotterie?
Cost. No, sir, I have not seen him.
Phil. Return at once to your aunt's.

Cost. Do you drive me from your house?

Phil. No, I do not drive you away, but I advise you—I entreat. Go quickly, I tell you.

Cost. I wish to know the reason.

Phil. You shall know it when you are at your aunt's.

Cost. Has anything new occurred?

Phil. Yes, there is something new.

Cost. Tell me what it is.

Phil. Monsieur de la Cotterie will tell you.

Cost. Where is he?

Phil. At your aunt's.

Cost. The Lieutenant has not been there.

Phil. He is this moment gone there.

Cost. What for?

Phil. Return; then you will know it.

Cost. Have you spoken to my father?

Phil. Yes; ask your husband that is to be.

Cost. My husband!

Phil. Yes, your husband.

Cost. Monsieur de la Cotterie?

Phil. Monsieur de la Cotterie.

Cost. May I rely on it?

Phil. Go directly to your aunt's.

Cost. Please tell me what has happened.

Phil. Time is precious; if you lose time, you lose your husband.

Cost. Ah me! I will run with all speed; would that I had wings to my feet. [*Exit.*

Enter Mademoiselle Giannina.

Phil. Two words from the Lieutenant are worth more than a thousand from me.

Gian. Is what Monsieur de la Cotterie has told me true, sir?

Phil. What has he told you?

Gian. That you advised him to marry the girl without the consent of her father.

Phil. Did he tell you this in confidence?

Gian. Yes, sir.

Phil. [*Aside.*] I am displeased at his indiscretion.

Gian. And that you gave him five hundred guineas to aid him in the scheme.

Phil. [*Aside.*] Imprudent! I am almost sorry I did so.

Gian. Your silence confirms it; it is true, then?

Phil. Well, what do you say to it?

Gian. Nothing, sir. It is enough for me to know you did it. Your humble servant, sir.

Phil. Where are you going?

Gian. To amuse myself.

Phil. In what manner?

Gian. With the marriage of Monsieur de la Cotterie.

Phil. But it has not taken place yet.

Gian. I hope it soon will.

Phil. Be cautious—mention it to no one.

Gian. Never fear; it will be known as soon as it is over. You will have the credit of contriving it, and I shall be most happy when it is done. [*Exit.*

Phil. [*Alone.*] I hope she will not imitate this bad example; but there is no danger. She is a good girl, and, like me, can distinguish between cases, and understands what is proper; and as I know how she has been brought up, under my own care, I have no apprehensions such a misfortune may befall me.

END OF THE SECOND ACT.

ACT III.

Scene I.—Philibert *and* Marianna.

Mar. Excuse me for interrupting you again.

Phil. I suppose you have some new piece of nonsense?

Mar. I hope you will not again call me blockhead.

Phil. Not unless you utter more absurdities.

Mar. I have only to tell you I am just going to be married, and to bespeak your kindness.

Phil. Then you have determined to marry before your mistress?

Mar. No, sir; she is to be married to-day, and I shall be married to-morrow.

Phil. And you do not wish me to call you blockhead?

Mar. You still persist in concealing it from me?

Phil. Concealing what?

Mar. The marriage of my young lady.

Phil. Are you out of your senses?

Mar. Now, to show you I am not so foolish, I will own a fault I have committed, from curiosity. I stood behind the hangings, and heard Monsieur de la Cotterie talking with your daughter, and it is fixed on that they are to be married privately this evening, and you have given five hundred guineas on account of her portion.

Phil. On account of her portion! [*Laughing.*]

Mar. Yes, I think on account of her portion; I saw the guineas with my own eyes.

Phil. Yes, you are foolish, more foolish, most foolish.

Mar. [*Aside.*] He vexes me so I hardly know what to do.

Phil. The Lieutenant, however, has acted very improperly; he ought not to have mentioned it to my daughter, especially when there was danger of being overheard.

Mar. If you hide it from me for fear I shall make it public, you do wrong to my discretion.

Phil. Your discretion, indeed! you conceal yourself, listen to what people are talking about, misunderstand them, and then report such nonsense.

Mar. I was wrong to listen, I admit; but as to misunderstanding, I am sure I heard right.

Phil. You will force me to say or do something not very pleasant.

Mar. Well, well! where did Mademoiselle Giannina go just now?

Phil. Where did she go?

Mar. Did she not go out with Monsieur de la Cotterie?

Phil. Where?

Mar. I heard they went to Madame Gertrude's.

Phil. To my sister's?

Mar. Yes, sir.

Phil. Giannina may have gone there, not the Lieutenant.

Mar. I know they went out together, sir.

Phil. The Lieutenant may have accompanied her; my sister's house is near the place where he was to go; my daughter might choose to be at hand to hear the news. I know all; everything goes on well, and I say again you are a blockhead.

Mar. [*Aside.*] This is too bad; I can scarcely keep my temper.

Phil. See who is in the hall—I hear some one.

Mar. [*Aside.*] Oh, it will be excellent if a trick has been played on the old gentleman! but it is impossible.

[*Exit.*

Phil. [*Alone.*] Heaven grant it may end well! The imprudence of the Lieutenant might have ruined the plot, but young persons are subject to these indiscretions.

I fortunately had sense enough when I was a young man, and have more now I am old.

Enter Gascoigne.

Gas. Your servant, Monsieur Philibert.

Phil. Good-day, my friend. What news have you?

Gas. My master sends his best compliments.

Phil. Where is the Lieutenant? What is he doing? How go his affairs?

Gas. I believe this note will give you full information.

Phil. Let us see. [*Opens it.*]

Gas. [*Aside.*] As he does not send me away, I will remain here.

Phil. [*To himself.*] There is a paper enclosed, which seems to be written by my daughter. Let us first know what my friend says.

Gas. [*Aside.*] Marianna is listening behind the hangings; she is as curious as I am.

Phil. [*Reading.*] "Monsieur: Your advice has encouraged me to a step which I should not have had the boldness to venture on, however urged by the violence of my love." Yes, indeed, he wanted courage. "I have carried Mademoiselle to a respectable and secure house, that is to say, to her aunt's."

He must have met Costanza, and they have gone together. I did well to send her quickly; all my own work!

"The tears of the girl softened the good old lady, and she assented to our marriage." Excellent, excellent! it could not be better done.

"Orders were given for a notary to be called in, and the marriage service was performed in the presence of two witnesses."

Admirable—all has gone on well. "I cannot express to you my confusion, not having the courage to ask anything but your kind wishes; the rest will be added in the writing of your daughter, whom you will more readily pardon. I kiss your hand."

What does he want of me that he has not the courage to ask, and gets my daughter to intercede? Let me read the enclosed. He must have gone immediately to my sister's, to let Giannina know when the marriage was over. Well, what says my daughter?

"Dear father." She writes well—a good mercantile hand; she is a fine girl, God bless her. "Permit me, through this letter, to throw myself at your feet, and to ask your pardon." Oh, Heavens! what has she done?

"Informed by yourself of the advice you had given to Monsieur de la Cotterie, and of the money you furnished him with to carry it into execution, I have yielded to my affection, and married the Lieutenant."

Oh, infamous! Deceiver! traitress! abandoned! They have killed me!

Enter Marianna.

Mar. What has happened, sir?

Phil. Help me! support me! for Heaven's sake do not leave me!

Mar. How can such a blockhead help you?

Phil. You are right; laugh at me—abuse me—show me no mercy. I deserve it all, and I give you full liberty to do so.

Mar. No; I feel compassion for you.

Phil. I am not worthy of your compassion.

Gas. Do not, sir, abandon yourself to despair; my master is an honourable gentleman, of a noble family.

Phil. He has ruined my daughter; he has destroyed my hopes.

Mar. You are able to provide handsomely for him.

Phil. And shall my estate go in this way?

Gas. Pardon me, sir; the same arguments you urged to convince Monsieur Riccardo may serve to convince yourself.

Phil. Ah, traitor! do you amuse yourself at my folly?

Mar. Gascoigne speaks to the purpose, and you have no right to complain of him. [*With warmth.*]

Phil. Yes, insult me, rejoice at my disgrace!

Mar. I have pity on you, blinded as you are by anger.

Gas. Condemn yourself for the fruits of your own bad advice.

Phil. Why deceive me? why make me believe the love of the officer was for Mademoiselle Costanza?

Gas. Because love is full of stratagems, and teaches lovers to conceal their passion, and to contrive schemes for their own happiness.

Phil. And if Monsieur Riccardo had agreed to the marriage of his daughter, what a figure I should have made in the affair!

Gas. My master never asked you to interfere for him.

Phil. No, but he let me do it.

Gas. Say, rather, that you did not understand him.

Phil. In short, they have betrayed and cheated me; the conduct of my daughter is treacherous, and that of the Lieutenant infamous.

Gas. You should speak more respectfully, sir, of an officer.

Mar. Remember, soldiers swear swords.

Phil. Yes, that is right; all he has to do now is to kill me.

Gas. My master has no such cruel design; you will soon see him come to ask your pardon.

Phil. I do not wish to see him at all.

Gas. Your daughter, then, shall come instead of him.

Phil. Name her not to me.

Mar. Your own flesh and blood, sir!

Phil. Ungrateful! she was my love—my only joy.

Gas. What is done cannot be undone.

Phil. I know it, insolent—I know it too well.

Gas. Do not be offended with me, sir.

Mar. Have compassion on him, his anger overpowers him. My poor master! he hoped to marry his daughter to a man of his own choice—to have her always near him—to see his grandchildren around him—to delight in their caresses, and to instruct them himself.

Phil. All my hopes are gone; no consolation is left for me.

Gas. Do you think, sir, your excellent son-in-law, a worthy Frenchman, and a good soldier, cannot provide grandchildren for you?

Mar. Not a year shall pass, but you will see the finest boy in the world gambolling around your feet.

Phil. My hatred for the father will make me hate the child.

Mar. Oh, the sense of consanguinity will cause you to forget every injury.

Gas. You have one only daughter in the world; can you have the heart to abandon her—never to see her more?

Phil. My anguish of mind will kill me. [*Covers his face with his hands.*]

Mar. Gascoigne!

Gas. What do you say?

Mar. Do you understand me? [*Makes a sign for him to go out.*]

Gas. I understand.

Mar. Now is the time.

Gas. So it may prove.

Phil. What do you say?

Mar. I am telling Gascoigne to go away, to disturb you no longer, and not to abuse your patience.

Phil. Yes, let him leave me.

Gas. Your servant, sir. Excuse me, if, after having committed such an offence in your house, you see me no more. My master, as things appear at present, will be forced to leave this, and to carry his wife to France. Have you no message to your poor daughter?

Phil. Do you think he will go away so soon?

Gas. He told me, if he received no kind answer from you, to order horses immediately.

Mar. It is a great grief to a father never to see his daughter again.

Phil. Is your master a barbarian? is he so ungrateful? Could I have done more for him? And he has used me with the greatest inhumanity; to seduce the heart of my daughter, and the whole time to conceal it from me.

Gas. He would willingly have brought her to you before now, but for the fear of your resentment.

Phil. Perfidious! I have to applaud him for his handsome action,—I have to be grateful for his treachery; he shuns the reproaches of an offended father,—he cannot bear to hear himself called traitor.

Gas. I understand; by your leave. [*Going.*]

Phil. Tell him he must never dare to come in my presence; I do not wish to see him,—I do not desire it.

Gas. [*Aside.*] I understand perfectly; nature never fails. [*Exit.*

Mar. [*Aside.*] Matters will soon be accommodated.

Phil. [*To himself.*] My own injury! this is good!— to my own injury!

Mar. To turn your thoughts from this subject, sir, may I now speak to you concerning my own affairs?

Phil. I need nothing else to torment me but for you to talk of your marriage. I hate the very word, and never wish to hear it again while I live.

Mar. It seems, then, you want the world to come to an end

Phil. For me it is ended.

Mar. My poor master! and where will your estate go—your riches?

Phil. May the devil take them!

Mar. You would die rich, and let your daughter live in want?

Phil. Poor unhappy girl!

Mar. And would you carry this hatred in your bosom, and feel remorse at your death?

Phil. Be silent, devil! torture me no more.

Enter Mademoiselle Costanza.

Cost. Monsieur Philibert, you have made sport of me.

Phil. [*Aside.*] This was wanting to complete all.

Cost. I have been waiting two hours, and no one has appeared.

Phil. [*Aside.*] I know not what answer to make.

Cost. Did you not urge me to return to my aunt's, telling me the Lieutenant would be there?

Mar. My young lady, you shall hear how it was. The Lieutenant had to go to the aunt's,—and to the aunt's he went. There he was to have an understanding with Mademoiselle,—and he had an understanding with Mademoiselle. But the poor gentleman mistook the house: instead of going to Aunt Hortensia's he found himself at Aunt Gertrude's, and instead of marrying Mademoiselle Costanza, he has married Mademoiselle Giannina.

Cost. Can it be possible they have laughed at and deceived me in this manner? Speak, Monsieur Philibert; tell me truly what has been done, and do not suppose me patient enough to submit to such an injury.

Phil. Oh, if I submit to it, you must submit too.

Cost. And what have you to submit to?

Phil. On your account I have been accessory to the ruin of my daughter.

Cost. On my account?

Phil. Yes; the machine I contrived for you has fallen on my own head.

Mar. Fortunately my master's skull is reasonably thick.

Cost. I understand nothing of all this.

Phil. I will tell you plainly and distinctly the whole affair. Know then—

Enter Monsieur Riccardo.

Ric. [*To* Costanza.] What are you doing here?

Phil. [*To himself.*] Another torment!

Cost. Sir, you have never forbidden my coming here.

Ric. Well, now I forbid it. I know what you have come for; I know your love for the foreigner, and your schemes against my authority and your own honour.

Phil. [*To* Riccardo, *with asperity.*] You know nothing. If you knew as much as I do, you would not speak so.

Ric. I speak so in consequence of what you told me this morning, and no light matter it is; enough to make me forbid my daughter's coming to your house.

Mar. Are you afraid they will marry her against your wishes?

Ric. I may well fear it.

Mar. Listen to me: if she does not marry my master, there is nobody else here for her to marry.

Ric. Where is the Frenchman—the officer?

Mar. Shall I tell him, sir?

Phil. Ah! he will hear it soon enough.

Mar. Know, then, the officer has presumed to marry my young mistress.

Ric. Ah! [*With surprise.*]

Phil. Oh! [*With vexation.*]

Cost. This is the wrong I apprehended. Ah, my father, resent the insult they have offered to me! They have made use of me to accomplish their designs; they have flattered me to expose me to ridicule; and the injury I have received is an insult to our family.

Ric. Yes, I will resent the insult they have offered to me. You I will send to a convent; and Monsieur Philibert makes amends for his offence by his own shame.

Phil. [*Aside.*] Quite right—I deserve yet more.

Cost. [*Aside.*] Wretched me! to what am I brought by my passion, my wretchedness, and disobedience!

Phil. My dear friend, excuse my impatient manner. I acknowledge the injustice I have done you, and Heaven punishes me rightly for my improper intentions. Ah, Monsieur Riccardo, I have lost my daughter!—I contrived my own disgrace!

Ric. Lost! she is only married—not entirely lost.

Phil. I fear I shall never see her again. Who knows but that monster has already carried her away? I gave him five hundred guineas to carry away my heart—my daughter—my only daughter—my love—my only love! Ah, could I embrace her once more! I wish to know if she is gone; I want to see her again. If she is gone, I will kill myself with my own hand. [*Going, meets his daughter.*]

Enter Mademoiselle Giannina, *and a little after,* De la Cotterie.

Gian. Ah, dearest father!

Phil. Ah, most ungrateful daughter!

Gian. For mercy's sake, pardon me! [*Throws herself on her knees.*]

Phil. Do you deserve pardon?

Gian. Your anger is most just.

Phil. [*Aside.*] I shall not survive it; I must die.

Ric. Both are to be pitied.

Cost. [*Aside.*] I shall be revenged if her father refuses to forgive her.

Phil. Rise.

Gian. I will not rise without your pardon.

Phil. How could you have the heart to cause me so great an affliction?

Gian. Ah, sir, your advice—

Phil. Not a word of it! torture me no more; never mention again my own folly and weakness. Rise; on that condition I pardon you.

Gian. Oh, dearest father! [*Rises.*]

Cost. [*Aside.*] She obtains forgiveness on easy terms.

Gian. Ah, sir, let your grace extend—

Phil. Do not speak to me of your husband!

Gian. Oh, give him a place in your heart, or I shall be forced to leave you.

Phil. Perfidious! to talk so to your father!

Gian. Conjugal duty will oblige me to take this step.

Phil. Oh, hard fate of a father! but it is just—I deserve more.

Ric. My friend, the act is done, there is no remedy. I advise you to be reconciled to him before your curious mishap is known throughout the whole city.

Phil. [*To* Costanza.] I entreat you, Mademoiselle—I entreat you not to make it known, for the sake of my honour and reputation. [*To* Marianna.] I tell you not to speak of it. My daughter, mention it to no one.

Gian. No, for the love of Heaven, let nobody hear of it. Quick! let everything be settled before any one leaves this room. Quick, my dear husband, come here; throw yourself at my father's feet, ask his pardon, kiss his hand; and do you pardon him, receive him for a son-in-law and for a son. Quick! hush! that no one may hear of it. [*She rapidly does everything as she says it.*]

Phil. [*Aside.*] I am confounded; I know not what to say.

Cost. He has not the firmness to resist the sight of his ungrateful daughter. [*Exit.*

De la Cot. Have I your pardon, sir?

Phil. Do you think you deserve it?

Gian. For Heaven's sake, say no more! We must take care that nobody shall know what has happened. My father is anxious to save the honour of his family; and, above all things, I charge you never to urge in your justification that he advised the scheme, and gave you five hundred guineas to carry it into execution.

Phil. [*To* Giannina, *with asperity.*] I commanded you not to mention it.

Gian. I was only informing my husband of your commands.

Ric. Well, Monsieur Philibert, are you reconciled?

Phil. What can I do? I am constrained by necessity, by affection, by my own kind disposition, to be reconciled to them. You are husband and wife, you are in my house, remain here, and may Heaven bless you!

Gian. Oh, perfect happiness!

De la Cot. I hope, sir, you will never repent of your pardon and kindness to me.

Mar. Hush! quick! that nobody may know it.

Phil. What now?

Mar. Hush! quick! There is a little affair of mine to be finished. Gascoigne is to be my husband, with the permission of our masters.

Gas. [*To his master.*] By your leave, sir. [*Gives her his hand.*]

Mar. Hush! quick! that nobody may know it.

Gian. Against your marriage nothing can be said;

mine may be condemned. I confess that I have exceeded the limits of duty, that I have been wanting in respect to my father, and have exposed to hazard my own honour and the reputation of my family. Those who now see me happy, and not punished, must be cautious not to follow a bad example; let them rather say it has pleased Heaven to mortify the father, and not that the daughter is exempt from remorse and regret. Most kind spectators, let the moral of this representation be a warning to families, and may whatever enjoyment you derive from it be consistent with the principles of duty and of virtue.

THE END OF "A CURIOUS MISHAP."

THE BENEFICENT BEAR*

(*IL BURBERO BENEFICO*)

(*LE BOURRU BIENFAISANT*)

A COMEDY IN THREE ACTS

[* In order to render the exact shade of meaning of the Italian title, it has been necessary to adopt the colloquial phrase.]

DRAMATIS PERSONÆ.

GERONTE.
DALANCOURT, *his nephew.*
DORVAL, *the friend of Geronte.*
VALERIO, *the lover of Angelica.*
PICCARDO, *the servant of Geronte.*
A SERVANT *of Dalancourt.*
MADAME DALANCOURT.
ANGELICA, *sister of Dalancourt.*
MARTUCCIA, *housekeeper to Geronte.*

The Scene is in Paris, at the house of GERONTE.

THE BENEFICENT BEAR.

——o——

ACT I.

SCENE I.—Martuccia, Angelica, *and* Valerio.

Ang. Valerio, leave me, I entreat you; I fear for myself, I fear for you. Ah! if we should be surprised—

Val. My dear Angelica!

Mar. Do go, sir.

Val. [*To* Martuccia.] One moment more. If I could be well assured—

Mar. Of what?

Val. Of her love—of her constancy.

Ang. Ah, Valerio! can you doubt it?

Mar. Go, go, sir; she loves you but too well.

Val. This is the happiness of my life—

Mar. Quick, go away. If my master should come in suddenly!

Ang. [*To* Martuccia.] He never leaves his room so early.

Mar. That is true; but you know he walks and amuses himself in this room. Here are his chessmen, and here he often plays. Oh, don't you know Signor Geronte?

Val. Pardon me, he is Angelica's uncle. I know my father was his friend, but I have never spoken to him.

Mar. He is a man, sir, of a most singular character.

At bottom a most worthy man, but impatient, and peculiar to the last degree.

Ang. Yes, he tells me he loves me, and I believe him; but while he tells me so, he makes me tremble.

Val. [*To* Angelica.] What have you to fear? you have neither father nor mother. You are at your brother's disposal, and he is my friend; I will speak to him.

Mar. Ah! Exactly! Trust to Signor Dalancourt.

Val. Well, can he refuse me?

Mar. Indeed, I think he can.

Val. Why so?

Mar. Listen; I will explain the whole matter in a few words. My nephew, your brother the lawyer's new clerk, has told me what I will now tell you. He has been with him only a fortnight, I heard it from him this morning; but he confided it to me as the greatest secret: for Heaven's sake do not betray me!

Val. Do not fear.

Ang. You know me.

Mar. [*Speaking in a low tone to* Valerio, *and looking towards the door.*] Signor Dalancourt is a ruined man, overwhelmed. He has run through all his fortune, and perhaps his sister's dowry too. Angelica is a burden too great for him to bear, and to free himself from it, he means to shut her up in a convent.

Ang. Oh, Heavens! What do you tell me?

Val. Can it be possible? I have known him a long time. Dalancourt always appeared to me a young man of good sense and honourable principles; sometimes impetuous, and apt to take offence, but—

Mar. Impetuous—oh, most impetuous!—a match for his uncle, but far from having his uncle's excellent feelings.

Val. He is esteemed, beloved by every one. His father was perfectly satisfied with him.

Mar. Ah, sir, since his marriage he is no longer the same man.

Val. Can it be that Madame Dalancourt—

Mar. Yes, she, they say, is the cause of this great change. Signor Geronte is deeply offended with his nephew for his foolish compliance with the whims of his wife, and—I know nothing, but I would lay a wager that this plan of the convent is of her contrivance.

Ang. [*To* Martuccia.] You surprise me. My sister-in-law, whom I looked on as so discreet, who showed me so much friendship! I never could have thought it.

Val. I know her, and cannot believe it.

Mar. Surely you are not serious? Does any lady dress more elegantly? Is there any new fashion that she does not immediately adopt? At balls and plays, is she not always the first?

Val. But her husband is ever at her side.

Ang. Yes, my brother never leaves her.

Mar. Well, they are both fools, and both will be ruined together.

Val. It is impossible.

Mar. Very well, very well. I have told you what you wanted to know. Now go at once, and do not expose my mistress to the danger of losing her uncle's favour. He alone can be of any service to her.

Val. Keep calm, Angelica. No question of interest shall ever form an obstacle.

Mar. I hear a noise. Go at once. [*Exit* Valerio.

Ang. How miserable I am!

Mar. There's your uncle coming. Did I not tell you so?

Ang. I am going.

Mar. No, remain here, and open your heart to him.

Ang. I would as soon put my hand in the fire.

Mar. Come, come; he is sometimes a little hasty, but he has not a bad heart.

Ang. You direct his household, you have influence with him; speak to him for me.

Mar. No, you must speak to him yourself; all I can do is to hint at the matter, and dispose him to listen to you.

Ang. Yes, yes, say something to him, and I will speak to him afterwards. [*Going.*]

Mar. Remain here.

Ang. No, no; when it is time, call me. I shall not be far off. [*Exit* Angelica.

Martuccia, *alone.*

Mar. How gentle she is—how amiable. I have been with her from her babyhood. I love her; I am distressed for her, and wish to see her happy. Here he is.

Enter Geronte.

Ger. [*To* Martuccia.] Where's Piccardo?

Mar. Signor—

Ger. Call Piccardo!

Mar. Yes, sir. But may I say one word to you?

Ger. [*Very impatiently.*] Piccardo, Piccardo!

Mar. [*In the same tone.*] Piccardo, Piccardo!

Enter Piccardo.

Pic. Here, sir; here, sir.

Mar. [*To* Piccardo *angrily.*] Your master—

Pic. [*To* Geronte.] Here I am, sir.

Ger. Go to my friend Dorval, and tell him I am waiting to play a game of chess with him.

Pic. Yes, sir, but—

Ger. But what?

Pic. I have a commission—

Ger. To do what?

Pic. From your nephew.

Ger. [*In a passion.*] Go to Dorval's.

Pic. He wishes to speak to you.

Ger. Begone, sir!

Pic. What a man! [*Exit.*

Ger. A madman—a miserable creature! No, I will not see him; I will not permit him to come and disturb my tranquillity. [*Goes to the table.*]

Mar. [*Aside.*] There, he is in a rage at once. Most unfortunate for me.

Ger. [*Sitting down.*] What a move that was I made yesterday! what a fatality! How in the world could I be checkmated with a game so well arranged? Let me see; this game kept me awake the whole night. [*Looking over the game.*]

Mar. May I speak to you, sir?

Ger. No.

Mar. No! But I have something important to say to you.

Ger. Well, what have you to say? let me hear it.

Mar. Your niece wishes to speak to you.

Ger. I have no time now.

Mar. Really! Is what you are about, then, of such very great importance?

Ger. Yes, of the utmost importance; I don't often amuse myself, and then I do not choose to be plagued to death. Do you hear?

Mar. This poor girl—

Ger. What has happened to her?

Mar. They want to shut her up in a convent.

Ger. In a convent!—To shut my niece in a convent!

to dispose of my niece without my approbation, without my knowing anything about it!

Mar. You know your nephew's embarrassments.

Ger. I have nothing to do with my nephew's embarrassments, nor his wife's follies. He has his own property; if he squanders it, if he ruins himself, so much the worse for him. But as for my niece, I am the head of the family, I am the master; it is for me to provide for her.

Mar. So much the better for her, sir, so much the better. I am glad to see you get so warm in the dear girl's behalf.

Ger. Where is she?

Mar. She is near, sir. Wait a moment—

Ger. Let her come in.

Mar. Yes, she most earnestly desires to do so, but—

Ger. But what?

Mar. She is timid.

Ger. Well, what then?

Mar. If you speak to her—

Ger. I must speak to her.

Mar. Yes, but in this tone of voice—

Ger. The tone of my voice hurts nobody; let her come and rely on my heart, not on my tone of voice.

Mar. That is true, sir. I know you; you are good, humane, charitable; but I entreat you, do not frighten the poor girl; speak to her with a little gentleness.

Ger. Yes, I will speak to her with gentleness.

Mar. You promise me?

Ger. I promise you.

Mar. Do not forget it.

Ger. [*Beginning to be impatient.*] No.

Mar. Above all, do not get impatient.

Ger. [*Impatiently.*] I tell you, no.

Mar. I tremble for Angelica. [*Exit.*

Geronte, *alone.*

Ger. She is right; I sometimes suffer myself to be carried away by my irritable temper. My niece deserves to be treated with tenderness.

Enter Angelica.—*She remains at a distance.*

Ger. Come near.

Ang. Sir? [*Timidly advancing one step.*]

Ger. [*Warmly.*] How can you expect me to hear you when you are three miles off?

Ang. Excuse me, sir. [*She approaches him, trembling.*]

Ger. What have you to say to me?

Ang. Has not Martuccia told you something?

Ger. [*At first gently, then by degrees he gets excited.*] Yes, she has spoken to me of you, of that insensate brother of yours, that extravagant fellow, who suffers himself to be led by the nose by his silly wife, who is ruined, utterly lost, and has no longer any respect for me. [*Angelica moves as though to go away.*] Where are you going? [*Very impetuously.*]

Ang. You are angry, sir.

Ger. Well, what is that to you? If I get angry at a blockhead, I am not angry with you. Come near; speak; you must not be afraid of my anger.

Ang. My dear uncle, I can't speak to you unless I see you calm.

Ger. What martyrdom! Well, I am calm. Speak. [*Trying to compose himself.*]

Ang. Martuccia, sir, has told you—

Ger. I don't mind what Martuccia says. I want to hear it from yourself.

Ang. My brother—

Ger. Your brother—

Ang. Wishes to shut me up in a convent.

Ger. Well, do you wish to go into a convent?

Ang. But, sir—

Ger. [*With warmth.*] Well! Speak.

Ang. It is not for me to decide.

Ger. [*With a little more warmth.*] I do not say it is for you to decide, but I want to know your inclination.

Ang. You make me tremble, sir.

Ger. [*Aside, restraining himself.*] I shall burst with rage.—Come near. I understand, then, a convent is not to your liking?

Ang. No, sir.

Ger. For what have you an inclination?

Ang. Sir—

Ger. Do not be afraid. I am calm. Speak freely.

Ang. Ah! I have not the courage.

Ger. Come here. Do you wish to be married?

Ang. Sir—

Ger. Yes or no?

Ang. If you desire—

Ger. Yes or no?

Ang. Well, yes—

Ger. Yes! you wish to be married! to lose your liberty, your tranquillity! Very well; so much the worse for you. Yes, I will marry you.

Ang. [*Aside.*] How good he is for all his hasty temper!

Ger. Have you an inclination for any one in particular?

Ang. [*Aside.*] Now, if I had the courage to speak to him of Valerio!

Ger. Well, have you any lover?

Ang. [*Aside.*] This is not the opportune moment. I will get Martuccia to speak to him.

Ger. Come, come, let us end the matter. The house in which you live, the persons you see, may perhaps have led you to form an attachment. I wish to know the truth. Yes, I will do something handsome for you, but on the condition that you deserve it. Do you understand? [*With great warmth.*]

Ang. [*Trembling.*] Yes, sir.

Ger. Speak openly, frankly. Have you any attachment? [*In the same tone.*]

Ang. [*Hesitating and trembling.*] But—no, sir.—No, sir, I have none.

Ger. So much the better. I will find a husband for you.

Ang. Oh, God! I should not like, sir—

Ger. What is it?

Ang. You know my timidity.

Ger. Yes, yes, your timidity. I know womankind; now you are a dove, but get married, and you will be a hawk.

Ang. Ah, my uncle! since you are so good—

Ger. Yes, too good.

Ang. Let me tell you—

Ger. Dorval not come yet! [*Going to the table.*]

Ang. Hear me, my dear uncle.

Ger. Don't disturb me now. [*Intent on the chessboard.*]

Ang. One single word—

Ger. [*Impatiently.*] Enough has been said.

Ang. [*Aside.*] Oh, Heaven! I am more unhappy than ever. Ah, my dear Martuccia will not abandon me!

[*Exit.*

Geronte, *alone.*

Ger. She is a good girl; I would willingly do all I can for her. If she had any attachment, I would endeavour to please her, but she has none. I will see, I will look about. But what in the world detains Dorval? Is he never coming? I long to try that

cursed combination again that made me lose the last
game. Certainly, I ought to have won it—he did not
beat me, I beat myself. I must have lost my senses.
Let us see a little. My pieces were placed so, and
Dorval's so. I moved the king to his castle's square;
Dorval placed his bishop on his king's second square. I
—check—yes, I take the pawn—Dorval—he takes my
bishop,—Dorval—yes, he takes my bishop, and I—give
check with my knight. By Jove! Dorval loses his
queen. He plays his king, and I take his queen. Yes,
the fellow, with his king, has taken my knight. But
so much the worse for him. Now he is in my nets;
his king is fast. Here is my queen; Yes, here she is.
Checkmate. It is clear. Checkmate, and the game
is won. Ah! if Dorval would come, he should see it.
—[*Calls.*] Piccardo!

Enter Dalancourt.

Dal. [*Apart, and in much confusion.*] My uncle is
alone; if he will listen to me!

Ger. I will place the pieces as they were at first.
[*Not seeing* Dalancourt, *he calls loudly.*] Piccardo!

Dal. Sir—

Ger. [*Without turning, and supposing he is speaking to*
Piccardo.] Well, have you found Dorval?

Enter Dorval.

Dor. Here I am, my friend.

Dal. [*With resolution.*] My uncle.

Ger. [*Turning, sees* Dalancourt, *rises quickly, throws
down the chair, and goes out without speaking.*]

SCENE II.—Dalancourt *and* Dorval.

Dor. [*Laughing.*] What is the meaning of this scene?
Dal. It is dreadful! All this because he has seen me.

Dor. [*In the same manner.*] Geronte is my friend. I know his disposition perfectly.

Dal. I am sorry on your account.

Dor. Indeed, I came at an unlucky time.

Dal. Excuse his violence.

Dor. [*Smiling.*] Oh, I'll scold him; I'll scold him.

Dal. Ah, my friend, you are the only person who can do anything for me with him.

Dor. I will do what I can, with all my heart, but—

Dal. I agree that, from appearances, my uncle has reason to be offended with me; but if he could read the bottom of my heart, all his affection for me would return, and he would never repent it.

Dor. Yes, I know your character, and I believe everything might be hoped from you; but your wife—

Dal. My wife, sir! Ah, you do not know her. All the world is mistaken about her, and my uncle especially. I must do her justice, and let the truth be known. She knows nothing of the embarrassments by which I am overwhelmed. She thought me richer than I was, and I have always concealed my affairs from her. I love her. We were married very young. I have never permitted her to ask for anything—to want anything. I have always endeavoured to anticipate her wishes, and to provide for her pleasures. In this way I have ruined myself. [*Earnestly.*]

Dor. To please a lady—to anticipate her desires! That is no easy task.

Dal. I am certain, had she known my situation, she would have been the first to forbid the expenses I have indulged in to please her.

Dor. Yet she did not forbid them.

Dal. No, because she had no fear—

Dor. My poor friend!

Dal. [*Afflicted.*] Indeed I am poor.

Dor. [*Still smiling.*] I pity you.

Dal. [*With warmth.*] You are making a jest of me.

Dor. [*Still laughing.*] By no means; but—you love your wife prodigiously?

Dal. Yes, I love her; I have always loved her, and shall love her as long as I live; I know her, know all her worth, and will not suffer any one to accuse her of faults which she has not.

Dor. [*Seriously.*] Gently, my friend, gently; you have a little too much of the family hastiness.

Dal. [*With much warmth.*] Pardon me, I would not for the world offend you; but when my wife is spoken of—

Dor. Well, well, let us speak of her no more.

Dal. But I wish you to be convinced.

Dor. [*Coldly.*] Yes, I am convinced.

Dal. [*With much earnestness.*] No, you are not.

Dor. [*A little excited.*] Excuse me, I tell you I am.

Dal. Very well, I believe you, and am delighted that you are. Now, my dear friend, speak to my uncle on my behalf.

Dor. Most willingly will I do so.

Dal. How much obliged to you I shall be!

Dor. But we must be able to give him some reasons. How have you managed to ruin yourself in so short a time? It is only four years since your father died, leaving you a handsome fortune, and it is said you have spent it all.

Dal. If you knew all the misfortunes that have happened to me! Seeing my affairs were in disorder, I wished to remedy them, and the remedy was worse than the disease: I listened to new schemes, engaged in new speculations, pledged my property, and have lost everything.

Dor. Here lies the error—new projects; the ruin of many another man.

Dal. And my condition is utterly hopeless.

Dor. You have been very wrong, my friend, especially as you have a sister.

Dal. Yes; and it is now time to think of providing for her.

Dor. Every day she grows more beautiful. Madame Dalancourt receives much company in her house, and youth, my dear friend, sometimes—you understand me?

Dal. Regarding this point, I have on reflection found an expedient; I think of placing her in a convent.

Dor. Place her in a convent! A good plan; but have you consulted your uncle?

Dal. No; he will not hear me; but you must speak to him for me and for Angelica. My uncle esteems and loves you, listens to you, confides in you, and will refuse you nothing.

Dor. I have great doubts of this.

Dal. I am sure of it. Pray try to see him, and speak to him at once.

Dor. I will do so; but where is he gone?

Dal. I will find out.—Let us see—Is any one there?
[*Calls.*

Enter Piccardo.

Pic. [*To Dalancourt.*] Here, sir.

Dal. Is my uncle gone from home?

Pic. No, sir; he went into the garden.

Dal. Into the garden! at this time of day?

Pic. For him it is all the same. When he is a little

out of temper, he walks about and goes out to take the air.

Dor. I will go and join him.

Dal. I know my uncle, sir; you must give him time to get calm. It is better to wait for him here.

Dor. But if he goes out, he may not return here again.

Pic. [*To* Dorval.] Pardon me, sir, it will not be long before he is here: I know his temper, a few minutes will be sufficient. I can assure you he will be much pleased to see you.

Dal. Well, my dear friend, go into his room. Do me the favour to wait for him there.

Dor. Willingly; I understand perfectly how cruel your situation is. Some remedy must be provided; yes, I will speak to him, but on condition—

Dal. [*With warmth.*] I give you my word of honour.

Dor. It is sufficient.

[*Exit into* Geronte's *room.*

Dal. You did not tell my uncle what I told you to tell him?

Pic. Pardon me, sir, I have told him, but he drove me away, according to his custom.

Dal. I am sorry for it; let me know when the moment is favourable for me to speak to him. Some day I will reward you for your services.

Pic. I am much obliged to you, sir; but, thank Heaven, I am in want of nothing.

Dal. You are rich, then?

Pic. I am not rich, but I have a master who will not let me want for anything. I have a wife and four children, and ought to be in the greatest straits of any man in the world; but my master is so good, that I support them without difficulty, and distress is unknown in my house. [*Exit.*

Dalancourt, *alone.*

Dal. Ah, my uncle is an excellent man. If Dorval can have any influence over him—If I can hope to receive assistance equal to my wants—If I can keep it concealed from my wife—Ah, why have I deceived her? Why have I deceived myself? My uncle does not return. Every minute is precious for me. In the meantime, I will go to my lawyer's. Oh, with what pain I go to him! It is true, he flatters me that, notwithstanding the decree, he will find means to gain time; but quibbles are so odious, my feelings suffer, and my honour is affected. Wretched are they who are forced to resort to expedients so discreditable.

Enter Madame Dalancourt.

Dal. Here comes my wife. [*Seeing her.*]

Mad. Ah, my husband! are you here? I have been looking everywhere for you.

Dal. I was going out.

Mad. I met that savage just now; he is scolding and scolding wherever he goes.

Dal. Do you mean my uncle?

Mad. Yes. Seeing a ray of sunshine, I went to walk in the garden, and there I met him. He was stamping his feet, talking to himself, but in a loud voice. Tell me, has he any married servants in his house?

Dal. Yes.

Mad. It must have been this. He said a great many bad things of the husband and wife; very bad, I assure you.

Dal. [*Aside.*] I can easily imagine of whom he spoke.

Mad. He is really insupportable.

Dal. You must treat him with respect.

Mad. Can he complain of me? I have failed in nothing; I respect his age, and his quality as your uncle. If I laugh at him sometimes when we are alone, you pardon it. Except this, I have for him all possible respect. But tell me sincerely, has he any for you or for me? He treats us with the greatest asperity; he hates us as much as he can, and now his contempt for me has become excessive: yet I must caress him and pay court to him.

Dal. [*Embarrassed.*] But—when it is so easy to do so—he is our uncle. Besides, we may have need of him.

Mad. Need of him! we! how? Have we not means of our own to live in decency? You are not extravagant; I am reasonable. For myself, I desire no more than for you to provide for me as you have done. Let us continue to live with the same moderation, and we shall be independent of every one.

Dal. [*In a passionate manner.*] Let us continue to live with the same moderation!

Mad. Yes, indeed; I have no vanity. I ask nothing more of you.

Dal. [*Aside.*] How unhappy I am!

Mad. But you seem to me to be disturbed—thoughtful. What is the matter? you are not easy.

Dal. You are mistaken, there is nothing the matter.

Mad. Pardon me, I know you. If you have any sorrow, why hide it from me?

Dal. [*More embarrassed.*] I am thinking of my sister. I will tell you the whole.

Mad. Your sister! But why of her? She's the best girl in the world—I love her dearly. Hear me. If you will trust her to me, I will relieve you of this burden, and at the same time make her happy.

Dal. How?

Mad. You think of placing her in a convent, and

I know, on good authority, it will be against her wishes.

Dal. [*A little warmly.*] At her age, ought she to be asked what she wishes or does not wish?

Mad. No; she has understanding enough to submit to the will of her friends; but why not marry her?

Dal. She is too young.

Mad. Good! was I older than she when we were married?

Dal. [*Excitedly.*]. Well, must I go about from door to door looking for a man to wed her?

Mad. Listen to me, my husband, and do not disturb yourself, I pray. If I guess aright, I am sure Valerio loves her, and that she too is attached to him.

Dal. [*Aside.*] Heavens, how much I have to suffer!

Mad. You know him. Can there be a better match for Angelica?

Dal. [*Much embarrassed.*] We will see—we will talk of it.

Mad. Do me the favour to leave the management of this affair to me; I have a great desire to succeed in it.

Dal. [*In the greatest embarrassment.*] Madame?

Mad. What say you?

Dal. It cannot be.

Mad. No! why not?

Dal. Will my uncle consent to it?

Mad. And if he does not? I do not wish that we should be wanting in our duty to him, but you are the brother of Angelica. Her fortune is in your hands— whether it is more or less depends on you alone. Let me assure myself of their inclination, and on the subject of interest, I would soon arrange that.

Dal. [*Anxiously.*] No; if you love me, do not meddle with it.

Mad. Are you then averse to marrying your sister?

Dal. On the contrary.

Mad. What then?

Dal. I must go now. I will talk with you about it on my return. [*Going.*]

Mad. Are you displeased at my interference?

Dal. Not at all.

Mad. Hear me. Perhaps it is concerning her fortune?

Dal. I know nothing about it. [*Exit.*

Mad. What does this conduct mean? I do not comprehend it. It is impossible that my husband— No, he is too wise to have anything to reproach himself with.

Scene III.—*Enter* Angelica.

Ang. If I could speak with Martuccia! [*Not seeing* Madame D.]

Mad. Sister!

Ang. [*Uneasily.*] Madame!

Mad. Where are you going, sister?

Ang. [*Uneasily.*] I am going away, Madame.

Mad. Ah! then you are offended?

Ang. I have reason to be so.

Mad. Are you angry with me?

Ang. Why, Madame?

Mad. Hear me, my child; if you are disturbed about the affair of the convent, do not think I have any hand in it. It is just the reverse; I love you, and will do all I can to render you happy.

Ang. [*Aside, weeping.*] What duplicity!

Mad. What's the matter? you are weeping.

Ang. [*Aside.*] How much she has deceived me! [*Wipes her eyes.*]

Mad. What cause have you for sorrow?

Ang. Oh, the embarrassments of my brother.

Mad. The embarrassments of your brother!

THE BENEFICENT BEAR.

Ang. Yes; no one knows them better than you.

Mad. What do you say? Explain yourself, if you please.

Ang. It is needless.

Enter Geronte, *and then* Piccardo.

Ger. [*Calls.*] Piccardo!

Pic. Here, sir. [*Coming out of* Geronte's *apartment.*]

Ger. [*With impatience.*] Well, where is Dorval?

Pic. He is waiting for you, sir, in your room.

Ger. He in my room, and you said nothing about it?

Pic. You did not give me time, sir.

Ger. [*Seeing* Angelica *and* Madame D., *he speaks to* Angelica, *turning as he speaks towards* Madame D., *that she may hear him.*] What are you doing here? I wish to have none of your family. Go away.

Ang. My dear uncle—

Ger. I tell you, go. [*Exit* Angelica, *mortified.*

Mad. I ask your pardon, sir.

Ger. [*Turning towards the door by which* Angelica *has gone out, but from time to time looking at* Madame D.] This is strange. This is impertinent. She wants to annoy me. There is another staircase for going down into the other apartment. I will shut up this door.

Mad. Do not be offended, sir; as to myself, I assure you—

Ger. [*He wants to go into his room, but not to pass* Madame D., *and says to* Piccardo.] Tell me, is Dorval in my room?

Pic. Yes, sir.

Mad. [*Perceiving the embarrassment of* Geronte, *steps back.*] Pass on, sir; I will not be in your way.

Ger. [*Passing, salutes her.*] My lady—I will shut up the door. [*Goes into his room, and* Piccardo *follows him.*]

Mad. What a strange character! but it is not this

that disturbs me. What distresses me is the anxious manner of my husband, and Angelica's words. I doubt; I fear; I wish to know the truth, and dread to discover it.

END OF THE FIRST ACT.

ACT II.

Scene I.—Geronte *and* Dorval.

Ger. Let us go on with our game, and talk no more of it.

Dor. But it concerns your nephew.

Ger. A blockhead! A helpless creature, who is the slave of his wife, and the victim of his vanity.

Dor. More gentleness, my friend, more gentleness.

Ger. And you, with your calmness, you will drive me mad.

Dor. What I say is right.

Ger. Take a chair. [*Sits down.*]

Dor. [*In a compassionate tone, while he is going to the chair.*] Poor young man!

Ger. Let us see the game of yesterday.

Dor. [*In the same tone.*] You will lose—

Ger. Perhaps not; let us see—

Dor. I say you will lose—

Ger. No, I am sure not.

Dor. Unless you assist him, you will certainly lose him.

Ger. Lose whom?

Dor. Your nephew.

Ger. [*With impatience.*] Eh! I was speaking of the game. Sit down.

Dor. I will play willingly, but first listen to me —
Ger. You are always talking to me of Dalancourt.
Dor. Well, if it be so?
Ger. I will not listen to you.
Dor. Then you hate him—
Ger. No, sir, I hate nobody.
Dor. But if you do not wish—
Ger. No more—play. Let us go on with the game, or I shall go away.
Dor. One single word, and I have done.
Ger. Very well.
Dor. You have some property?
Ger. Yes, thank Heaven!
Dor. More than you want?
Ger. Yes, some over with which I can serve my friends.
Dor. And you will give nothing to your nephew?
Ger. Not a farthing.
Dor. It follows—
Ger. It follows?
Dor. That you hate him.
Ger. It follows that you do not know what you say. I hate, I detest his manner of thinking, his abominable conduct; to give him money would be only to nourish his vanity, his prodigality, his folly. Let him change his system, and I will change when he does. I wish repentance to deserve favours, not favours to prevent repentance.
Dor. [*After a moment's silence, he seems convinced, and says, with much gentleness*] Let us play.
Ger. Let us play.
Dor. I am distressed at it.
Ger. Check to the king. } [*Playing.*]
Dor. And this poor girl!
Ger. Who?

Dor. Angelica.

Ger. [*Leaving the game.*] Ah, as to her, it is another affair. Speak to me of her.

Dor. She must suffer, too.

Ger. I have thought of it, and have foreseen it. I shall marry her.

Dor. Excellent! she deserves it.

Ger. Is she not a most engaging young lady?

Dor. Yes, truly.

Ger. Happy is the man who shall possess her. [*Reflects a moment, and then calls*] Dorval!

Dor. My friend?

Ger. Hear me.

Dor. [*Rising.*] What would you say?

Ger. If you wish her, I will give her to you.

Dor. Who?

Ger. My niece.

Dor. What?

Ger. What! what! are you deaf? Do you not understand me? [*Animated.*] I speak clearly—if you wish to have her, I give her to you.

Dor. Ah! ah!

Ger. And if you marry her, besides her fortune, I will give her of my own a hundred thousand francs. Eh! what say you to it?

Dor. My friend, you do me much honour.

Ger. I know who you are; I am certain by this step to secure the happiness of my niece.

Dor. But—

Ger. But what?

Dor. Her brother?

Ger. Her brother! Her brother has nothing to do with it; it is for me to dispose of her; the law, the will of my brother—I am master here. Come, make haste, decide upon the spot.

Dor. Your proposal is not to be decided on in a moment. You are too impetuous.

Ger. I see no obstacle; if you love her, if you esteem her, if she suits you, it is all done.

Dor. But—

Ger. But—but—Let us hear your but.

Dor. Does the disproportion between sixteen and forty-five years appear to you a trifle?

Ger. Nothing at all. You are still a young man; and I know Angelica, she has no foolish notions.

Dor. She may have a liking for some other person?

Ger. She has none.

Dor. Are you sure of it?

Ger. Most certain; quick—let us conclude it. I will go to my notary's; he shall draw up the contract: she is yours.

Dor. Softly, my friend, softly.

Ger. [*With heat.*] What now? Do you wish still to vex me—to annoy me with your slowness—with your cold blood?

Dor. Then you wish—

Ger. Yes, to give you a sensible, honest, virtuous girl, with a hundred thousand crowns for her fortune, and a hundred thousand livres at her marriage. Perhaps I affront you?

Dor. By no means; you do me an honour I do not deserve.

Ger. [*With warmth.*] Your modesty on this occasion is most inopportune.

Dor. Do not get angry; do you wish me to take her?

Ger. Yes.

Dor. Then I take her—

Ger. [*With joy.*] Indeed!

Dor. But on condition—

Ger. Of what?

Dor. That Angelica consents to it.

Ger. Do you make no other obstacle?

Dor. No other.

Ger. I am delighted. I answer for her.

Dor. So much the better if you are sure.

Ger. Most sure—most certain. Embrace me, **my** dear nephew.

Dor. Let us embrace, my dear uncle.

    [Dalancourt *enters by the middle door; sees his uncle; listens as he passes; goes towards his own apartment, but stops at his own door to listen.*]

Ger. This is the happiest day of my life.

Dor. My dear friend, how very kind you are!

Ger. I am going to the notary's. This very day it shall all be concluded. [*Calls.*] Piccardo!

Enter Piccardo.

Ger. My cane and hat.   [*Exit* Piccardo.

Dor. I will now go home.

    [Piccardo *returns, and gives his master his cane and hat, and withdraws.* Dalancourt *is still at his door.*]

Ger. No, no, you must wait here for me; I will soon return. You must dine with me.

Dor. I have to write; I must send for my agent, who is a league from Paris.

Ger. Go into my room and write; send your letter by Piccardo. Yes, Piccardo will carry it himself; Piccardo is an excellent young man—sensible—faithful. Sometimes I scold him, but I am very fond of him.

Dor. Well, since you are determined, it shall be so; I will write in your room.

Ger. Now it is all concluded.

Dor. Yes, we agree.

Ger. [*Taking his hand.*] Your word of honour?
Dor. [*Giving his hand.*] My word of honour.
Ger. My dear nephew!
[*Exit at the last words, showing joy.*]

Scene II.—Dalancourt *and* Dorval.

Dor. In truth, all this seems to me a dream. I marry!—I, who have never thought of such a thing!

Dal. Ah, my dear friend, I know not how to express my gratitude to you.

Dor. For what?

Dal. Did I not hear what my uncle said? He loves me, he feels for me; he has gone to his notary; he has given you his word of honour. I see plainly what you have done for me; I am the most fortunate man in the world.

Dor. Do not flatter yourself so much, my dear friend, for the good fortune you imagine has not the least foundation in truth.

Dal. How then?

Dor. I hope, in time, to be able to do you a service with him; and hereafter I may have some title to interest myself in your behalf; but till then—

Dal. [*With warmth.*] For what, then, did he give you his word of honour?

Dor. I will tell you at once; he did me the honour to propose your sister to me as a wife.

Dal. [*With joy.*] My sister! Do you accept?

Dor. Yes, if you approve it.

Dal. You overwhelm me with joy; you surprise me. As regards her fortune, you know my situation.

Dor. About that we will say nothing.

Dal. My dear brother, let me, with all my heart, embrace you.

Dor. I flatter myself that your uncle on this occasion —

Dal. Here is a connection to which I shall owe my happiness. I am in great need of it. I have been to my lawyer's, and did not find him.

Enter Madame Dalancourt.

Dal. [*Seeing his wife.*] Ah, Madame!

Mad. [*To* Dalancourt.] I have been waiting for you with impatience. I heard your voice.

Dal. My wife, here is Signor Dorval; I present him to you as my brother-in-law, as the husband of Angelica.

Mad. [*With joy.*] Indeed!

Dor. I shall be highly pleased, Madame, if my happiness meets with your approbation.

Mad. I am rejoiced at it, sir; I congratulate you with all my heart. [*Aside.*] What did he mean by speaking of the embarrassments of my husband?

Dal. [*To* Dorval.] Is my sister informed of it?

Dor. I think not.

Mad. [*Aside.*] Then it was not Dalancourt who made the match.

Dal. Do you wish me to bring her here?

Dor. No, do not bring her; there may still be a difficulty.

Dal. What is it?

Dor. Her consent.

Dal. Fear nothing; I know Angelica, and your circumstances and merit. Leave it to me; I will speak to my sister.

Dor. No, my dear friend, do not, I beg you, do not let us spoil the affair; leave it to Signor Geronte.

Dal. As you please.

Mad. [*Aside.*] I comprehend nothing of all this.

Dor. I am going into your uncle's room to write; he

has given me permission, and he has told me expressly to wait for him there, so excuse me; we shall soon see each other again. [*Exit into* Geronte's *apartment.*

Scene III.—Dalancourt *and* Madame Dalancourt.

Mad. From what I hear, it appears you are not the person who marries your sister?

Dal. [*Embarrassed.*] My uncle marries her.

Mad. Has your uncle mentioned it to you? Has he asked your consent?

Dal. [*With a little warmth.*] My consent! Did you not see Dorval? Did he not tell me of it? Do you not call this asking my consent?

Mad. [*A little warmly.*] Yes. It is an act of civility on the part of Dorval, but your uncle has said nothing to you.

Dal. [*Embarrassed.*] What do you mean by that?

Mad. I mean, he thinks us of no account.

Dal. [*Warmly.*] You take the worst view of everything. This is terrible! You are insupportable.

Mad. [*Mortified.*] I insupportable! you find me insupportable! [*With much tenderness.*] Ah, my husband! this is the first time such an expression has ever escaped from your lips. You must be in a state of great uneasiness so to forget your affection for me.

Dal. [*Aside.*] Ah! too true.—My dear wife, I ask your pardon with all my heart. But you know my uncle; do you desire to offend him still more? Do you wish me to hinder my sister? The match is a good one; nothing can be said against it. My uncle has chosen it; so much the better. Here is one embarrassment the less for you and me. [*With joy.*]

Mad. Come, come, I am glad you take it in good part; I praise and admire your conduct. But permit me to make one suggestion: Who is to attend to the necessary preparations for a young lady going to be married? Is your uncle to have this trouble? Will it be proper? will it be correct?

Dal. You are right; but there is time, we will talk of it.

Mad. Hear me: you know I love Angelica. The ungrateful girl does not deserve I should care for her; but she is your sister.

Dal. How! you call my sister ungrateful! Why so?

Mad. Do not let us speak of it now; some other time, when we are alone, I will explain to you. And then—

Dal. No; I wish to hear it now.

Mad. Have patience, my dear husband.

Dal. No, I tell you; I wish to know at once.

Mad. Well, as you wish it, I must satisfy you.

Dal. [*Aside.*] How I tremble!

Mad. Your sister—

Dal. Proceed.

Mad. I believe she is too much on your uncle's side.

Dal. Why?

Mad. She told me—yes, me—that your affairs were embarrassed, and that—

Dal. That my affairs were embarrassed;—and do you believe it?

Mad. No. But she spoke to me in such a manner as to make me think she suspected I was the cause of it, or at least, that I had contributed to it.

Dal. [*A little excitedly.*] You! she suspects you!

Mad. Do not be angry, my dear husband. I know very well her want of judgment.

Dal. [*With feeling.*] My dear wife!

Mad. Do not be distressed. Believe me, I shall think no more of it. It all arises from him; your uncle is the cause of it all.

Dal. Oh no! my uncle has not a bad heart.

Mad. He not a bad heart? Heavens! the worst in the world! Has he not shown it to me?—But I forgive him.

Enter a Servant.

Ser. Here is a letter for you, sir.

Dal. Give it to me. [*He takes the letter. Exit Servant.*] Let us see it. [*Agitated.*] This is the hand of my lawyer. [*Opens the letter.*]

Mad. What does he write?

Dal. Excuse me for a moment. [*He retires apart, reads, and shows displeasure.*]

Mad. [*Aside.*] There must be some bad news.

Dal. [*Aside, after reading the letter.*] I am ruined!

Mad. [*Aside.*] My heart beats!

Dal. [*Aside.*] My poor wife! what will become of her? How can I tell her?—I have not the courage.

Mad. [*Weeping.*] My dear Dalancourt, tell me, what is it? Trust your wife: am I not the best friend you have?

Dal. Take it and read: this is my situation. [*Gives her the letter.*] [*Exit.*

Madame Dalancourt, *alone.*

Mad. I tremble.—[*Reads.*] "*Sir, all is lost; the creditors will not subscribe. The decree was confirmed. I inform you of it as soon as possible; be on your guard, for your arrest is ordered.*"—What do I read! what do I read! My husband in debt, in danger of losing his liberty! Can it be possible? He does not gamble, he has no bad habits; he is not addicted to unusual luxury. —By his own fault—may it not then be my fault? Oh, God! what a dreadful ray of light breaks in upon me! The reproofs of Angelica, the hatred of Signor

Geronte, the contempt he shows for me, day after day! The bandage is torn from my eyes: I see the errors of my husband, I see my own. Too much love has been his fault, my inexperience has made me blind. Dalancourt is culpable, and I perhaps am equally so. What remedy is there in this cruel situation? His uncle only—yes—his uncle can help him;—but Dalancourt—he must be now in a state of humiliation and distress—and if I am the cause of it, though involuntarily, why do I not go myself? Yes—I ought to throw myself at Geronte's feet—but, with his severe, unyielding temper, can I flatter myself I shall make any impression on him? Shall I go and expose myself to his rudeness? Ah! what matters it? Ah! what is my mortification compared to the horrible condition of my husband? Yes, I will run! This thought alone ought to give me courage. [*She goes towards* Geronte's *apartment.*]

Enter Martuccia.

Mar. Madame, what are you doing here? Signor Dalancourt is in despair.

Mad. Heavens! I fly to his assistance. [*Exit.*

Mar. What misfortunes!—what confusion! If it be true she is the cause of it, she well deserves— Who comes here?

Enter Valerio.

Mar. Why, sir, do you come here now? You have chosen an unfortunate time. All the family is overwhelmed with sorrow.

Val. I do not doubt it. I just come from Signor Dalancourt's lawyer. I have offered him my purse and my credit.

Mar. This is a praiseworthy action. Nothing can be more generous than your conduct.

Val. Is Signor Geronte at home?

Mar. No; the servant told me he saw him with his notary.

Val. With his notary?

Mar. Yes; he is always occupied with some business. But do you wish to speak with him?

Val. Yes, I wish to speak with them all. I see with sorrow the confusion of Dalancourt's affairs. I am alone. I have property, and can dispose of it. I love Angelica, and am come to offer to marry her without a portion, and to share with her my lot and my fortune.

Mar. This resolution is worthy of you. No one could show more esteem, more love, and more generosity.

Val. Do you think I may flatter myself?—

Mar. Yes, and especially as she enjoys the favour of her uncle, and he desires to marry her.

Val. [*With joy.*] He desires to marry her?

Mar. Yes.

Val. But if he wishes to marry her, he also wishes to propose a match that is to his taste?

Mar. [*After a moment's silence.*] It may be so.

Val. And can this be any comfort to me?

Mar. Why not? [*To* Angelica, *who enters timidly.*] Come in, my young lady.

Ang. I am terribly frightened.

Val. [*To* Angelica.] What is the matter?

Ang. My poor brother—

Mar. Is he just the same?

Ang. Rather better. He is a little more tranquil.

Mar. Hear me. This gentleman has told me something very consoling for you and for your brother.

Ang. For him too?

Mar. If you knew what a sacrifice he is disposed to make!

Val. [*Aside to* Martuccia.] Say nothing of it. [*Turn-*

ing to Angelica.] Can any sacrifice be too great for you?

Mar. But it must be mentioned to Signor Geronte.

Val. My dear friend, if you will take the trouble.

Mar. Willingly. What shall I say to him? Let us see. Advise me. But I hear some one. [*She goes towards the apartment of* Signor Geronte.] [*To* Valerio.] It is Signor Dorval. Do not let him see you. Let us go into my room, and there we can talk at our ease.

Val. [*To* Angelica.] If you see your brother—

Mar. Come, sir, let us go—quick. [*She goes out and takes him with her.*]

Scene IV.—Angelica, *and then* Dorval.

Ang. [*Aside.*] What have I to do with Signor Dorval? I can go away.

Dor. Mademoiselle Angelica!

Ang. Sir?

Dor. Have you seen your uncle? Has he told you nothing?

Ang. I saw him this morning, sir.

Dor. Before he went out of the house?

Ang. Yes, sir.

Dor. Has he returned?

Ang. No, sir.

Dor. [*Aside.*] Good. She knows nothing of it.

Ang. Excuse me, sir. Is there anything new in which I am concerned?

Dor. Your uncle takes much interest in you.

Ang. [*With modesty.*] He is very kind.

Dor. [*Seriously.*] He thinks often of you.

Ang. It is fortunate for me.

Dor. He thinks of marrying you. [Angelica *appears*

modest.] What say you to it? Would you like to be married?

Ang. I depend on my uncle.

Dor. Shall I say anything more to you on the subject?

Ang. [*With a little curiosity.*] But — as you please, sir.

Dor. The choice of a husband is already made.

Ang. [*Aside.*] Oh, heavens! I tremble.

Dor. [*Aside.*] She seems to be pleased.

Ang. [*Trembling.*] Sir, I am curious to know—

Dor. What, Mademoiselle?

Ang. Do you know who is intended for me?

Dor. Yes, and you know him too.

Ang. [*With joy.*] I know him too?

Dor. Certainly, you know him.

Ang. May I, sir, have the boldness—

Dor. Speak, Mademoiselle.

Ang. To ask you the name of the young man?

Dor. The name of the young man?

Ang. Yes, if you know him.

Dor. Suppose he were not so young?

Ang. [*Aside, with agitation.*] Good Heavens!

Dor. You are sensible—you depend on your uncle—

Ang. [*Trembling.*] Do you think, sir, my uncle would sacrifice me?

Dor. What do you mean by sacrificing you?

Ang. Mean—without the consent of my heart. My uncle is so good—But who could have advised him—who could have proposed this match? [*With temper.*]

Dor. [*A little hurt.*] But this match—Mademoiselle—Suppose it were I?

Ang. [*With joy.*] You, sir? Heaven grant it!

Dor. [*Pleased.*] Heaven grant it?

Ang. Yes, I know you; I know you are reasonable. You are sensible; I can trust you. If you have given my uncle this advice, if you have proposed this match, I hope you will now find some means of making him change his plan.

Dor. [*Aside.*] Eh! this is not so bad.—[*To* Angelica.] Mademoiselle—

Ang. [*Distressed.*] Signor?

Dor. [*With feeling.*] Is your heart engaged?

Ang. Ah, sir—

Dor. I understand you.

Ang. Have pity on me!

Dor. [*Aside.*] I said so, I foresaw right; it is fortunate for me I am not in love—yet I began to perceive some little symptoms of it.

Ang. But you do not tell me, sir.

Dor. But, Mademoiselle—

Ang. You have perhaps some particular interest in the person they wish me to marry?

Dor. A little.

Ang. [*With temper and firmness.*] I tell you I shall hate him.

Dor. [*Aside.*] Poor girl! I am pleased with her sincerity.

Ang. Come, have compassion; be generous.

Dor. Yes, I will be so, I promise you; I will speak to your uncle in your favour, and will do all I can to make you happy.

Ang. [*With joy and transport.*] Oh, how dear a man you are! You are my benefactor, my father. [*Takes his hand.*]

Dor. My dear girl!

Enter Geronte.

Ger. [*In his hot-tempered manner, with animation.*] Excellent, excellent! Courage, my children, I am delighted with you. [Angelica *retires, mortified;* Dorval *smiles.*] How! does my presence alarm you? I do not condemn this proper show of affection. You have done well, Dorval, to inform her. Come, my niece, embrace your future husband.

Ang. [*In consternation.*] What do I hear?

Dor. [*Aside and smiling.*] Now I am unmasked.

Ger. [*To* Angelica, *with warmth.*] What scene is this? Your modesty is misplaced. When I am not present, you are near enough to each other; when I come in, you go far apart. Come here.—[*To* Dorval, *with anger.*] And do you too come here.

Dor. [*Laughing.*] Softly, my friend.

Ger. Why do you laugh? Do you feel your happiness? I am very willing you should laugh, but do not put me in a passion; do you hear, you laughing gentleman? Come here and listen to me.

Dor. But listen yourself.

Ger. [*To* Angelica, *and endeavouring to take her hand.*] Come near, both of you.

Ang. [*Weeping.*] My uncle!

Ger. Weeping! What's the matter, my child? I believe you are making a jest of me. [*Takes her hand, and carries her by force to the middle of the stage; then turns to* Dorval, *and says to him, with an appearance of heat*] You shall escape me no more.

Dor. At least let me speak.

Ger. No, no!

Ang. My dear uncle—

Ger. [*With warmth.*] No, no. [*He changes his tone and becomes serious.*] I have been to my notary's, and have arranged everything; he has taken a note of it in my presence, and will soon bring the contract here for us to subscribe.

Dor. But will you listen to me?

Ger. No, no. As to her fortune, my brother had the

weakness to leave it in the hands of his son; this will no doubt cause some obstacle on his part, but it will not embarrass me. Every one who has transactions with him suffers. The fortune cannot be lost, and in any event I will be responsible for it.

Ang. [*Aside.*] I can bear this no longer.

Dor. [*Embarrassed.*] All proceeds well, but—

Ger. But what?

Dor. The young lady may have something to say in this matter. [*Looking at* Angelica.]

Ang. [*Hastily and trembling.*] I, sir?

Ger. I should like to know if she can say anything against what I do, what I order, and what I wish. My wishes, my orders, and what I do, are all for her good. Do you understand me?

Dor. Then I must speak myself.

Ger. What have you to say?

Dor. That I am very sorry, but this marriage cannot take place.

Ger. Not take place! [Angelica *retreats frightened;* Dorval *also steps back two paces.*] [*To* Dorval.] You have given me your word of honour.

Dor. Yes, on condition—

Ger. [*Turning to* Angelica.] It must then be this impertinent. If I could believe it! if I had any reason to suspect it! [*Threatens her.*]

Dor. [*Seriously.*] No, sir, you are mistaken.

Ger. [*To* Dorval. Angelica *seizes the opportunity and makes her escape.*] It is you, then, who refuse? So you abuse my friendship and affection for you!

Dor. [*Raising his voice.*] But hear reason—

Ger. What reason? what reason? There is no reason. I am a man of honour, and if you are so too, it shall be done at once. [*Turning round, he calls*] Angelica!

Dor. What possesses the man? He will resort to violence on the spot. [*Runs off.*]

Geronte, *alone.*

Ger. Where is she gone? Angelica! Hallo! who's there? Piccardo! Martuccia! Pietro! Cortese!— But I'll find her. It is you I want. [*Turns round, and, not seeing Dorval, remains motionless.*] What! he treat me so! [*Calls.*] Dorval! my friend! Dorval— Dorval! my friend! Oh, shameful—ungrateful! Hallo! Is no one there? Piccardo!

Enter Piccardo.

Pic. Here, sir.
Ger. You rascal! Why don't you answer?
Pic. Pardon me, sir, here I am.
Ger. Shameful! I called you ten times.
Pic. I am sorry, but—
Ger. Ten times! It is scandalous.
Pic. [*Aside, and angry.*] He is in a fury now.
Ger. Have you seen Dorval?
Pic. Yes, sir.
Ger. Where is he?
Pic. He is gone.
Ger. How is he gone?
Pic. [*Roughly.*] He is gone as other people go.
Ger. Ah, insolent! do you answer your master in this manner? [*Very much offended, he threatens him and makes him retreat.*]

Pic. [*Very angrily.*] Give me my discharge, sir.
Ger. Your discharge—worthless fellow! [*Threatens him and makes him retreat. Piccardo falls between the chair and the table. Geronte runs to his assistance and helps him up.*]

Pic. Oh! [*He leans on the chair, and shows much pain.*]

Ger. Are you hurt? Are you hurt?

Pic. Very much hurt; you have crippled me.

Ger. Oh, I am sorry! Can you walk?

Pic. [*Still angry.*] I believe so, sir. [*He tries, and walks badly.*]

Ger. [*Sharply.*] Go on.

Pic. [*Mortified.*] Do you drive me away, sir?

Ger. [*Warmly.*] No. Go to your wife's house, that you may be taken care of. [*Pulls out his purse and offers him money.*] Take this to get cured.

Pic. [*Aside, with tenderness.*] What a master!

Ger. Take it. [*Giving him money.*]

Pic. [*With modesty.*] No, sir, I hope it will be nothing.

Ger. Take it, I tell you.

Pic. [*Still refusing it.*] Sir—

Ger. [*Very warmly.*] What! you refuse my money? Do you refuse it from pride, or spite, or hatred? Do you believe I did it on purpose? Take this money. Take it. Come, don't put me in a passion.

Pic. Do not get angry, sir. I thank you for all your kindness. [*Takes the money.*]

Ger. Go quickly.

Pic. Yes, sir. [*Walks badly.*]

Ger. Go slowly.

Pic. Yes, sir.

Ger. Wait, wait; take my cane.

Pic. Sir—

Ger. Take it, I tell you! I wish you to do it.

Pic. [*Takes the cane.*] What goodness! [*Exit.*

Enter Martuccia.

Ger. It is the first time in my life that—Plague on

my temper! [*Taking long strides.*] It is Dorval who put me in a passion.

Mar. Do you wish to dine, sir?

Ger. May the devil take you! [*Runs out and shuts himself in his room.*]

Mar. Well, well! He is in a rage: I can do nothing for Angelica to-day; Valerio can go away. [*Exit.*

END OF THE SECOND ACT.

ACT III.

SCENE I.—Piccardo *and* Martuccia.

Mar. What, have you returned already?

Pic. [*With his master's cane.*] Yes, I limp a little: but I was more frightened than hurt; it was not worth the money my master gave me to get cured.

Mar. It seems misfortunes are sometimes profitable.

Pic. [*With an air of satisfaction.*] Poor master! On my honour, this instance of his goodness affected me so much, I could hardly help shedding tears; if he had broken my leg, I should have forgiven him.

Mar. What a heart he has! Pity he has so great a failing.

Pic. But what man is there without defects?

Mar. Go and look for him; you know he has not dined yet.

Pic. Why not?

Mar. My son, there are misfortunes, terrible misfortunes, in this house.

Pic. I know all; I met your nephew, he told me all: this the reason I have returned so soon. Does my master know it?

Mar. I think not.

Pic. Ah, how it will distress him!

Mar. Certainly—and poor Angelica.

Pic. But Valerio?

Mar. Valerio—Valerio is here now; he will not go away. He is still in the apartment of Signor Dalancourt: encourages the brother, takes care of the sister, consoles Madame;—one weeps, another sighs, the other is in despair; all is in confusion.

Pic. Did you not promise to speak to my master?

Mar. Yes, I should have spoken to him, but he is too angry just now.

Pic. I am going to look for him, to carry him his cane.

Mar. Go; and if you see the tempest a little calmed, tell him something concerning the unhappy state of his nephew.

Pic. Yes, I'll speak to him, and I'll let you know what passes. [*Opens the door softly, enters the room, and then shuts it.*]

Mar. Yes, dear friend, go softly.—This Piccardo is an excellent young man, amiable, polite, obliging; he is the only person in the house to my liking. I do not so easily become friends with everybody.

Enter Dorval.

Dor. [*In a low tone, and smiling.*] Ah, Martuccia!

Mar. Your servant, sir.

Dor. Is Signor Geronte still angry?

Mar. It would not be strange if the storm were over. You know him better than any one else.

Dor. He is very angry with me.

Mar. With you, sir? He angry with you!

Dor. [*Smiling.*] There is no doubt of it; but it is

nothing; I know him. I am sure as soon as we meet he will be the first to embrace me.

Mar. Nothing is more likely. He loves you, esteems you, you are his only friend. It is singular—he, a man always in a passion, and you—I say it with respect—the most tranquil man in the world.

Dor. It is exactly for this reason our friendship has continued so long.

Mar. Go and look for him.

Dor. No; it is too soon. I want first to see Angelica. Where is she?

Mar. With her brother. You know the misfortunes of her brother?

Dor. [*With an expression of sorrow.*] Ah, too well: everybody is talking of them.

Mar. And what do they say?

Dor. Don't ask me: the good pity him, the hardhearted make a jest of him, and the ungrateful abandon him.

Mar. Oh, Heaven! And the poor girl?

Dor. Must I speak of her too?

Mar. May I ask how she will fare in this confusion? I take so much interest in her, that you ought to tell me.

Dor. [*Smiling.*] I have learned that one Valerio—

Mar. Ah, ah! Valerio!

Dor. Do you know him?

Mar. Very well, sir; it is all my own work.

Dor. So much the better; will you aid me?

Mar. Most willingly.

Dor. I must go and be certain if Angelica—

Mar. And also if Valerio—

Dor. Yes, I will go to him too.

Mar. Go then into Dalancourt's apartment; you will there kill two birds with one stone.

Dor. How?

Mar. He is there.

Dor. Valerio?

Mar. Yes.

Dor. I am glad of it; I will go at once.

Mar. Stop; shall I not tell him you are coming?

Dor. Good! such ceremony with my brother-in-law!

Mar. Your brother-in-law?

Dor. Yes.

Mar. How?

Dor. Do you not know?

Mar. Nothing at all.

Dor. Then you shall know another time. [*Goes into* Dalancourt's *apartment.*]

Mar. He is out of his senses.

Enter Geronte.

Ger. [*Speaking while he is turning towards the door of his room.*] Stop there, I will send the letter by some one else; stop there, it shall be so. [*Turning to* Martuccia.] Martuccia!

Mar. Sir?

Ger. Get a servant to take this letter directly to Dorval. [*Turning towards the door of his apartment.*] He is not well, he walks lame, and yet he would take it. [*To* Martuccia.] Go.

Mar. But, sir—

Ger. Well, let us hear.

Mar. But Dorval—

Ger. [*Impatiently.*] Yes, to Dorval's house.

Mar. He is here.

Ger. Who?

Mar. Dorval.

Ger. Where?

Mar. Here.

Ger. Dorval here?

Mar. Yes, sir.

Ger. Where is he?

Mar. In Signor Dalancourt's room.

Ger. [*Angrily.*] In Dalancourt's room! Dorval in Dalancourt's room! Now I see how it is, I understand it all. Go and tell Dorval from me—but no—I do not want you to go into that cursed room; if you set your foot in it, I will discharge you. Call one of the servants of that fellow—no, I don't want any of them—go yourself—yes, yes, tell him to come directly—do you hear?

Mar. Shall I go, or not go?

Ger. Go! don't make me more impatient. [*Martuccia goes into Dalancourt's room.*]

Geronte, *alone.*

Ger. Yes, it must be so; Dorval has discovered into what a terrible abyss this wretched man has fallen; yes, he knew it before I did, and if Piccardo had not told me, I should be still in the dark. It is exactly so. Dorval fears a connection with a ruined man; that is it. But I must look further into it to be more certain. Yet why not tell me? I would have persuaded him—I would have convinced him.—But why did he not tell me? He will say, perhaps, that my violence did not give him an opportunity. This is no excuse: he should have waited, he should not have gone away; my resentment would have been over, and he might have spoken to me. Unworthy, treacherous, perfidious nephew! you have sacrificed your happiness and your honour. I love you, culpable as you are. Yes, I love you too much; but I will discard you from my heart and from my thoughts. Go hence—go and perish in some other place. But where can he go? No matter, I'll think of him no more;—your sister alone interests me; she only deserves my tenderness, my kindness. Dorval is my friend; Dorval shall marry her. I will give them all my estate—I will leave the guilty to their punishment, but will never abandon the innocent.

SCENE II.—*Enter* Dalancourt.

Dal. Ah, my uncle, hear me for pity's sake! [*He throws himself in great agitation at Geronte's feet.*]

Ger. [*Sees Dalancourt, then draws back a little.*] What do you want? Rise.

Dal. [*In the same posture.*] My dear uncle, you see the most unhappy of men; have mercy! listen to me!

Ger. [*A little moved, but still in anger.*] Rise, I say.

Dal. [*On his knees.*] You, who have a heart so generous, so feeling, will you abandon me for a fault which is the fault of love only, and an honest, virtuous love? I have certainly done wrong in not profiting by your advice, in disregarding your paternal tenderness; but, my dear uncle, in the name of your brother, to whom I owe my life, of that blood which flows in the veins of us both, let me move you—let me soften your feelings.

Ger. [*By degrees relents, wipes his eyes, yet not letting* Dalancourt *see, and says in a low tone*] What! you have still the courage?

Dal. It is not the loss of fortune that afflicts me; a sentiment more worthy of you oppresses me—my honour. Can you bear the disgrace of a nephew? I ask nothing of you; if I can preserve my reputation, I give you my word, for myself and my wife, that want shall have no terrors for us, if, in the midst of our misery, we can have the consolation of an unsullied character, our mutual love, and your affection and esteem.

Ger. Wretched man! you deserve—but I am weak;

this foolish regard for blood speaks in favour of this ingrate. Rise, sir; I will pay your debts, and perhaps place you in a situation to contract others.

Dal. [*Moved.*] Ah, no, my uncle! I promise you, you shall see in my conduct hereafter—

Ger. What conduct, inconsiderate man? That of an infatuated husband who suffers himself to be guided by the caprices of his wife, a vain, presumptuous, thoughtless woman—

Dal. No, I swear to you, my wife is not in fault; you do not know her.

Ger. [*Still more excited.*] You defend her? You maintain what is false in my presence? Take care! but a little more, and on account of your wife I will retract my promise; yes, yes, I will retract it—you shall have nothing of mine. Your wife!—I cannot bear her. I will not see her.

Dal. Ah, my uncle, you tear my heart!

Enter Madame Dalancourt.

Mad. Ah, sir! you think me the cause of all the misfortunes of your nephew; it is right that I alone should bear the punishment. The ignorance in which I have lived till now, I see, is not a sufficient excuse in your eyes. Young, inexperienced, I have suffered myself to be guided by a husband who loved me. The world had attractions for me; evil examples seduced me. I was satisfied, and thought myself happy, but I am guilty in appearance, and that is enough. That my husband may be worthy of your kindness, I submit to your fatal decree. I will withdraw from your presence, yet I ask one favour of you: moderate your anger against me; pardon me—my youth—have compassion on my husband, whom too much love—

Ger. Ah, Madame, perhaps you think to overcome me?

Mad. Oh, Heaven! Is there no hope? Ah, my dear Dalancourt, I have then ruined you! I die. [*Falls on a sofa.*]

Ger. [*Disturbed, moved with tenderness.*] Hallo! who's there? Martuccia!

Enter Martuccia.

Mar. Here, sir.

Ger. Look there—quick—go see to her; do something for her assistance.

Mar. My lady! What's the matter?

Ger. [*Giving a phial to* Martuccia.] Take it. Here's Cologne water. [*To* Dalancourt.] What is the matter?

Dal. Ah, my uncle!

Ger. [*To* Madame D., *in a rough tone.*] How are you?

Mad. [*Rising languidly, and in a weak voice.*] You are too kind, sir, to interest yourself in me. Do not mind my weakness—feelings will show themselves. I shall recover my strength. I will go, my—I will resign myself to my misfortunes.

Ger. [*Affected, does not speak.*]

Dal. [*Distressed.*] Ah, my uncle! can you suffer—

Ger. [*With warmth to* Dalancourt.] Be silent!—[*To* Madame D., *roughly.*] Remain in this house with your husband.

Mad. Ah, sir! ah!

Dal. [*With transport.*] Ah, my dear uncle!

Ger. [*In a serious tone, but without anger, taking their hands.*] Hear me: my savings are not on my own account; you would one day have known it. Make use of them now; the source is exhausted, and henceforth you must be prudent. If gratitude does not influence you, honour should at least keep you right.

Mad. Your goodness—

Dal. Your generosity—

Ger. Enough! enough!

Mar. Sir—

Ger. Do you be silent, babbler!

Mar. Now, sir, that you are in a humour for doing good, don't you mean to do something for Mademoiselle Angelica?

Ger. Well thought of. Where is she?

Mar. She is not far off.

Ger. And where is her betrothed?

Mar. Her betrothed?

Ger. He is perhaps offended at what I said, and will not see me. Is he gone?

Mar. Sir—her betrothed—he is still here.

Ger. Let him come in.

Mar. Angelica and her betrothed?

Ger. Yes, Angelica and her betrothed.

Mar. Admirable! Directly, sir, directly. [*Going towards the door.*] Come, come, my children; have no fear.

Enter Valerio, Dorval, *and* Angelica.

Ger. [*Seeing* Valerio.] What's this? What is this other man doing here?

Mar. They are, sir, the betrothed and the witness.

Ger. [*To* Angelica.] Come here.

Ang. [*Trembling, speaking to* Madame D.] Ah, sister! I ought indeed to ask your pardon.

Mar. And I too, Madame.

Ger. [*To* Dorval.] Come here, Signor Betrothed. What say you? Are you still angry? Will you not come?

Dor. Do you speak to me?

Ger. Yes, to you.

Dor. Pardon me, I am only the witness.

Ger. The witness!

Dor. Yes. I will explain the mystery. If you had permitted me to speak—

Ger. The mystery! [*To* Angelica.] Is there any mystery?

Dor. [*Serious, and in a resolute tone.*] Hear me, friends: you know Valerio; he was informed of the misfortune of the family, and had come to offer his fortune to Dalancourt, and his hand to Angelica. He loves her, and is ready to marry her with nothing, and to settle on her an annuity of twelve thousand livres. Your character is known to me, and that you delight in good actions. I have detained him here, and have undertaken to present him.

Ger. You had no attachment, eh? You have deceived me. I will not consent that you shall have him. This is a contrivance on both your parts, and I will never submit to it.

Ang. [*Weeping.*] My dear uncle!

Val. [*In a warm and suppliant manner.*] Sir!

Dor. You are so good!

Mad. You are so generous!

Mar. My dear master!

Ger. Plague on my disposition! I cannot continue angry as long as I would. I could willingly beat myself. [*All together repeat their entreaties, and surround him.*] Be silent! let me alone! May the devil take you all! let him marry her.

Mar. [*Earnestly.*] Let him marry her without a portion!

Ger. What, without a portion! I marry my niece without a portion! Am I not in a situation to give her a portion? I know Valerio; the generous action he has just proposed deserves a reward. Yes, let him have her portion, and the hundred thousand livres I have promised Angelica.

Val. What kindness!

Ang. What goodness!

Mad. What a heart!

Dal. What an example!

Mar. Bless my master!

Dor. Bless my good friend!

[*All surround him, overwhelm him with caresses, and repeat his praises.*]

Ger. [*Trying to rid himself of them, shouts*] Peace! peace! Piccardo!

Enter Piccardo.

Pic. Here, sir.

Ger. We shall sup in my room; all are invited. Dorval, in the meantime we'll have a game of chess.

THE FAN

(IL VENTAGLIO)

A COMEDY IN THREE ACTS

DRAMATIS PERSONÆ.

Count Rocca Marina.
Baron del Cedro.
Signor Evarist.
Signora Geltrude, *a widow.*
Candida, *her niece.*
Coronato, *an innkeeper.*
Moracchio, *a peasant.*
Nina, *his sister.*
Susanna, *a small shopkeeper.*
Crispino, *a shoemaker.*
Timoteo, *an apothecary.*
Limonato, *a waiter.*
Tognino, *servant to the two ladies.*
Scavezzo, *boots to the innkeeper.*

Scene of action, a little village near Milan.

THE FAN.

―o―

ACT I.

[An open space bounded at the back by a house bearing the inscription *Osteria* (*Inn*). Houses to right and left; on the left a gentleman's mansion with a low projecting terrace. The foremost house has the word Café upon a swinging shield; before its main door and windows stand small tables and chairs. It has also a back door which adjoins a little pharmacy. At the end of the right-hand side of houses, a small general store. The inn has a restaurant on the ground-floor, and on the left a small shoemaker's workshop. Right and left, between the inn and the side houses, runs the street.]

Scene I.

[*Evarist* and the *Baron* sit towards the front at a little table drinking coffee. *Limonato* serves them. *Crispino* is cobbling in his booth, near to him *Coronato* sitting beside his door, writing in a notebook. The *Boots* cleans the restaurant windows. In the middle of the stage sits the *Count* reading a book. He is dressed in a white summer costume, while the *Baron* and *Evarist* are in shooting dress, with their guns beside them. *Geltrude* and

Candida on the terrace, knitting. To the right *Tognino* is sweeping the square, *Nina* is spinning before her house door, beside her stands *Moracchio* holding two hunting dogs by a cord. Every now and again *Timoteo* puts his head out of the pharmacy; in the background *Susanna*, sewing before her shop. A pause after the rise of the curtain. All absorbed in their occupations. *Crispino* hammers energetically upon a shoe at which he is working. *Timoteo* is pounding loudly in a mortar, therefore invisible.]

Evarist. How do you like this coffee?
Baron. It is good.
Evarist. I find it excellent. Bravo, Limonato! to-day you have surpassed yourself.
Limonato. I thank you for the praise, but I do beg of you not to call me by this name of Limonato.
Evarist. I like that! Why, all know you by that name! You are famed by the name of Limonato. All the world says, "Let us go to the village and drink coffee at Limonato's." And that vexes you?
Limonato. Sir, it is not my name.
Baron. Eh, what! From to-day onwards I will call you Mr. Orange.
Limonato. I will not be the butt of all the world
[Candida *laughs aloud.*]
Evarist. What think you, Signorina Candida? [*He takes up a fan which* Candida *has put down on the parapet of the terrace and fans himself, replacing it.*]
Candida. What should I think? Why, it makes one laugh.
Geltrude. Leave the poor creature in peace; he makes good coffee, and is under my patronage.
Baron. Oh, if he is under the patronage of the

Signora Geltrude, we must respect him. [*Whispers to* Evarist.] Do you hear? The good widow protects him.

Evarist. [*Softly to the* Baron.] Do not speak evil of the Signora Geltrude. She is the wisest and most reputed lady in all the world.

Baron. [*As above.*] As you like; but she has the same craze for patronizing as the Count over there, who is reading with the very mien of a judge.

Evarist. Oh, as regards him, you are not wrong. He is a very caricature, but it would be unjust to compare him with the Signora Geltrude.

Baron. For my part, I think them both ridiculous.

Evarist. And what do you find ridiculous in the lady?

Baron. Too much instruction, too much pride, too much self-sufficiency.

Evarist. Excuse me, then you do not know her.

Baron. I much prefer Signorina Candida.

[*After having carried on this talk in half tones, they both rise to pay. Each protests to the other, the* Baron *forestalls* Evarist. *Limonato returns to the shop with the cups and money.* Timoteo *pounds yet louder.*]

Evarist. Yes, it is true. The niece is an excellent person. [*Aside.*] I would not have him as a rival.

Count. Hi, Timoteo!

Timoteo. Who called me?

Count. When will you cease pounding?

Timoteo. Excuse me. [*Pounds on.*]

Count. I cannot read, you crack my skull.

Timoteo. Excuse me, I shall have done directly [*Continues yet louder.*]

Crispino. [*Laughs aloud as he works.*] Hi, Coronato!

Coronato. What would you, Master Crispino?

Crispino. [*Beating hard on a sole he has in hand.*] The

Count does not wish us to make a noise. [*Beats ye louder on his shoe.*]

Count. What impudence! Will you never end this worry?

Crispino. Does not the Count see what I am doing?

Count. And what are you doing?

Crispino. Mending your old shoes.

Count. Quiet, impudent fellow. [*Continues to read.*]

Crispino. [*Beats on and* Timoteo *also.*] Host!

Count. Now, I can bear it no longer. [*He rises from his seat.*]

Scavezzo. Hi, Moracchio!

Moracchio. What is it, Boots?

Scavezzo. The Count.

[*Both laugh and mock at the* Count.]

Moracchio. Quiet, quiet! after all, he is a gentleman.

Scavezzo. A strange one.

Nina. Moracchio!

Moracchio. What do you want?

Nina. What did Scavezzo say?

Moracchio. Nothing, nothing. Attend to your own affairs, and spin.

Nina. [*Turns away her chair with contempt, and goes on spinning.*] My good brother is truly as amiable as ever. He always treats me thus. I can hardly await the hour when I shall marry.

Susanna. What is the matter, Nina?

Nina. Oh, if you knew! In all the world I don't think there is a greater boor than my brother.

Moracchio. I am as I am, and as long as you are under me—

Nina. [*Pouts and spins.*] Not much longer, I hope.

Evarist. [*To* Moracchio.] Now, what is it all about again? You are always teasing that poor child, and she does not deserve it, poor thing.

Nina. He makes me wild with anger.

Moracchio. She wants to know everything

Evarist. Come, come, it will do now.

Baron. [*To* Candida.] Signor Evarist is kind-hearted.

Candida. [*With disdain.*] It seems so also to me.

Geltrude. [*To* Candida.] Look to yourself, child. We do nought but criticise the actions of others, and do not take care of our own.

Baron. [*Aside.*] There, these are the sort of doctrines I can't abide to hear.

Crispino. [*Aside while he works.*] Poor Nina! But once she is my wife, he won't tease her any more.

Coronato. [*Aside.*] Yes, I will marry her, and if it were only to free her from the brother.

Evarist. Well, Baron, shall we go?

Baron. To tell you the truth, this morning I do not feel like going shooting. I am tired from yesterday.

Evarist. Do as you like. You will excuse me if I go?

Baron. Do not let me detain you. [*Aside.*] So much the better for me. I will try my luck with Signorina Candida.

Evarist. Moracchio! we will go. Call the dogs and take your gun.

Baron. [*To* Evarist.] You come back to dinner?

Evarist. Certainly. I have ordered it already.

Baron. Then I will await you. *Au revoir,* ladies. [*Aside.*] I will go to my room, so as to rouse no suspicions.

Scene II.

The above. Moracchio *comes back.*

Moracchio. Here I am, sir, with the dogs and the gun.

Evarist. If you allow, ladies, I will go shooting a while.

Geltrude. Pray do as you please, and enjoy yourself.

Candida. And good luck.

Evarist. Accompanied by your good wishes, I must be lucky. [*He busies himself with his gun.*]

Candida. [*Aside.*] Signor Evarist is really amiable.

Geltrude. Yes, amiable and well-mannered. But, niece, distrust all strangers.

Candida. Why should I mistrust him?

Geltrude. For some time since I have had my reasons for this.

Candida. I have always been reserved.

Geltrude. Yes, I am content with you. Continue to be reserved towards him.

Candida. [*Aside.*] This warning comes too late. I am deeply enamoured of him.

Evarist. All is right. Come, Moracchio. Once more, ladies, your humble servant.

> [Geltrude *bows.* Candida *the same. In doing so her fan falls into the street.* Evarist *picks it up.*]

Candida. Oh, never mind.

Geltrude. Do not trouble.

Evarist. The fan is broken. How sorry I am!

Candida. What does it matter?—an old fan!

Evarist. Well, if you allow. [*Gives the fan to* Tognino, *who takes it into the house.*]

Candida. There, aunt, you see how it vexes him that the fan is broken.

Geltrude. Good manners demand this. [*Aside.*] Here love is in play.

Scene III.

The above. Tognino *on the terrace. He hands the fan to* Candida.

Evarist. I am vexed that this fan broke on my

account, but I will make it good. [*To* Susanna.] I should like to speak to you, but inside the shop. [*To* Moracchio.] Go on ahead, and wait for me at the edge of the wood. [*With* Susanna *into the shop.*]

Moracchio. [*To himself.*] I call this waste of time. Out upon these gentlemen sportsmen. [*Exit.*

Nina. [*To herself.*] So much the better that my brother has at last gone. I can scarcely await the moment to be alone with Crispino. But this tiresome man, the host, is always around. He follows me perpetually, and I can't abide him.

Count. [*Reading.*] Oh, beautiful, beautiful! [*To* Geltrude.] Signora!

Crispino. What have you read that is interesting, Count?

Count. What does that matter to you? What do you understand about it?

Crispino. [*Hammering.*] Who knows who knows most?

Geltrude. You called me, Count?

Count. You a lady of taste, oh, if you heard what I have just read! A masterpiece!

Geltrude. Something historical?

Count. Bah!

Geltrude. A philosophical discussion?

Count. Bah!

Geltrude. A poem?

Count. Bah!

Geltrude. What then?

Count. Something astonishing, unheard of, translated from the French! A fable.

Crispino. A fable! Astonishing! Unheard of! [*He hammers hard.*]

Count. Would you like to hear?

Geltrude. Gladly.

Crispino. Why, he reads fables like little children! [*Hammers.*]

Count. Will you at last leave off your noise?

Crispino. [*Hammering on.*] I am putting a patch on your shoe.

[Timoteo *pestles.*]

Count. The devil's own noise! And you too?

Timoteo. [*Puts his head outside the pharmacy.*] It is my business.

Count. [*Reads.*] "There was once a lovely maiden"— [*To* Timoteo.] Go to the devil with your mortar! It is not to be borne.

Timoteo. I pay my rent, and have no better place in which to pound. [*Goes on.*]

Count. If you will allow, signora, I will take the liberty of coming up to you. You will then hear the beautiful fable. [*Goes into the house.*]

Geltrude. This chemist is too tiresome. Let us go and receive the Count.

Candida. I don't care to hear his fables.

Geltrude. But good manners demand it.

Candida. Out upon this Count!

Geltrude. Niece, honour that you may be honoured. Come. [*She goes into the house.*]

Candida. [*Rising to follow her.*] To please you.

Scene IV.

The above without the Count *and* Geltrude. Evarist *and* Susanna *come out of the shop.*

Candida. What! Signor Evarist still here? Not gone shooting? I should like to know the reason. [*Watches him from the back of the terrace.*]

Susanna. Do not complain, sir, the fan is cheap.

Evarist. [*Aside.*] Candida is no longer here. [*Aloud.*] I am sorry that the fan is not more beautiful.

Susanna. That was the last of those of the first quality. Now my shop is emptied. [*Smiling.*] I suppose it is a present?

Evarist. Certainly. I do not buy fans for myself.

Susanna. For Signorina Candida, because hers broke?

Evarist. [*Impatiently.*] No; for some one else.

Susanna. All right, all right. I am not curious. [*Reseats herself in front of the shop to work.*]

Candida. He has great secrets with the draper. I am curious to hear some details. [*Approaches to the front.*]

Evarist. [*Approaching* Nina.] Nina!

Nina. Your wishes, sir?

Evarist. A favour. I know Signorina Candida loves you.

Nina. Yes, she has pity on the poor orphan. But alas! I am subjected to my brother, who embitters my life.

Evarist. Listen to me.

Nina. [*Spinning on.*] Spinning does not make me deaf.

Evarist. [*To himself.*] Her brother is full of whims, but neither does she seem free of them.

[Susanna, Crispino, and Coronato *stretch out their heads to observe the couple.*]

Candida. Business with the shopwoman; business with Nina. I do not understand. [*Comes forward yet more.*]

Evarist. May I ask you a favour?

Nina. Have I not already answered you? Have I not told you to command? I am not deaf. If my spindle disturbs you, I will throw it aside. [*Does so.*]

Evarist. But how impetuous!

Candida. What does her anger signify?

Coronato. It seems to me they are getting hot. [*Creeps to the front, his note-book in hand.*]

Crispino. She throws aside her spindle. [*Does the same with his shoe and hammer.*]

Susanna. Would he give her a present were she less angry? [*She too approaches from out the background.*]

Nina. I am at your orders.

Evarist. You know that Signorina Candida broke her fan?

Nina. Why, certainly.

Evarist. I have bought a new one at the shop.

Nina. As you please.

Evarist. But Signora Geltrude must not know.

Nina. There you do wisely.

Evarist. And I wish that you should give her the fan secretly.

Nina. I cannot serve you.

Evarist. How unkind of you!

Candida. [*To herself.*] He told me he was going shooting, and he is still here.

Crispino. [*Approaches, pretending to be at work.*] If I could only hear something!

Coronato. [*Approaches also, pretending to do accounts.*] I can scarcely contain myself for curiosity.

Evarist. Why will you not do me this favour?

Nina. Because I want to know nothing about this matter.

Evarist. You take the matter too seriously. Candida loves you so much.

Nina. True, but in such matters—

Evarist. You told me you wanted to marry Crispino. [*Turns and sees the two listeners.*] What do you want here, you rogues?

Crispino. [*Seating himself hastily.*] I am working, sir.

Coronato. [*Does the same.*] Can I not reckon and walk around at the same time?

Candida. They are discussing important secrets.

Susanna. What is there about this Nina that all men are after her?

Nina. If you want nothing else of me, I will go on spinning. [*Does so.*]

Evarist. But listen, do! Candida has begged me to give you a dowry that you may wed your Crispino.

Nina. [*Suddenly grows friendly.*] Really?

Evarist. Yes; and I gave her my word that I would do all—

Nina. Where is the fan?

Evarist. Here.

Nina. Quick, quick, give it to me, but so that no one sees.

[Evarist *gives her the fan.*]

Crispino. [*Advancing his head, to himself.*] Ho, ho, he gave her something!

Susanna. [*The same.*] In very truth—he gives her the fan!

Coronato. [*Ditto.*] What could he have given her?

Candida. [*Ditto.*] Yes, he deceives me. The Count is right.

Evarist. But, mind, quite secretly.

Nina. Let me act, and do not fear.

Evarist. Addio.

Nina. My respects.

Evarist. Then I rely on you?

Nina. And I on you. [*Seats herself and resumes her spinning.*]

Evarist. [*About to go, sees* Candida *on the terrace.*] Ah, there she is again! I will tell her to be attentive. [*Calls.*] Signorina Candida!

[Candida *turns her back to him and goes away.*]

Evarist. What does this mean? Is it contempt? Does she despise me? Impossible! I know she loves me, and she knows my passion for her. And yet—no, now I understand! Her aunt will have seen and observed her, and she would not show before her. Yes, yes, it must be that, it cannot be anything else. But I must at last give up all this secrecy and talk with Signora Geltrude, and obtain from her the precious gift of her niece.

Nina. In truth, I owe the Signorina thanks that she interests herself in me. Shall I not repay her? These are little services one exchanges without any base thoughts in the rear.

Coronato. [*Gets up and goes to* Nina.] Hm, great secrets, great consultations with Signor Evarist?

Nina. What does not concern you, does not matter to you.

Coronato. Were that the case I should not interfere.

[Crispino *approaches the couple quietly to listen.*]

Nina. I am not subservient to you, Master Host.

Coronato. Not yet, but I hope soon.

Nina. Indeed! and who says so?

Coronato. He has said it and promised it and sworn it, and he can and may dispose of you.

Nina. [*Laughing.*] Perchance my brother?

Coronato. Yes, your brother; and I will tell him of all the secrets, the confidence, the presents—

Crispino. [*Comes between them.*] Ho, ho! what right have you to this girl?

Coronato. I owe you no answer.

Crispino. And you, what have you to discuss with Signor Evarist?

Nina. Leave me in peace, both of you.

Crispino. I will know!

Coronato. What, you will? Command where you may command. Nina is my betrothed, her brother has promised her to me.

Crispino. And I have her word, and the word of the sister is worth a thousand times more than that of the brother.

Coronato. She is as good as engaged to me.

Crispino. We will speak of this again. Nina, what did Signor Evarist give you?

Nina. Go to the devil with you!

Coronato. No answer! But stop, I saw him come out of Susanna's shop. She will tell me. [*Goes towards* Susanna.]

Crispino. He bought her a present. [*He too goes to* Susanna.]

Nina. [*To herself.*] I shall reveal nothing. But if Susanna—

Coronato. Neighbour, I beg you, what did Signor Evarist buy of you?

Susanna. [*Laughing.*] A fan.

Crispino. Do you know what he gave the girl?

Susanna. What could it be but the fan

Nina. That is not true.

Susanna. Why, certainly it is!

Coronato. [*To* Nina.] Produce the fan.

Crispino. [*Pushing him away.*] Here I command! I must see the fan.

Coronato. [*Raises his fist towards* Crispino.] Wait a while.

Crispino. [*Ditto.*] Yes, you wait too.

Nina. [*To* Susanna.] It is all your fault.

Susanna. Mine?

Nina. Chatterbox!

Susanna. Oh ho! [*Threatens her.*]

Susanna. I go. Peasant girl, consort with your likes. [*Retires into her shop.*]

Crispino. But now I will see the fan.

Nina. I have not got one.

Coronato. What did the gentleman give you?

Nina. Your curiosity is impertinent.

Coronato. I will know.

Crispino. [*To* Coronato.] I tell you that does not concern you.

Nina. This is not the way to treat a respectable girl. [*Goes towards her house.*]

Crispino. [*Approaching her.*] Tell me, Nina.

Nina. No.

Coronato. I must know. [*He pushes* Crispino *aside.*]

[*Nina hurries into the house and shuts the door in both their faces.*]

Coronato. It's your fault.

Crispino. Impudent fellow!

Coronato. Do not excite yourself.

Crispino. I do not fear you.

Coronato. Nina will be mine!

Crispino. We shall see about that. And should she be, I swear—

Coronato. What, threats! Do you not know to whom you speak?

Crispino. I am an honest man, as all know.

Coronato. And what am I, pray?

Crispino. I know nothing about it.

Coronato. I am an honoured innkeeper.

Crispino. Honoured?

Coronato. What! you doubt it?

Crispino. Oh, it is not I who doubt it.

Coronato. Who, then, may I ask?

Crispino. All the village.

Coronato. My good man, it is not about me that all talk. I do not sell old leather for new.

Crispino. Nor I water for wine; nor do I trap cats at night to sell them as lamb or hare.

Coronato. I swear to Heaven —[*Raises his hand.*]

Crispino. What! [*Does the same.*]
Coronato. The devil take me! [*Feels in his pocket.*]
Crispino. His hand in his pocket! [*Runs to his booth to fetch an implement.*]
Coronato. I have no knife.

> [Crispino *seizes the apothecary's chair and threatens to hurl it at his adversary.* Coronato *takes up a bench and swings it at Crispino.*]

Scene V.

The above. Timoteo, Scavezzo, Limonato, *the* Count.

> [Timoteo *hurrying out of his shop, pestle in hand.* Limonoto, *out of the café with a log of firewood.* Scavezzo, *out of the inn with a spit.*]

Count. [*Coming out of* Geltrude's *house.*] Peace, peace! quiet there, I command!—I, you villains, the Count Rocca Marina! Ho there, peace, I say, you rogues!

Crispino. [*To* Coronato.] Well, to please the Count.

Coronato. Yes, thank the Count, for but for him I would have broken all the bones in your body.

Count. Quiet, quiet, it is enough! I would know the reason of the strife. Go away, you others. I am here, no one else is needed.

Timoteo. Is no one hurt?

> [Limonato *and* Scavezzo *depart.*]

Count. You wish that they had cracked their skulls, contorted their arms, disjointed their legs, is it not so, Apothecary, to show us a specimen of your talents and powers?

Timoteo. I seek no one's ill; but if there were wounded to heal, cripples to succour, breakages to bind up, I would gladly help them. Above all, I would with all my heart serve your worship in such an eventuality.

Count. Impertinent fellow! I will have you removed.

Timoteo. Honest men are not removed so easily.

Count. Yes, one removes ignorant, impudent impostors of apothecaries like you.

Timoteo. I am astonished to hear you talk thus, Count —you who without my pills would be dead.

Count. Insolent fellow!

Timoteo. And those pills you have not yet paid for. [*Exit.*

Coronato. [*Aside.*] Here the Count might be of use to me.

Count. Well, now, my men, tell me what is the matter, what is the reason for your quarrels?

Crispino. I will tell you, sir—I will tell it before all the world. I love Nina.

Coronato. And Nina will be my wife.

Count. [*Laughing.*] Ah ha! I understand: a love quarrel; two champions of Cupid, two worthy rivals, two pretenders to the lovely Venus of our village.

Crispino. If you think to make fun of me—[*Moves to go away.*]

Count. No, stay.

Coronato. The matter is serious, I assure you.

Count. Yes, I believe it. You are lovers, you are rivals. By Jupiter, what a combination! Why, the very theme of the fable I was reading to Signora Geltrude just now. [*Points to his book.*] "There was a maiden of rare beauty"—

Crispino. I understand. With your permission—

Count. Where are you going? Come here!

Crispino. If you will allow me, I go to finish cobbling your shoes.

Count. Yes, go, that they may be ready by to-morrow.

Coronato. And be careful that they are not patched with old leather.

Crispino. I shall come to you when I want a fresh skin.

Coronato. Thank Heaven I am no cobbler nor shoemaker!

Crispino. It does not matter, you will give me a horse's skin or a cat's.

Coronato. [*Aside.*] I know I shall kill that man.

Count. What did he say of cats? Do you give us cats to eat?

Coronato. Sir, I am an honest man, and this person is a rogue who persecutes me unjustly.

Count. The effect of love, of rivalry. So you are in love with Nina?

Coronato. Yes, sir, and I was about to seek your protection.

Count. My protection? [*Gives himself an important air.*] Well, we will see. Are you sure she loves you in return?

Coronato. To tell the truth, I fancy she loves him better than me.

Count. That is bad.

Coronato. But I have her brother's word.

Count. A thing not much to be relied on.

Coronato. Moracchio has promised it to me most faithfully.

Count. So far so good, but you cannot force a woman.

Coronato. Her brother can dispose of her.

Count. [*Hotly.*] It is not true. Her brother cannot dispose of her.

Coronato. But your protection.

Count. My protection is all well and good. My protection is valid, my protection is powerful. But a nobleman, such as I, does not arbitrate nor dispose of a woman's heart.

Coronato. But, after all, she is a peasant.

Count. What does that matter? A woman's ever a woman. I distinguish the grades, the conditions, but as a whole I respect the sex.

Coronato. [*Aside.*] I understand. Your protection is worthless.

Count. How are you off for wine? have you a good supply?

Coronato. I have some that is quite perfect, good and exquisite.

Count. I shall come and taste it. Mine has turned out ill this year.

Coronato. [*Aside.*] It is two years that he has sold it.

Count. If yours is good, I will take a supply.

Coronato. [*Aside.*] I do not care for this patronage.

Count. Do you hear?

Coronato. Yes, I hear.

Count. Tell me one thing: if I were to speak to the girl, and induced her by explanations—

Coronato. Your words might do something in my favour.

Count. After all, you deserve to be preferred.

Coronato. It seems to me, too, that between me and Crispino—

Count. Oh, there is no comparison!—a man like you, educated, well dressed, a respectable person.

Coronato. You are too kind.

Count. I respect women, it is true, but just because of that, treating them as I treat them, I assure you, they do for me what they would do for no one else.

Coronato. It is that which I thought too, but you wanted to make me doubt.

Count. I do like the lawyers, who start by making difficulties. Friend, you are a man who has a good inn, who can afford to maintain a wife decently. Have confidence in me, I will take up your cause.

Coronato. I beg your protection.

Count. I accord it. I promise it.

Coronato. If you would put yourself out to come and taste my wine—

Count. Most gladly, good man. [*Puts his hand on his shoulder.*]

Coronato. [*Aside.*] Two or three barrels of wine will not be ill spent here.

END OF THE FIRST ACT.

ACT II.

Scene I.

Susanna *alone, comes out of her house and arranges her wares.*

Susanna. Bad times, little business to be done in this village. I have as yet sold but one fan, and that I have given for a price—really just to get rid of it. The people who can spend take their supplies in the city. From the poor there is little to earn. I am a fool to lose my time here in the midst of these peasants, without manners, without respect, who do not know the difference between a shopwoman of education and those who sell milk, salad, and eggs. My town education stands me no stead in the country. All equal, all companions, Susanna, Nina, Margherita, Lucia; the shopkeeper, the goatherd, the peasant, all one. The two ladies yonder are a little more considered, but little, very little. As for that impertinent Nina, because she is a little favoured by the gentry, she thinks she is something great. They have given her

a fan. What will a peasant girl do with such a fan?
Cut a dash, eh! the minx must fan herself, thus.
Much good may it do you! Why, it's ridiculous, and
yet these things at times make me rage. I, who have
been well educated, I can't tolerate such absurdities.
[*Seats herself and works.*]

Scene II.

Candida, *who comes out of the mansion.*

Candida. I shan't be at peace till I have cleared it
up. I saw Evarist coming out of the shop and go to
Nina, and certainly he gave her something. I must
see if Susanna can tell me something. Yes, aunt is
right, "Mistrust all strangers." Poor me! If he prove
unfaithful! It is my first love. I have loved none but
him. [*Advances towards* Susanna.]

Susanna. [*Rises.*] Ah, Signorina Candida, your
humble servant.

Candida. Good day, Susanna. What are you working
at so busily?

Susanna. I am making a cap.

Candida. To sell?

Susanna. To sell, but Heaven knows when.

Candida. It might be that I need a nightcap.

Susanna. I have some in stock. Will you see them?

Candida. No, no, there is no hurry. Another time.

Susanna. Will you take a seat? [*Offers her chair.*]

Candida. And you?

Susanna. Oh, I will fetch another chair. [*She goes
into the shop and brings out a second chair.*] Pray sit
here, you will be more comfortable.

Candida. You sit down also and go on working.

Susanna. [*Does so.*] What an honour you afford me!

One sees at once you are well-born. He who is well-born despises no one. The peasants here are proud, and Nina especially.

Candida. Speaking of Nina, did you notice her when Signor Evarist spoke to her?

Susanna. Whether I noticed? I should think so.

Candida. He had a long confab with her.

Susanna. Do you know what happened after? Such a fight as there was!

Candida. I heard a noise, an angry discussion. They told me Crispino and Coronato were at loggerheads.

Susanna. Precisely, and all because of this beauty, this treasure.

Candida. But why?

Susanna. Jealousy between themselves, jealousy because of Signor Evarist.

Candida. Do you think Signor Evarist has any friendship for Nina?

Susanna. I know nothing. I do not concern myself about others' affairs, and think ill of no one; but if the host and the shoemaker are jealous of him, they must have their reasons.

Candida. [*Aside.*] Alas! the argument is but too true, to my prejudice.

Susanna. Excuse me, I should not like to make a mistake.

Candida. In what?

Susanna. I hope that you take no interest in Signor Evarist?

Candida. I? Oh, none whatever! I know him because he sometimes comes to the house, and is a friend of my aunt's.

Susanna. Then I will tell you the truth. [*Aside.*] I do not think this can offend her. I almost thought that between you and Signor Evarist there was some understanding,—of course permissible and respectable,—but since he was with me this morning, I am of another opinion.

Candida. He was with you this morning?

Susanna. Yes. He came to buy a fan.

Candida. [*Eagerly.*] He bought a fan?

Susanna. Precisely; and as I had seen that you had broken yours, so to speak, on his account, I at once said to myself, He buys it to give it to the Signorina Candida.

Candida. So he bought it for me?

Susanna. Oh no, Signorina. I will confess to you I took the liberty of asking him if he were buying it for you. He replied in a manner as if I had offended him, "That is not my business; what is there between me and the Signorina Candida? I have destined it elsewhere."

Candida. And what did he do with this fan?

Susanna. What did he do with it? He gave it to Nina.

Candida. [*Aside.*] Oh, I am lost! I am miserable!

Susanna. [*Observing her agitation.*] Signorina Candida!

Candida. [*Aside.*] Ungrateful, unfaithful, and for whom?—for a peasant girl!

Susanna. [*With insistance.*] Signorina Candida!

Candida. [*Aside.*] The offence is insupportable.

Susanna. [*Aside.*] Poor me! What have I done?—Signorina Candida, calm yourself, it may not be thus.

Candida. Do you believe he gave the fan to Nina?

Susanna. Oh, as to that, I saw it with my own eyes.

Candida. And then you say it may not be thus?

Susanna. I do not know—I do not wish that by my fault—

Scene III.

The above. Geltrude *at the door of the villa.*

Susanna. See, there is your aunt.

Candida. For Heaven's sake, say nothing!

Susanna. Do not fear.—[*Aside.*] And she would have me believe she does not love him! It's her own fault. Why did she not tell me the truth?

Geltrude. What are you doing here, niece?

[Candida *and* Susanna *rise.*]

Susanna. She is condescending to accord me her company.

Candida. I came to see if she sold nightcaps.

Susanna. Yes, it is true, she asked me about some. Oh, do not fear that your niece is not safe with me. I am no chatterbox, and my house is most respectable.

Geltrude. Do not justify yourself without being accused.

Susanna. I am very sensitive, Signora.

Geltrude. Why did you not tell me you needed a nightcap?

Candida. You were in your writing-room, and I did not wish to disturb you.

Susanna. Would you like to see it? I will go and get it. I pray, sit down. [*Gives her chair to* Geltrude, *and goes into the shop.*]

Geltrude. [*Seating herself, to* Candida.] Have you heard nothing of this encounter between the shoemaker and the host?

Candida. They say it is a matter of love and jealousy. They say Nina is the cause.

Geltrude. I am sorry, for she is a good girl.

Candida. Oh, aunt, excuse me; I have heard things about her of a nature that would make it better we should no longer let her come to the house.

Geltrude. Why? What have they told you?

Candida. I will tell you after. Do as I do, aunt; don't receive her any more, and you will do well.

Geltrude. Since she came more often to see you than to see me, I leave you free to treat her as you please.

Candida. [*Aside.*] The minx! she will not have the impudence to appear before me.

Susanna. [*Returning.*] Here are the caps, ladies; see, choose, and content yourselves. [*All three occupied with the caps, and speaking softly among themselves.*]

Scene IV.

The above. The Count *and the* Baron *come out of the inn.*

Count. I am glad you have confided in me. Leave the rest to me, and do not fear.

Baron. I know you are Signora Geltrude's friend.

Count. Oh, friend!—well, I will tell you. She is a lady who has some talents; I like literature, I converse with her more willingly than with any other. For the rest, she is a poor city dame. Her husband left her this wretched house and some acres of ground, and, in order to be respected in this village, she needs my protection.

Baron. Long live the Count who protects widows and fair ladies!

Count. What would you have? In this world one must be good for something.

Baron. Then you will do me the favour—

Count. Do not fear, I will speak to her; I will ask her niece's hand for a cavalier, who is my friend, and when I have asked her I am sure she will not have the courage to say no.

Baron. Tell her who I am.

Count. To what purpose, when it is I who ask?
Baron. But you ask for me.
Count. For you.
Baron. You know precisely who I am.
Count. How should I not know your titles, your faculties, your honours! Oh, we members of the aristocracy all know each other.
Baron. [*Aside.*] How I should laugh at him if I had not need of him!
Count. My dear colleague!
Baron. What is it?
Count. Behold Signora Geltrude and her niece.
Baron. They are busy; I do not think they have seen us.
Count. Certainly not. If Signora Geltrude had seen me, she would have moved instantly.
Baron. When will you speak to her?
Count. At once if you like.
Baron. It is not well I should be there. Speak to her. I will wait at the apothecary's. I am in your hands.
Count. Good-bye, dear colleague and friend.
Baron. Good-bye, beloved colleague. [*Embraces him.*] [*Aside.*] He is the maddest March hare in the world.
Count. [*Calling aloud.*] Signora Geltrude!
Geltrude. [*Rising.*] Oh, Count, excuse me! I did not see you.
Count. I beg, give me a word.
Susanna. Pray approach. My shop is at your service.
Count. No, no; I have something private to say. Excuse the trouble, but I beg you come here.
Geltrude. In a moment. Allow me to pay for a cap I have bought, and then I am at your disposal. [*Pulls out a purse to pay* Susanna, *and to prolong the moment.*]
Count. What! you would pay at once! I never had that vice.

Scene V.

Coronato comes out of the inn with Scavezzo, *who carries a barrel of wine on his shoulders.*

Coronato. Honoured sir, this is the barrel of wine for you.

Count. And the second?

Coronato. After this I will bring the second. Where shall we take it?

Count. To my palace.

Coronato. To whom shall I consign it?

Count. To my steward, if he is there.

Coronato. I am afraid he is not there.

Count. Give it to any one you find.

Coronato. All right. Let us go.

Scavezzo. The Count will give me some drink money.

Count. Take care not to drink my wine, and don't put water to it.—[*To* Coronato.] Don't let him go alone.

Coronato. Never fear, never fear! I go too.

Scavezzo. [*Aside.*] No, no, don't fear; between the master and me we have prepared it by now. [*Exit.*

Geltrude. [*Who has paid, advances towards the* Count. Susanna *is seated, and works.* Candida *remains seated. They whisper together.*] Here I am, Count, and what is it you wish?

Count. In a few words, will you give me your niece?

Geltrude. Give? What do you mean by give?

Count. What? don't you understand? In marriage.

Geltrude. To you?

Count. Not to me, but to a person I know and propose.

Geltrude. I will tell you, Count: you know my niece has lost her parents, and, being the daughter of my only brother, I have undertaken to fill for her a mother's place.

Count. All these, excuse me, are useless discourses.

Geltrude. Excuse me. Let me come to my point.

Count. Well, what then?

Geltrude. Candida has not inherited enough from her father to suffice to marry her in her own rank.

Count. It does not matter; it is no question of that here.

Geltrude. Let me finish. My husband left me an ample provision.

Count. I know.

Geltrude. I have no children.

Count. And you will give her a dowry?

Geltrude. Yes, when the match shall meet her favour.

Count. Oh yes, that is the needful point. But I am proposing this match, and when I propose, it must meet her favour.

Geltrude. I am certain that the Count is incapable of proposing other than an acceptable person, but I hope he will do me the honour to tell me who this person is.

Count. A colleague of mine.

Geltrude. What! a colleague! What does that mean?

Count. A nobleman, like yourself.

Geltrude. Signore—

Count. Do not raise objections.

Geltrude. Pray let me speak. If you will not let me, I shall go.

Count. Come, come, be gracious! Speak, I listen. I am amiable, complaisant with ladies. I listen to you.

Geltrude. I will tell you what I feel in a few words. A title makes the honour of a house, but not of a person. I do not think my niece is ambitious, nor am I inclined to sacrifice her to the idol of vanity.

Count. [*Laughing.*] Ah, one sees that you read fables.

Geltrude. Such feelings are not learnt from fables nor novels. Nature inspires them and education cultivates them.

Count. Nature, education, all you will. He whom I propose is the Baron del Cedro.

Geltrude. The Baron is in love with my niece?

Count. Oui, Madame.

Geltrude. I know him and respect him.

Count. You see what a good match I propose to you.

Geltrude. He is a gentleman of merit.

Count. And my colleague.

Geltrude. He is perhaps a trifle free of speech, but without harm.

Count. Well, now, your answer, I beg?

Geltrude. Adagio, adagio, Count. Such matters are not decided all in a moment. I should like the Baron to have the goodness to speak to me.

Count. Excuse me, if I say a thing, there can be no doubt about it. I woo on his behalf, and he has begged my intercession, implored me—And I speak to you, beg you—that is to say, I do not beg you, I demand of you—

Geltrude. Let us admit that the Baron is in earnest.

Count. By Jupiter, what is this we are to admit? the thing is certain when I say so.

Geltrude. Admitted, then, that the thing is certain. The Baron desires her, you demand her. It is always needful I should ask Candida if she assents.

Count. She cannot know about it unless you tell her.

Geltrude. [*Ironically.*] Have the goodness to believe that I shall tell her.

Count. Here she comes. Speak to her about it.

Geltrude. I will speak to her.

Count. Go, then, and I will wait you here.

Geltrude. [*Bowing.*] Excuse me.—[*Aside.*] If the Baron is in earnest, it would indeed be a piece of good luck for my niece, but I doubt. [*Goes towards* Susanna.]

Count. Ha, ha! with my good manners I attain from

people all I want. [*Takes a book from his pocket, seats himself, and reads.*]

Geltrude. Candida, I have to speak to you. Let us take a turn.

Susanna. Will you go into my little garden? You will be quite free there.

Geltrude. Yes, let us go there, because I must come back here at once.

Candida. [*Aside.*] What can she want to tell me? I am too miserable to expect any good news. [*Both into the shop.*]

Count. She is capable of keeping me waiting here for an hour. It is well that I have this book to entertain me. What a beautiful thing is literature! A man with a good book to hand is never alone. [*Reads.*]

Scene VI.

Count. Nina *comes out of her house.*

Nina. Well, one good thing, the dinner is ready, so when that fellow Moracchio comes he can't scold me. No one is looking. I had better go now and take the fan to Signorina Candida. If I can give it her without her aunt seeing, I will; if not, I'll wait another chance.

Count. Why, Nina, Nina. Ho, here, my girl! [*Goes towards the villa.*]

Nina. Signore. [*Turns to look at him.*]

Count. A word.

Nina. [*Aside.*] I did not need this impediment.

Count. [*Aside.*] I must not neglect Coronato. I have promised him my protection, and he merits it. [*Gets up and puts aside his book.*]

Nina. Here I am. What would you, sir?

Count. Where were you going?

Nina. To do my own business, sir.

Count. What! You reply like that to me, with such audacity, such impertinence?

Nina. How would you have me speak? I speak as I know how; I am not used to converse. I speak like that with every one, and no one has told me I am impertinent.

Count. You must distinguish the people with whom you speak.

Nina. I don't know how to distinguish. If you want something, say it! If you want to amuse yourself, I have no time to lose with your worship.

Count. Come hither.

Nina. I am here.

Count. Would you like to marry?

Nina. Yes, sir.

Count. That is well; you please me now.

Nina. Oh, what I have in my heart, I have in my mouth.

Count. Would you like me to find you a husband?

Nina. No, sir.

Count. How no?

Nina. How no? Because it's no, because to marry I have no need of you.

Count. Do you not need my protection?

Nina. No, indeed, not a bit of it.

Count. Do you understand all I can do in this village?

Nina. You may be able to do all in the village, but you can do nothing in my marriage.

Count. I can do nothing?

Nina. [*Smiling gently.*] Nothing, in truth, nothing, nothing.

Count. You are in love with Crispino.

Nina. He is to my taste.

Count. And you prefer him to that worthy man, to that rich man, that admirable man, Coronato?

Nina. I would prefer him to others far better than Coronato.

Count. You would prefer him to any other?

Nina. [*Laughing, and making him understand that she refers to him.*] Oh, and if you knew to whom, for instance!

Count. And to whom would you prefer him, then?

Nina. To what end? Do not make me chatter.

Count. No, because you would be capable of saying some impertinence.

Nina. Do you want anything else of me?

Count. Simply this: I protect your brother, your brother has given his word for you to Coronato, and you must marry Coronato.

Nina. [*With affectation.*] Your worship protects my brother?

Count. Just so.

Nina. And my brother has given his word to Coronato?

Count. Just so.

Nina. Well, if things be so—

Count. Well?

Nina. Let my brother marry the host.

Count. I swear that you shall never marry Crispino.

Nina. No? And why?

Count. I shall send him away from this village.

Nina. I shall go and seek for him wherever he is.

Count. I shall have him beaten.

Nina. Oh, as for that, he will think about it.

Count. What would you do if he were dead?

Nina. I do not know.

Count. Would you take another?

Nina. It might be.

Count. Imagine that he is dead.
Nina. Sir, I can neither read, nor write, nor reckon.
Count. Saucy girl!
Nina. Do you want anything else?
Count. Go to the devil!
Nina. Show me the road!
Count. I swear, were you not a woman—
Nina. What would you do?
Count. Go hence, I say!
Nina. I obey at once, for I am well bred.
Count. Well bred? and goes off and does not salute!
Nina. Oh, pardon me. I am till death your worship's obedient servant. [*Laughs and runs towards the villa.*]

Count. [*With scorn.*] Rustica progenies nescit habere modum. I do not know what to do. If she does not want Coronato, I can't force her. It is not my fault. What on earth does he want a wife for, who does not want him? Are women scarce? I will find him one better than this. He shall see what my protection is worth.

Scene VII.

The above, and Geltrude *and* Candida *outside the shop.*

Count. Well, Signora Geltrude?
Geltrude. Count, my niece is a prudent girl.
Count. Well, then, briefly?
Geltrude. Count, permit me.
Count. Pardon me, but if you knew what I have endured with a woman—it is true, another woman— [*Aside.*] But all women are alike.—Well, then, what does niece Candida say?
Geltrude. If the Baron really—
Count. Really! out upon your suspicions!

Geltrude. Admitting the condition and the circumstances, my niece is content to marry the Baron.

Count. Bravo! [*Aside.*] This time at least I have had a success.

Candida. [*Aside.*] All to revenge myself on that false Evarist!

Geltrude. [*Aside.*] I certainly did not think she would consent. I fancied another affection held her, but I see I erred.

Scene VIII.

Nina *on the terrace. The above.*

Nina. She is not here, and I can find her nowhere. Oh, there she is!

Count. Consequently the Signorina Candida marries the Baron del Cedro.

Nina. [*Aside.*] What do I hear? What will she answer?

Geltrude. She will do it as soon as the conditions—

Count. [*To* Candida.] What conditions do you put?

Candida. None, sir; I marry him in any case.

Count. Excellent Signorina Candida! I like you thus. [*Aside.*] Ah, when I have to do with matters, all goes swimmingly.

Nina. [*Aside.*] But this is a terrible business! Poor Signor Evarist! It is useless for me to give the fan to Signorina Candida. [*Exit.*

Geltrude. [*Aside.*] I deceived myself. She loves the Baron, and I thought her attracted to Signor Evarist.

Count. If you will allow me, I will go and give this good news to the Baron, to my dear friend, my dear colleague.

Geltrude. And where is the Baron?

Count. He expects me at the apothecary's. Do as I

beg. Go to the house, and I will conduct him to you at once.

Geltrude. What do you say, niece?

Candida. Yes, he can speak with you.

Count. And with you?

Candida. I will do whatever my aunt wishes.—[*Aside.*] I shall die, but I shall die avenged.

Count. I go at once. Expect us, we will come to you. As the hour is so advanced, it would not be amiss if you invited him to dinner.

Geltrude. What! the first time!

Count. Oh, these are exaggerated considerations. He will gladly accept, I answer for him, and to induce him, I will stay too. [*Exit.*

Geltrude. Let us go, then, and await them.

Candida. Yes, let us go.

Geltrude. What is the matter with you? Do you do it willingly?

Candida. Yes, willingly.—[*Aside.*] I have given my word, it is irremediable.

Geltrude. [*Aside.*] Poor child, I pity her. In these cases, notwithstanding one's love, one feels confused. [*Goes towards the villa.*]

Scene IX.

Nina on the terrace, and the above.

Nina. Oh, Signorina Candida!

Candida. [*Angrily.*] What are you doing here?

Nina. I came to look for you.

Candida. Go away, and do not presume to set foot in our house again!

Nina. What! this affront to me?

Candida. What affront? You are an unworthy

creature, and I cannot and will not tolerate you longer. [*Enters the villa.*]

Geltrude. [*Aside.*] This is a little too severe.

Nina. I am amazed, Signora Geltrude.

Geltrude. I am indeed sorry for the mortification you have had, but my niece is a person of good judgment, and if she has treated you ill, she must have her reasons.

Nina. What reasons can she have? I am astonished at her.

Geltrude. Come, come, do not forget your respect; do not raise your voice.

Nina. I will go and seek justification.

Geltrude. No, no, stay here. It is no good now, do it after.

Nina. And I tell you, I will go now!

Geltrude. Do not presume to pass this door. [*Places herself on the threshold.*]

Scene X.

The above. Count *and* Baron *going from the apothecary's to the villa.*

Count. Come, come, let us go.

Baron. I must go.

Geltrude. [*To* Nina.] Impudent lass! [*Goes in and throws to the door at the moment that the* Count *and* Baron *are about to enter. She does not see them.*]

[Nina *goes away angered.* Count *remains speechless, looking at the closed door.*]

Baron. What, they shut the door in our faces!

Count. In our faces? No, it is impossible!

Baron. Impossible, you say! But it is a fact

Nina. This insult to me! [*Walks up and down trembling.*]

Count. Let us go and knock.

Nina. [*Aside.*] If they go in, I will get in too.

Baron. No, stay; I want to know no more. I do not wish to expose myself to fresh insults. You have served me but ill. They have laughed at you, and made fun of me on your account.

Count. [*Hotly.*] What way of speaking is this?

Baron. And I demand satisfaction!

Count. From whom?

Baron. From you.

Count. In what manner?

Baron. Sword in hand!

Count. With the sword! But it's twenty years that I am in this village, and that I no longer use a sword.

Baron. With pistols, then. [*Draws two pistols from his pocket.*]

Nina. [*Running towards the house.*] Pistols! hi, folks, here! pistols! They are murdering each other.

Scene XI.

The above. Geltrude *on the terrace.*

Geltrude. But, gentlemen, what is this?

Count. Why did you bolt the door in our faces?

Geltrude. I? Excuse me, I am incapable of such a vile action with whomsoever it should be; how little, then, with you and the Baron, who deigns to condescend to my niece!

Count. [*To the* Baron.] You hear!

Baron. But, Madame, at the very moment we wanted to come to you, the door was closed in our faces.

Geltrude. I assure you I did not see you. I closed the door to hinder that saucy girl Nina from entering.

Nina. [*Puts her head out of her own door.*] What? saucy! saucy yourself!

Count. Quiet the impudent lass!

Geltrude. Will you enter, pray? I will give orders that the door be opened.

Count. [*To the Baron.*] You hear?

Baron. I have nothing more to say.

Count. What will you do with these pistols?

Baron. Excuse my acute sense of honour. [*Puts away the pistols.*]

Count. And you mean to present yourself to two ladies with two pistols in your pocket?

Baron. I always carry them in the country for self-defence.

Count. But if they knew you had these pistols,—you know what women are,—they would not come near you.

Baron. You are right. Thank you for warning me, and, as a sign of good friendship, allow me to present you with them. [*Draws one from his pocket and presents it.*]

Count. [*Nervously.*] A present to me?

Baron. Yes; surely you will not refuse it?

Count. I accept it because it comes from your hands. But they are not loaded?

Baron. What a question! Do you expect me to carry empty pistols?

Count. Wait! Ho there, café!

Limonato. [*From out his shop.*] What would you, sir?

Count. Take these pistols and keep them till I ask you for them.

Limonato. At your service. [*Takes the pistols from the Baron.*]

Count. Take care, they are loaded!

Limonato. [*Laughing*]. Oh, I know how to manage them.

Count. Take care, no follies!

Limonato. [*Aside.*] The Count is courageous, truly.

Count. I thank you, and shall value them.—[*Aside.*] To-morrow I will sell them.

Tognino. [*From the villa.*] Gentlemen, my mistress expects you.

Count. Let us go.

Baron. Yes, let us go.

Count. Well, what do you say? Am I a man of my word? Ah, dear colleague, we noblemen—our protection is worth something.

> [Nina *comes out of her house softly, and goes behind them to enter.* Tognino *has let the* Count *and* Baron *pass, and remains on the threshold.* Nina *wants to enter.* Tognino *stops her.*]

Tognino. You have nothing to do here.

Nina. Yes, but I have.

Tognino. My orders are not to let you pass. [*Goes in and shuts the door.*]

Nina. I am furious!—I feel choking with rage! This insult to me—to a girl of my kind! [*Stamps with rage*].

Scene XII.

Evarist *from the street, his gun on his shoulder, and* Moracchio *with a gun in his hand and bag with game, and the dogs tied by a cord. The above.*

Evarist. Here, take my gun, and keep those partridges till I dispose of them. [*Seats himself before the cafe.*]

Moracchio. Never fear, I will take care of them.—[*To* Nina.] Is dinner ready?

Nina. Quite ready.

Moracchio. What on earth is the matter? You are always angry with all the world, and then complain of me.

Nina. Oh, it's true, we are relations, there is no gainsaying it.

Moracchio. Come, let us go in and dine. It is time.

Nina. Yes, yes, go. I will come after.—[*Aside.*] I want to speak to Signor Evarist.

Moracchio. Yes, come; if not, I shall eat all. [*Goes into the house.*]

Nina. If I ate now, I should eat poison.

Evarist. [*Aside.*] No one on the terrace! Doubtless they are at dinner. It is better I go to the inn, the Baron expects me. [*Rises.*] Well, Nina, nothing new to tell me?

Nina. Oh yes, sir, I have something to tell you.

Evarist. Have you given my fan?

Nina. Here it is, your accursed fan!

Evarist. What does this mean? Could you not give it?

Nina. I have received a thousand insults, a thousand impertinences, and have been chased from the house like a good-for-nothing.

Evarist. Then Signora Geltrude noticed it?

Nina. Oh, not only Signora Geltrude. The greatest insults came from Signorina Candida.

Evarist. But why? What did you do to her?

Nina. I did nothing to her, sir.

Evarist. You told her you had a fan for her?

Nina. How could I tell her when she never gave me time, but sent me off like a thief?

Evarist. But there must be some reason.

Nina. For my part, I know I have done nothing to her. But all this ill-treatment, I am sure, I am certain, has been done to me because of you.

Evarist. Because of me? The Signorina Candida, who loves me so much!

Nina. Does the Signorina Candida love you so much?

Evarist. There is no doubt about it. I am sure of it.

Nina. Oh yes, I too can assure you that she loves you much, much, much.

Evarist. You put me into a terrible agitation.

Nina. [*Ironically.*] Go, go and seek your lady-love, your dear one.

Evarist. And why should I not go?

Nina. Because the place is taken!

Evarist. [*Anxiously.*] By whom?

Nina. By Baron del Cedro.

Evarist. The Baron is in the house?

Nina. Why should he not be in the house, seeing he is to marry the Signorina Candida?

Evarist. Nina, you dream—you are raving! you do nothing but talk absurdities!

Nina. You don't believe me? Well, go and see, and you will know if I speak the truth.

Evarist. In Signora Geltrude's house?

Nina. And in Signorina Candida's.

Evarist. The Baron!

Nina. Del Cedro.

Evarist. Marries Signorina Candida!

Nina. I have seen it with these eyes, and heard it with these ears.

Evarist. It cannot be! It is impossible! You talk nonsense.

Nina. Go, see for yourself. Listen, and you will soon learn if I talk nonsense.

Evarist. I will see at once! [*Runs to the villa and knocks.*]

Nina. Poor fool, he trusts in the love of a city girl. The city girls are not as we are.

[Evarist *goes on knocking.* Tognino *opens and looks out of the door.*]

Evarist. Well, what is it?

Tognino. Excuse me, I can let no one pass.
Evarist. Have you told them it is I?
Tognino. I have.
Evarist. To Signorina Candida?
Tognino. To Signorina Candida.
Evarist. And Signora Geltrude does not wish that I should come in?
Tognino. Yes, Signora Geltrude had said you might pass, but Signorina Candida did not wish it.
Evarist. Did not wish it? I swear to Heaven I will come in! [*Tries to push aside* Tognino, *who bolts the door.*]
Nina. Well, and what did I tell you?
Evarist. I am beside myself! I do not know in what world I am. To shut the door in my face!
Nina. Oh, do not be amazed! They treated me in the same beautiful way.
Evarist. How is it possible Candida could thus deceive me?
Nina. What is a fact cannot be doubted.
Evarist. I still do not believe it—I cannot believe it—I will never believe it!
Nina. You do not believe it?
Evarist. No; there must be some mistake, some mystery. I know Candida's heart. She is incapable of this!
Nina. All right. Console yourself that way, and enjoy your consolation. Much good may it do you!
Evarist. I absolutely must speak to Candida.
Nina. But since she won't receive you?
Evarist. It does not matter. There must be some other reason! I will go into the café. It will be enough for me to see her, to hear a word from her. A sign alone from her will suffice to assure me of life or to give me my death-blow.
Nina. Well, take it.

Scene XIII.

Coronato *and* Scavezzo *return.* Scavezzo *goes straight to the inn.* Coronato *remains aside to listen.* The above.

Evarist. What do you want to give me?
Nina. Why, your fan!
Evarist. Keep it. Don't torment me.
Nina. You give me this fan?
Evarist. Yes, yes, keep it, I give it you.—[*Aside.*] I am beside myself!
Nina. If it is so, I thank you.
Coronato. [*Aside.*] Ho, ho! now I know what the present was! A fan. [*Goes to the inn without being seen.*]
Evarist. But if Candida won't let me see her—if by chance she does not look out of the window—if seeing me she refuses to listen to me—if her aunt forbids her! I am in a sea of confusion, of agitation.

[Crispino, *with a sack full of leather and shoes on his shoulder, goes towards his booth. Seeing the two, he stops to listen.*]

Nina. Dear Signor Evarist, you make me sad; I am deeply grieved for you.
Evarist. Yes, my good girl, I deserve your pity.
Nina. So good, amiable, and polite a gentleman.
Evarist. You know my heart, you bear testimony to my love.
Crispino. [*Aside.*] Nice things these! I see I came in time.
Nina. Indeed, if I knew how to comfort you—
Crispino. [*Aside.*] Better and better!
Evarist. Well, at all costs I will try my luck. I will not have to reproach myself that I neglected to clear up the matter. I go to the café, Nina; I go and tremble.

Retain to me your friendship and good-will. [*He takes her hand, and goes into the café.*]

Nina. On the one hand he makes me laugh, on the other I am sorry for him.

[Crispino *puts down his sack, pulls out some shoes, puts them on the bench, and goes into his shop without speaking.*]

Nina. Why, here is Crispino! Welcome back! Where have you been till now?

Crispino. Don't you see, to buy leather and to take shoes for mending.

Nina. But you do nothing but mend old shoes. I would not have people say—you know they are so ill-natured here—

Crispino. The evil tongues will find more to say about you than about me.

Nina. About me! What can they say?

Crispino. What do I care what they say—that I am more of a cobbler than a shoemaker? It is enough for me to be an honest man, and to earn my bread righteously. [*He sits down and works.*]

Nina. But I don't want to be called the cobbleress.

Crispino. When?

Nina. When I shall be your wife.

Crispino. Eh?

Nina. Eh! What does this eh! mean? what does this eh! mean?

Crispino. It means that Signorina Nina will be neither cobbleress nor shoemakeress; she has aims most vast and grand.

Nina. Are you mad, or have you drunk this morning?

Crispino. I am not mad, I have not drunk, but I am neither blind nor deaf.

Nina. Then what the devil do you mean? Explain yourself if you would have me understand you.

Crispino. I am to explain myself! You would have me explain myself? Do you think I have not heard your fine words with Signor Evarist?

Nina. With Signor Evarist?

Crispino. [*Imitating* Evarist.] Yes, my good girl, you know my heart; you bear testimony to my love.

Nina. [*Laughing.*] You silly fellow!

Crispino. [*Imitating* Nina.] Indeed, if I knew how to comfort you—

Nina. [*Laughing.*] Silly fellow, I say!

Crispino. [*Imitating* Evarist.] Nina, retain to me your friendship and good-will.

Nina. [*Laughing yet more.*] Sillier than ever!

Crispino. I?

Nina. Yes, absurd; madly absurd!

Crispino. But, by Jove, did I not see, did I not hear your beautiful conversation with Signor Evarist?

Nina. Silly boy, I tell you!

Crispino. And what you replied.

Nina. Silly boy!

Crispino. Nina, have done with this "silly," or I shall go silly in very deed. [*Threatens her.*]

Nina. Eh! eh! [*Becomes serious, and changes her tone.*] But do you really think Signor Evarist loves me?

Crispino. I know nothing about it.

Nina. Come here. Listen. [*Speaks rapidly.*] Signor Evarist loves Signorina Candida; and Signorina Candida has planted him, and wants to marry the Baron. And Signor Evarist is desperate, and came to pour out his heart to me; and I pretended to be sympathetic to make fun of him, and he let himself be comforted that way. Do you understand now?

Crispino. Not a word.

Nina. Are you persuaded of my innocence?

Crispino. Not entirely.

Nina. Then, if things are thus, go to the devil with you! Coronato desires me, seeks me; my brother has promised me to him. The Count, who respects me, implores—I shall marry Coronato.

Crispino. Come, come, don't be so angry instantly. Can you assure me you speak the truth—that there is nothing between you and Signor Evarist?

Nina. And you do not wish me to call you silly! But, my own good Crispino, whom I love so much, my dear betrothed! [*She caresses him.*]

Crispino. [*Gently.*] And what did Signor Evarist give you?

Nina. Nothing.

Crispino. Nothing? nothing? nothing?

Nina. When I tell you nothing, nothing.—[*Aside.*] I do not want him to know about the fan, or he will suspect me again.

Crispino. Can I be sure?

Nina. Come, come, you tease me.

Crispino. You love me?

Nina. Yes, I love you.

Crispino. Well, then, let us make peace. [*He takes her hand.*]

Nina. [*Laughing.*] Silly fellow.

Crispino. [*Laughing.*] But why silly?

Nina. Because you are.

Scene XIV.

Coronato, *who comes out of the inn. The above.*

Coronato. At last I know what present Signorina Nina has had.

Nina. What business is that of yours?

Crispino. [*To* Coronato.] From whom has she had a present?

Coronato. From Signor Evarist.

Nina. It is not true.

Crispino. It is not true?

Coronato. But it is, and I know, too, what it is.

Nina. Well, be it what it be, it does not concern you. I love Crispino, and shall be the wife of my Crispino.

Crispino. [*To* Coronato.] Well, what is the present?

Coronato. A fan.

Crispino. [*Angrily to* Nina.] A fan?

Nina. [*Aside.*] Confound that fellow!

Crispino. [*To* Nina.] Did you receive a fan?

Nina. It is not true.

Coronato. It is so true, that you have it in your pocket.

Crispino. I wish to see that fan.

Nina. No, no!

Coronato. I will find the means to make her show it.

Nina. You are an interfering fellow.

Scene XV.

Moracchio *from out the house, a table napkin in his hand, eating.*

Moracchio. What's all this noise about?

Coronato. Your sister has had a fan given her, it is in her pocket, and she denies it.

Moracchio. [*Sternly.*] Give me that fan.

Nina. Leave me alone.

Moracchio. Give me that fan, or, I swear by Heaven— [*Threatens her.*]

Nina. Confound you all! Here it is.

Crispino. [*Wants to take it.*] I want it.

Coronato. No; I.

Nina. Leave me alone, I say!

THE FAN.

Moracchio. Quick, give it here. I want it.

Nina. No; rather than to you or Coronato, I will give it to Crispino.

Moracchio. Give it to me, I say!

Nina. To Crispino! [*Gives the fan to* Crispino, *and runs into the house.*]

Coronato. Give it here.

Moracchio. Give it here.

Crispino. You shall not have it.

[*Both fall on* Crispino *to get it from him. He escapes from the scene, they follow him.*]

Scene XVI.

The Count *on the terrace.* Timoteo *outside his shop.*

Count. Hi! Signor Timoteo!

Timoteo. What do you command?

Count. Quick, quick, bring spirits and cordials! Signorina Candida has fainted!

Timoteo. Instantly. [*Returns into the shop.*]

Count. What was she looking at? One would think some poisonous plants grew in the garden of the café.

[*Exit.*

[Crispino *crosses the stage, running.* Coronato *and* Moracchio *run after him, and all three disappear.*]

Baron. [*From the villa to the apothecary.*] Quick, quick, Signor Timoteo!

Timoteo. [*Advancing with various phials and cups.*] Here I am.

Baron. Quick, quick!

Timoteo. All right, all right. [*Goes up to the door.*]

[Crispino, Coronato, Moracchio, *from outside the scene, run furiously across the stage, knock against* Timoteo, *throw him down, breaking all his bottles.* Crispino *falls over him and loses hold of the fan.* Coronato *snatches it up and runs off.* Timoteo *gets up and returns to his shop.*]

Coronato. [*To* Moracchio.] Here it is, here it is! I have got it! [*Exit.*

END OF THE SECOND ACT.

ACT III.

Scene I.

Crispino comes out of his shop, with bread, cheese, and a bottle of wine, seats himself on the bench, and breakfasts. *Tognino* comes out of *Geltrude's* villa with a broom, and crosses to the pharmacy. *Coronato* and *Scavezzo* come out of the inn; the latter carries a barrel on his shoulders; the former passes *Crispino*, looks at him and laughs. Then both go off. *Crispino* looks after him and clenches his fist. *Tognino*, issuing from the pharmacy, sweeps the square. *Timoteo* with glasses and bottles hurries across to the villa. *Crispino* has emptied his wine-bottle, and goes into the inn. *Susanna* comes out of her shop, seats herself to do some needlework. *Tognino* off into the villa. *Crispino* comes back, his bottle refilled. He draws the fan from his pocket, looks at it smiling, and seats himself again. *Nina* also seats herself outside her door to spin. *Crispino* hides the fan under his leather apron, and goes on eating. *Coronato* comes back, passes *Crispino*, and smiles. *Crispino* smiles also. *Coronato*, arrived at his own door, turns round once more to look at *Crispino* and smile, then enters. *Crispino* laughs too, takes up the fan, looks at it with pleasure, and then hides it again.

Count and Baron coming out of Geltrude's villa.

Count. No excuse! my friend, that should not vex you.

Baron. I assure you it can't please me either.

Count. If Signorina Candida felt ill, that was an accident; you must excuse. You know women are subject to vapours and nervous attacks.

Baron. But when we went in she was not ill, and scarcely did she see me than she retired to her room.

Count. Because she felt it coming on.

Baron. And then, did you notice Signora Geltrude when she came out of her niece's room, with what attention, what interest she read some papers that seemed letters.

Count. She is a woman who has much business on her hands, and a large correspondence. Doubtless they were letters just arrived.

Baron. No; they were old papers. I bet anything they were something she had found either on the table or on the person of Signorina Candida.

Count. Dear friend, your suspicions are strange! Your imagination runs away with you!

Baron. I imagine that which doubtless is the case. I suspect that an understanding exists between Signorina Candida and Evarist.

Count. Impossible! Were it so, I should know it. I know everything! There is nothing done in the village that I do not know! And further, were it as you think, do you suppose Signorina Candida would ever have accepted your proposal? How can you suppose she would thus compromise the mediation of a nobleman of my standing?

Baron. Oh, for that a good reason can be found. She was forced to say "Yes;" but Signora Geltrude was not as amiable to me after reading those letters; indeed, she seemed to me to show pleasure that we should go.

Count. Well, I think that all we have to complain of against Signora Geltrude is, that she did not ask us to stay to dinner with her.

Baron. To that I am indifferent.

Count. I gave her some hints, but she pretended not to understand.

Baron. I assure you she was most anxious we should leave.

Count. I am sorry for you. Where will you dine to-day?

Baron. I told the host to prepare dinner for two.

Count. For two?

Baron. I expect Evarist, who has gone shooting.

Count. If you will come and dine with me—

Baron. With you?

Count. But my dinner is half a mile from here.

Baron. Thank you, but the dinner is already ordered. Hi there, Coronato!

Scene II.

Coronato *from out the inn.* The above.

Coronato. You called me?

Baron. Has Signor Evarist returned?

Coronato. I have not seen him yet, sir. I am sorry, because the dinner is ready, and the food will get spoilt.

Count. Evarist is capable of amusing himself shooting till evening, and making you lose your dinner.

Baron. What can I do? I promised to wait for him.

Count. Well, it's all very well to wait for him up to a certain point. But, my dear friend, it does not seem to me you should wait long for a person who is your social inferior. I admit the demands of politeness, of humanity; but, my dear colleague, let us also preserve our aristocratic decorum.

Baron. I feel half inclined to ask you to come and take Evarist's place.

Count. If you do not wish to wait for him, or if you dislike eating alone, come to my house and take pot-luck.

Baron. No, no, my dear Count. Do me the pleasure of dining with me. Let us go to table, and if Evarist is not punctual, that is his loss.

Count. [*Content.*] It will teach him politeness.

Baron. [*To* Coronato.] Tell them to serve.

Coronato. Yes, sir. [*Aside.*] H'm, h'm! there'll be little left for the kitchen now.

Baron. I will go and see that they have prepared for our dinner. [*Enters.*]

Count. [*To* Coronato.] Have you taken the second barrel of wine?

Coronato. Yes, sir, I sent it to your house.

Count. You sent it! without going with it? I fear mischief.

Coronato. I will tell you. I accompanied the man until the turn of the road, where we met your servant.

Count. My steward?

Coronato. No, sir.

Count. My footman?

Coronato. No, sir.

Count. My lackey?

Coronato. No, sir.

Count. Who then?

Coronato. That man who lives with you, and sells your fruit, salad, vegetables.

Count. What! that man?

Coronato. Just so. I met him, showed him the barrel, and he accompanied my servant.

Count. [*Aside.*] The devil! that fellow, who never sees wine, is capable of drinking up half the barrel. [*Goes towards the door.*]

Coronato. Excuse me.

Count. What is it?

Coronato. Have you spoken for me to Nina?

Count. [*Embarrassed.*] All right, all right!

Coronato. All right?

Count. [*Advancing towards the door.*] We will speak about it after.

Coronato. But tell me one thing.

Count. Come, come, let me go in, so as not to keep the Baron waiting.

Coronato. [*Aside.*] I have good hopes. He is a man, if he takes up a cause, to succeed with it—sometimes.— [*In loving yet harsh tones.*] Nina! Nina!

[Nina *spins on and does not reply.*]

Coronato. Allow me at least to salute you.

Nina. [*Without looking up.*] You would do better to give me back my fan.

Coronato. Indeed!—[*Aside*]. Oh, by the bye, I left that fan in the cellar!—Yes, yes, let us speak of that fan.—[*Aside.*] I hope no one has carried it off. [*Goes into the house.*]

[Crispino *laughs aloud.*]

Susanna. You seem to have a light heart, Crispino, you laugh so merrily.

Crispino. I laugh because I have my reasons for laughing.

Nina. [*To* Crispino.] You laugh, and I feel gnawed with anger.

Crispino. Anger? And what are you angry about?

Nina. That that fan should be in Coronato's hands.

Crispino. [*Laughing.*] Yes, it is in Coronato's hands.

Nina. Then why do you laugh?

Crispino. I laugh because it is in Coronato's hands. [*Gets up and carries the remains of his meal into his workshop.*]

Nina. What silly laughter!

Susanna. I never thought my fan would pass through so many hands.

Nina. [*Looking at her with amazement.*] Your fan?

Susanna. Oh, I say my fan because it came from my shop.

Nina. I suppose you were paid for it?

Susanna. Of course, else I should not have given it.

Nina. And it will also have been paid double its worth?

Susanna. Not so; and even were it so, what does it matter to you? For what it cost you, you can accept it.

Nina. How do you know what it costs me?

Susanna. [*Sarcastically and pointedly.*] Oh, I don't know what it cost you, nor whether he who gave it you has great obligations towards you.

Nina. What obligations? What do you mean by obligations? Do I meddle in your affairs?

Susanna. There, there, don't excite yourself! You don't intimidate me with your fury!

Crispino. [*From out the shop.*] What's the matter? Incessant bickerings, incessant high words.

Susanna. She makes side hits and expects one to keep silent.

Crispino. Are you angry, Nina?

Nina. I angry? I am never angry!

Susanna. Oh, she loves peace, and never excites herself!

Nina. Never, except when I am teased, if I have to hear impertinences, if I am trampled under foot.

[Susanna *mutters to herself.*]

Crispino. Is it I who ill-treat you, tease you, trample you under foot?

Nina. [*Spinning sulkily.*] I am not speaking of you.

Susanna. No, she does not refer to you, she refers to me.

Crispino. One might really say it is an art to live for five minutes in peace on this square.

Nina. When evil tongues are abroad.

Crispino. Quiet! it is shameful.

Susanna. One is to be insulted, and then not speak.

Nina. I speak reasonably.

Susanna. Better I should be silent.

Nina. Certainly it is better to be silent than say foolish things.

Crispino. You will always have the last word.

Nina. Yes; and were I in my grave—

[Timoteo *from out the villa with cups and bottles.*]

Nina. He who wants me, takes me as I am, and who does not want me, leaves me alone!

Crispino. Do be quiet at last!

Timoteo. [*Aside.*] I won't go again into that house. Is it my fault that these waters don't help? I can only give what I have. They expect to find all the refinements of town in a village. And then what are spirits, cordials, essences? So many quack remedies. The corner-stones of an apothecary are, water, quinine, mercury. [*Goes into his shop.*]

Crispino. Some one must be ill at the villa.

Nina. [*With contempt.*] Yes, that dear jewel of a Signorina Candida!

Susanna. Poor Signorina Candida!

Crispino. What is the matter with her?

Susanna. [*Pointedly.*] Nina should know something about it.

Nina. I? What have I to do with it?

Susanna. Because she is ill on your account.

Nina. On my account! [*Springs to her feet.*]

Susanna. Oh, one cannot speak quietly with you.

Crispino. I should like to know what all this means. [*Gets up from his work.*]

Nina. [*To* Susanna.] You are only able to say silly things!

Susanna. There, there, don't excite yourself.

Crispino. [*To* Nina.] Let her speak.

Nina. Well, speak, then.

Susanna. I won't say anything more to you!

Nina. If you have any sense of honour, speak.

Susanna. If matters are thus, well, I will.

Crispino. Quiet there! Signora Geltrude is approaching. No scenes before her.

Nina. She shall give me an explanation!

Scene III.

Geltrude *from the villa. The above.*

Geltrude. [*Gravely.*] Is your brother returned?

Nina. [*Ungraciously, and turning away.*] Yes, he is.

Geltrude. [*As above.*] Has Signor Evarist returned also?

Nina. [*As above.*] Yes, he has.

Geltrude. Do you know where he is?

Nina. [*With annoyance.*] I know nothing! Good day. [*Enters the house.*]

Geltrude. What manners!—Crispino!

Crispino. [*Rises.*] Madame?

Geltrude. Do you know where to find Signor Evarist?

Crispino. No, Madame, in truth I do not.

Geltrude. Do me the favour to go and see if he is in the inn.

Crispino. Certainly. [*Goes towards the inn.*]

Susanna. [*Softly.*] Signora Geltrude!

Geltrude. What would you?

Susanna. One word.

Geltrude. Do you know nothing about Signor Evarist?

Susanna. Ah, Madame, I know many things. I have many things to tell you.

Geltrude. Alas! I too have much to disquiet me; I have seen letters that surprise me! Speak, enlighten me if you can.

Susanna. But here, in public! Shall I not come to your house?

Geltrude. I first want to see Signor Evarist.

Susanna. Will you then step into my shop?

Geltrude. Yes, rather let us do that. But first let us await Signor Evarist.

Susanna. There he is!

Crispino. [*From the inn.*] He is not there. They expected him to dinner, and he has not come.

Geltrude. Yet he must have come back from shooting.

Crispino. Oh yes, he came back; I saw him.

Geltrude. Where can he be?

Susanna. He is not at the café either.

Crispino. Nor at the apothecary's.

Geltrude. Let us search a little. The village is not so large. Look about, we must discover him.

Crispino. I will set off at once!

Geltrude. If you find him, tell him I want much to speak to him, and that I wait for him in Susanna's shop.

[Crispino *goes.*]

Geltrude. [*Enters* Susanna's *shop.*] Now I am ready and anxious to hear you.

Susanna. Well, well, you will hear nice things.

Crispino. There is something wrong about this Signor Evarist. And then this fan—I am glad I have got it. Coronato noticed it was gone, I suppose. He is scarcely likely to suspect me. No one will have told him that I went to buy some wine. I went just in time. I found the fan a-top of the barrel. Silly fellow! And while his man filled my flask, I pocketed the fan! I shall take pretty good care not to confess that I took it. He is capable of calling me a thief. But where am I to look for this gentleman? Not at the Count's, for he is dining in there. In the village? I am sorry I am not enlightened as to Susanna's meaning. But I will get to the bottom of it. And if I find Nina guilty— Well, and what shall I do then? Cast her off? I don't know. I love her too much. What can it all be?

SCENE IV.

Crispino *and* Limonato *from the café.* Then Coronato.

Crispino. Do you know where Signor Evarist is?

Limonato. I! why should I? I am not his servant.

Crispino. Don't excite yourself thus. Might he not happen to be at your place?

Limonato. Then you would see him.

Crispino. Out upon you, you lemonade manufacturer!

Limonato. What does this mean?

Crispino. Wait till your shoes want cobbling again.
[*Exit.*

Limonato. The wretch! Shall I tell him Signor Evarist is in our garden? No, he is only just comforted, why disturb him again? Hi, host!

Coronato. [*At his door.*] What would you?

Limonato. Signor Evarist sends me. Tell the Baron he is not to wait dinner for him; he is busy, and does not wish to be disturbed.

Coronato. Tell him the notice comes too late. The Baron has nearly done his dinner.

Limonato. All right. [*About to go.*]

Coronato. And if you hear that some one has found a fan, let me know.

Limonato. With pleasure. Have you lost one?

Coronato. Yes; I don't know how. A rogue carried it off, and my stupid cellarman can't tell me who came to fetch wine. But if I discover him, then—Good-day. [*Exit.*

Limonato. I will do my best. [*Exit.*

Scene V.

The Count *at the window of the inn. The above.*

Count. I heard Limonato's voice. Hi, Limonato!

Limonato. Sir?

Count. Two cups of coffee!

Limonato. Excuse me, for whom?

Count. For me and the Baron. [*Disappears.*]

Limonato. At once!—[*Aside.*] Now I know the Baron is inside and pays, he shall have the coffee.

Nina. Hi, Limonato!

Limonato. And what do you want?

Nina. Is Signor Evarist still with you?

Limonato. How with me?

Nina. Yes, with you.

Limonato. There is the café, if he were there, you would see him.

Nina. Bah! I mean in the garden.

Limonato. Bah! I don't know anything. [*Exit.*

Nina. Rude fellow! And people say I am irritable! How can I help it, when all tease, all maltreat me?—those ladies, that creature over there, Coronato, Moracchio, Limonato, and Crispino. I can bear it no longer.

Scene VI.

Evarist *running excitedly out of the café.* The above.

Evarist. [*To* Nina.] There she is, there she is! Now I am happy!

Nina. What does this joy mean?

Evarist. Oh, Nina, I am the happiest, the most contented man in the world!

Nina. I am glad to hear it. I hope, then, you will make up to me for all I have had to endure on your account.

Evarist. Anything you wish! Know, Nina, that they suspected that I loved you. Signorina Candida knew I had given you the fan, thought I had bought it for you, was jealous of me, was jealous of you!

Nina. Was jealous of me?

Evarist. Precisely; and to avenge herself, and in despair, she was about to marry another. She saw me, and fell down lifeless in a faint. Happily, a moment after her aunt left the house, Candida went into the garden. I climbed over the hedge, sprang over the wall, fell at her feet, wept, swore, implored, called all the saints to witness, and convinced her. She is mine, is mine, and will be mine in all eternity!

Nina. I congratulate you. I am glad to hear it, sir.

Evarist. One only condition she makes in order to be quite convinced of my love.

Nina. And that is?—

Evarist. In order that I may justify myself and you also, it is needful that you give her the fan.

Nina. Oh dear, oh dear!

Evarist. My honour and your own are at stake. It would seem otherwise as if I had really bought the fan for you. She must be relieved of every suspicion. I know you are a sensible girl, therefore give me back that fan.

Nina. But, sir, I have it no longer.

Evarist. Why tell this lie? I gave it you, and I would not ask it back did not my whole life's happiness hang on it. I will buy you another, far better and more beautiful. But, for Heaven's sake, give me back that fan, and quickly too!

Nina. Oh, if I but had it!

Evarist. Nina, I repeat, our honour is at stake.

Nina. I swear I no longer have the fan!

Evarist. Oh, heavens! And what did you do with it?

Nina. Oh, they knew I had the fan, and forced me to give it up by violence.

Evarist. Who?

Nina. My brother.

Evarist. [*Goes towards the house and calls.*] Moracchio!

Nina. No, stop! He has not got it!

Evarist. Who, then?

Nina. He gave it to Crispino.

Evarist. [*Runs towards the workshop.*] Crispino!

Nina. Stop and listen, I say!

Evarist. I am beside myself.

Nina. Crispino no longer has it either.

Evarist. Heaven and hell, who has it then? Quick!

Nina. That rogue of a Coronato.

Evarist. Coronato! hi, host, Coronato!

Coronato. Yes, sir?

Evarist. Give here that fan.
Coronato. What fan?
Nina. That which you stole.
Evarist. Out with it! Quick!
Coronato. Sir, I am sincerely sorry, but—
Evarist. How so? What is this?
Coronato. I can no longer find it.
Evarist. Not find it!
Coronato. I stupidly forgot it in the cellar, and went away. When I came back, it had vanished. Some one must have stolen it.
Evarist. Look for it!
Coronato. I have searched the whole house, in vain.
Evarist. I will pay you whatever you like for it!
Coronato. But if it is gone—I tell you it is gone.
Evarist. I am in despair!
Coronato. I am most sorry, but I can do nothing. [*Exit.*
Evarist. It is all your fault! You are my misfortune!
Nina. I? And how am I to blame in it all?

Scene VII.

Candida *on the terrace.* *The above.*

Candida. [*Calling him.*] Signor Evarist!
Evarist. There she is, there she is! Oh, I am in despair!
Nina. What, what! the world is not come to an end because of this!
Candida. [*Calls more loudly.*] Signor Evarist!
Evarist. Oh, Candida, my dearest! I am the most miserable, the most wretched man in the world!

Candida. What! you can't get the fan?

Nina. [*Aside.*] She guesses it at once!

Evarist. If you knew what a coil of complications, and all to my injury! It is too true, the fan is lost, and it is not possible to find it as yet.

Candida. Oh, I know where it is!

Evarist. Where? where? If you could give us some hint!

Nina. [*To* Evarist.] Who knows? Some one may have found it.

Candida. The fan will be in the hands of her to whom you gave it, and who will not give it up, and she is right.

Nina. [*To* Candida.] This is not true.

Candida. Be silent!

Evarist. I swear to you on my honour—

Candida. It is enough! My decision is made! I am astonished at you, to prefer a peasant girl to me.

[*Exit.*

Nina. Peasant girl! What does she mean?

Evarist. I swear to Heaven, you are the cause of all my miseries, which will be my death! She has decided! Well, I have decided too; I will await my rival here, and will challenge him. Either he or I must fall! And all this is your fault, Nina!

Nina. I go, or I shall lose my reason. [*She turns slowly towards her house.*]

Evarist. How passion consumes me! My heart thumps, my brain is in a whirl, my breath comes heavily. I can scarcely stand! Oh, who will help me? [*He staggers towards a chair.*]

Nina. [*Turns round and sees him.*] What is this? What do I see? He is dying! Help, help! Here, Moracchio! here, Limonato!

Scene VIII.

Limonato *from the café with two cups on a tray.* Moracchio *runs from his house to succour* Evarist.

Crispino. [*Comes out of the side street.*] Oh, there is Signor Evarist. But what is the matter?
Nina. Water, water!
Crispino. Wine, wine!
Limonato. Give him wine. I will just carry these cups to the inn.
Moracchio. Courage, courage, sir! He is in love; that is his malady.
Timoteo. [*Comes out of his shop.*] What is the matter?
Moracchio. Come here, Timoteo.
Nina. Yes, do you help.
Timoteo. What is the matter?
Nina. He has fainted.
Timoteo. There I can help.
Nina. The poor gentleman, he is in love.
Crispino. [*With a bottle of wine.*] Here, here! that will restore him to life—five-year-old wine.
Nina. He is reviving!
Crispino. Oh, this wine would make the dead rise!
Moracchio. Courage, courage, sir, I say!
Timoteo. [*With bottles, glasses, and a razor.*] Here I am. Quick, undress him!
Moracchio. What is the razor for?
Timoteo. In case of need, it is better than a lancet.
Crispino. A razor?
Nina. What?
Evarist. [*Gets up.*] Oh ho! who wants to cut my throat with a razor?
Nina. The apothecary.

Timoteo. Excuse me; I am an honest man, and no assassin. When one has the best intentions, it is not right to make one appear ridiculous. See whether I will come another time. [*Exit.*

Moracchio. Won't you step into my house, sir, and rest on my bed?

Evarist. Wherever you like.

Moracchio. Take my arm and lean on me.

Evarist. Oh, how much rather I would that my miserable life were ended! [*Walks off, leaning on* Moracchio.]

Nina. [*Aside.*] If he wanted to die, he could not have done better than give himself up to the apothecary.

Moracchio. Here we are at the door. Let us go in.

Evarist. Useless kindness to him who only asks to die. [*They enter.*]

Moracchio. Nina, get the bed ready for Signor Evarist.

Crispino. [*As she is going to enter, calls her.*] Nina!

Nina. What is it?

Crispino. You are wonderfully compassionate for this gentleman.

Nina. I do my duty, because you and I are the cause of his illness.

Crispino. Speak for yourself, there I can't answer. But I? What have I to do with him?

Nina. Because of that accursed fan. [*Goes in.*]

Crispino. Accursed fan, indeed! I have now heard it named millions of times! But I am glad to think I did Coronato. He is my enemy, and will be so till Nina is my wife. But what now? I could bury this fan in the ground; but if it be trodden on, it will break. What shall I do with it. [*Pulls out the fan.*]

[Limonato *crosses from his café to the inn.*]

Count. [*From out the inn.*] The dinner was excellent! For once I have eaten my fill.

Crispino. [*Aside.*] Ho, ho, the Count. Shall I— Yes, that will be the best way. [*Advances towards him, fan in hand.*]

Count. What is that you have in your hand?

Crispino. A fan. I found it on the ground.

Count. [*Takes it.*] A lady must have lost it in passing by. What will you do with it?

Crispino. I really don't know.

Count. Do you want to sell it?

Crispino. Sell it? I should not know what to ask for it. What may it be worth?

Count. I don't know, for I don't understand such things. There are figures painted on it; but a fan found in the country can't be worth much.

Crispino. I wish it were worth very much.

Count. In order to sell it well?

Crispino. No, certainly not; but only in order to offer it to your honour.

Count. To me! You want to give it to me?

Crispino. But as it seems of no value—

Count. Oh no; it is not bad, and seems quite decent. Thank you, my friend. Whenever I can be of use to you, count on my protection.—[*Aside.*] I shall give it away.

Crispino. But one thing I beg of you.

Count. [*Aside.*] Didn't I think so! This class of people gives nothing for nothing!—Well, what is it? Speak.

Crispino. I beg you to tell no one that I gave it to you.

Count. Is that all?

Crispino. All.

Count. If it's nothing but that— [*Aside.*] He is

cautious. But, my good friend, why should people not know? Have you perchance stolen it?

Crispino. Excuse me. I am not capable of that.

Count. Then why should no one know it comes from you? If you have found it, and the owner does not turn up, I don't see why—

Crispino. [*Laughing.*] And yet I have my reasons.

Count. And they are?—

Crispino. Well, I am in love.

Count. I know it. With Nina.

Crispino. And if Nina knew I had this fan, and did not give it to her, she would be angry.

Count. Just as well for her not to have it. This is no fan for a country girl. Do not fear; I shall not betray you. But that reminds me, how do matters stand with you and Nina? Do you really mean to marry her?

Crispino. I confess I desire her as my wife.

Count. Well, then, you shall have her. This **very** evening, if you like, we will celebrate the wedding.

Crispino. Really, you are in earnest?

Count. In earnest. Who am I? What is meant by my protection? I am almighty!

Crispino. But Coronato wants her also.

Count. Coronato! Who is Coronato? A stupid fellow! Does she love you?

Crispino. Yes, dearly.

Count. Good, then: you are loved, Coronato **is** not. Depend on my protection.

Crispino. Most certainly. But—her brother?

Count. Brother! what brother? what of him? If the sister is satisfied, the brother has nothing to say. Depend entirely on my protection.

Crispino. By Saint Crispin!

Count. There now, go back to **your** work, that **my** shoes may get done at last.

Crispino. As your Honour desires.

[Count *examines the fan.*]

Crispino. [*Aside.*] The devil a bit! I forgot that Signora Geltrude sent me to look for Signor Evarist, and now I have found him and not told her. But his illness—the fan—in short, I forgot! I will call him, but I don't like to go to Moracchio's house. I will go to the Signora Geltrude and tell her Signor Evarist is found, and she is to have him called, only not by me. [*Goes off towards the draper's shop.*]

Count. What can it cost? Not much. Were it more choice, I would give it to Signorina Candida, who broke her own. But why should I not? It is not half bad.

Nina. [*At the window.*] Where is Crispino? Not there!

Count. The figures are badly painted, but it seems to me they are well drawn.

Nina. Oh, what do I see! The fan is in the Count's hands! Quick, quick, to wake Signor Evarist!

Count. And who refuses a gift? She shall have it.

Scene IX.

Count. Baron *from the inn.* Then Tognino.

Baron. What! you abandon me?

Count. I saw you were not inclined to talk.

Baron. Yes, it is true. I can't resign myself. Tell me, do you think we might go now and try to see those ladies once more.

Count. Why not? I have a happy thought! Shall I make you a present,—a present that will make you cut a good figure in Signorina Candida's eyes?

Baron. What is this present?

Count. You know she broke her fan this morning.

Baron. Yes, I heard of it.

Count. Here is a fan. Let us go and find her and give her this one from you. [*Gives it to the* Baron.] Look, it is not ugly.

Baron. You want me then to—

Count. Yes, you give it. I do not want to have any merit in the matter. I leave all the honour to you.

Baron. I gladly accept this excuse, but you will at least let me know what it cost?

Count. Oh, a trifle.

Baron. Nevertheless, kindly tell me the price.

Count. But to what end? Did you not give me a present of two pistols?

Baron. I do not know what to say. Well, I accept your present gratefully.—[*Aside.*] Where did he find this fan? It seems to me impossible that he bought it.

Count. Well, what do you say to it? Isn't it a pretty thing? And just in the nick of time! Oh, I understand these things, I have much experience. I am well provided. There is a whole room full of nick-nacks for ladies. But do not let us waste time. Let us go. [*Rings at* Signora Geltrude's *house.*]

Tognino. [*From the terrace.*] What do you wish, gentlemen?

Count. Will the ladies receive us?

Tognino. Signora Geltrude is out, and Signorina Candida is resting in her room.

Count. Let us know as soon as she is awake.

Tognino. Yes, sir. [*Exit.*

Count. Did you hear?

Baron. Well, we must just wait. I have to write a letter to Milan; I will go and write it at the apothecary's. If you will come too—

Count. No; I don't like going to that man's house.

Go and write your letter, and I will wait here till the servant calls us.

Baron. Very well. As soon as you want me, I am at your service.

Count. Count on me, do not fear.

Baron. [*Aside.*] I do not count on him, and still less on the aunt, and yet less on the niece. [*Goes to* Timoteo's.]

Count. I will amuse myself with my book, with my beautiful collection of wonderful fables. [*Pulls out his book, seats himself, and reads.*]

Scene X.

Count. Evarist *comes out of* Nina's *house.*

Evarist. Oh, there he is still! I thought he was gone. I can't think how I was able to fall asleep amid so much distress of mind. Fatigue—exhaustion. Now I feel born anew with the hopes of having back the fan.— [*Calls.*] Count, your servant.

Count. [*Reading and smiling.*] Your servant, Signor Evarist.

Evarist. Will you permit me to say a few words?

Count. [*As above.*] In a moment I am at your disposal.

Evarist. [*Aside.*] If he has not got the fan in his hand, I don't know how to begin speaking about it.

Count. [*Gets up laughing, and pockets his book.*] Here I am, at your services.

Evarist. [*Searching with his eyes for the fan.*] I should be sorry if I have disturbed you.

Count. It does not matter, I will finish reading my fable another time.

Evarist. [*As above.*] I should not like you to think me impertinent.

Count. What are you looking at? Have I some spot about me?

Evarist. Excuse me, I was told you had a fan.

Count. [*Confused.*] A fan! It is true. Was it perchance you who lost it?

Evarist. Yes, sir, I lost it.

Count. But there are many fans in the world. How do you know it is yours?

Evarist. If you would have the kindness to show it to me?

Count. My friend, I am sorry you come too late.

Evarist. How too late?

Count. The fan is no longer in my possession.

Evarist. What?

Count. No; I gave it away.

Evarist. And pray to whom?

Count. That is just what I would rather not tell you.

Evarist. Count, I must know! I must have back that fan, and I will know who has it now!

Count. I will not tell!

Evarist. Heavens and earth, but you shall tell!

Count. Do not forget who I am!

Evarist. [*Angrily.*] I say it, and I will maintain it! This is an ungentlemanly action!

Count. Do you know that I have a couple of loaded pistols?

Evarist. What do I care about your pistols? I want my fan!

Count. How absurd! So much eagerness and noise for a bit of a fan which is worth perhaps five paoli!

Evarist. Let it be worth whatever it is worth, you cannot know that for me it is priceless. I would give twenty ducats to have it!

Count. You would give twenty ducats!

Evarist. If I tell you so, I promise it! If you can get it back I will gladly sacrifice twenty ducats.

Count. [*Aside.*] The devil! It must be painted by Titian or Raphael of Urbino.—I will see if I can get you back the fan.

Evarist. If the owner likes to sell it for twenty ducats, I repeat I am willing.

Count. Had I the fan, such a proposal would offend me.

Evarist. But perchance it will not offend its present owner.

Count. Perchance, who knows? My friend, I assure you, I am quite confused.

Evarist. Let us do like this, Count. This is a gold snuff-box whose weight alone represents a worth of over twenty ducats. Its workmanship makes it worth twice as much. Never mind; for that fan I will willingly give this box. Here it is!

Count. [*Holding the box in his hand.*] Are there perhaps diamonds on that fan? I noticed nothing.

Evarist. It is not of the faintest value, but it is of worth to me.

Count. Then I must try and satisfy you.

Evarist. I beg of you!

Count. Await me here.—[*Aside.*] I am quite confused.—But am I to give the box in exchange?

Evarist. Yes, yes, give it!

Count. Wait. [*Walks a few steps.*] And if the person gives me the fan, and does not want the box?

Evarist. I have given it to you. Do what you like with your property.

Count. In earnest?

Evarist. In earnest.

Count. [*Aside.*] After all, the Baron is a gentleman and my friend. Because of the twenty ducats I would not accept it, but a gold snuff-box—that gives an aristocratic, refined, well-to-do air.—[*Aloud.*] Wait for me here. [*Goes into the pharmacy.*]

Evarist. To justify myself in her eyes I would sacrifice my life, my heart's blood!

Scene XI.

Crispino *from out of* Susanna's *shop.* *The above.*
Then the Count, *after* Nina.

Crispino. Oh, there he is! Sir, your servant. Signora Geltrude wishes to speak with you. She is here in the shop, and begs you to have the kindness to step in there. She expects you.

Evarist. Tell her I am at her service in one moment. I must urgently speak to some one before.

Crispino. Yes, sir. And how are you now—better?

Evarist. Much better, I am glad to say.

Crispino. I am delighted to hear it. And Nina is well?

Evarist. I think so.

Crispino. She is a good girl, is Nina.

Evarist. Yes, indeed, and I know she loves you dearly.

Crispino. And I love her too, but—

Evarist. But what?

Crispino. I have been told certain things.

Evarist. Concerning me, perhaps?

Crispino. To say the truth, yes, sir.

Evarist. Friend, I am a gentleman, and your Nina is a good, honest girl.

Crispino. I think so too. There are always evil tongues about.

[Count, *coming out of the pharmacy.*]

Evarist. There now! Go to Signora Geltrude and tell her I shall come directly.

Crispino. Yes, sir. [*Walks away.*] I feel easy now that nothing is wrong here.—[*Aloud as he passes the Count.*] I commend myself to you on behalf of Nina.

Count. Count on my protection!

Crispino. I desire it earnestly. [*Goes into the shop.*]

Evarist. Well, Count?

Count. Here is the fan. [*He shows it him.*]

Evarist. [*Seizes it eagerly.*] Oh, what happiness! How greatly I am obliged to you!

Count. Look whether it be yours.

Evarist. Beyond a doubt. [*Wishes to move off.*]

Count. And the snuff-box?

Evarist. Do not let us name that. I am but too grateful. [*Off to* Susanna's *shop.*]

Count. What it means not to understand things perfectly! I thought it a common fan, and now it seems it is worth so much,—so much, in fact, that it is worth exchanging against a gold snuff-box. No doubt the Baron would have liked the box. He was vexed that I asked for the fan back, but when I said I would present it in his name, he was mollified a little. I will now go and buy one like it.

Crispino. [*Returning.*] Well, this job is done. I like to serve Signora Geltrude. So you give me good hopes, Count?

Count. Most excellent hopes! To-day is a fortunate day for me, and all I do in it succeeds.

Crispino. Let us hope this will succeed too.

Count. Most undoubtedly! Hi, Nina!

Nina. [*Comes out of her house testily.*] What do you want now?

Count. Do not be angered so quickly. I want to do you a service. I want to marry you.

Nina. I don't need you for that.
Count. With some one to your taste.
Nina. And I say no!
Count. With Crispino.
Nina. With Crispino?
Count. Aha, what do you say now?
Nina. With all my heart!
Count. There, Crispino, you see what my protection means!
Crispino. Yes, sir, I see.

Scene XII.

Moracchio *from the house.* *The above.*

Moracchio. What are you doing here?
Nina. What does it matter to you?
Count. Nina is going to be married under the ægis of my protection.
Moracchio. As you like, sir; and she must consent, whether she like it or no.
Nina. [*Gravely.*] Oh, I will consent dutifully.
Moracchio. The better for you!
Nina. And to show you I consent, I will give my hand to Crispino.
Moracchio. [*Amazed.*] But—Count—
Count. [*Placidly.*] Let them be.
Moracchio. But, Count, did you not give your word to Coronato?

Scene XIII.

Coronato *from the inn.* *The above.*

Coronato. Who is talking about me?
Moracchio. Come here, and behold! The Count wants my sister to marry—

Coronato. [*Anxiously.*] Count!

Count. I am a just man and a nobleman, a sensible protector and human. Nina does not want you, and I cannot, and must not, and will not use violence!

Nina. And I want Crispino, though the whole world oppose it!

Coronato. [*To* Moracchio.] And what say you?

Moracchio. [*To* Coronato.] And what say you?

Coronato. I don't care a fig! Who does not want me, does not deserve me!

Nina. That is the saying.

Count. [*To* Crispino.] See the results of my protection!

Coronato. Count, I have sent the second barrel of wine.

Count. Bring me the bill, and I will pay it. [*While speaking, he pulls out the gold snuff-box, and ostentatiously takes snuff.*]

Coronato. [*Aside.*] He has a gold snuff-box—he can pay. [*Exit.*

Moracchio. [*To* Nina.] Well, you have had your way after all.

Nina. So it seems.

Moracchio. And if you repent, it will be your affair.

Count. She will never need to repent. She has my protection.

Moracchio. Bread seems to me better than protection. [*Exit.*

Count. And when shall we hold the wedding?

Crispino. Soon.

Nina. Yes, soon.

Scene XIV.

Baron *from the pharmacy.* *The above.*

Baron. Well, Count, have you seen Signorina

Candida, and have you given her the fan? Why would you not let me have the pleasure of giving it her myself?

Nina. [*Aside.*] What! Signor Evarist has not got it!

Count. I have not yet seen Signorina Candida, and as for the fan, I have others, and have destined a better one for her. Oh, here is Signora Geltrude!

Scene XV.

Geltrude, Evarist, *and* Susanna, *all three come out of* Susanna's *shop.*

Geltrude. [*To* Susanna.] Do me the favour of telling my niece to come down. I must speak to her.

Susanna. I go at once. [*Goes to the villa, knocks, they open, she enters.*]

Geltrude. [*Softly to* Evarist.] I do not wish the Count and the Baron to go into the house.

Count. Signora Geltrude, the Baron and I were just about to visit you.

Geltrude. I am obliged for the polite intention. The evening is so fine, we can talk out of doors.

Baron. So you have come back, Signor Evarist?

Evarist. [*Curtly.*] As you see.

Scene XVI.

The above. Candida.

Candida. What does my aunt wish?
Geltrude. Let us take a few turns.
Candida. [*Aside.*] Why, there is the false Evarist!
Geltrude. But why have you got no fan?
Candida. Don't you remember I broke mine this morning?

Geltrude. Ah, yes, true; if we could find another.

Baron. [*Whispers to* Count.] Now is the time to give it.

Count. [*Aside.*] No, not in public.

Geltrude. Signor Evarist, you do not happen by chance to have one?

Evarist. Here it is, at your service. [*He shows it to* Geltrude, *but does not give it to her.*]

[Candida *turns aside contemptuously.*]

Baron. [*Softly to the* Count.] Your fan! out with your fan!

Count. [*As above.*] Don't poke me so!

Baron. [*As above.*] Out with it, I say!

Count. [*As above.*] Not now, not now!

Geltrude. Niece, won't you accept Signor Evarist's polite offer?

Candida. No, aunt, excuse me; I don't need it.

Count. [*To* Baron.] You see, she does not accept it!

Baron. [*To* Count.] Give it me at once!

Count. [*To* Baron.] Do you mean to pick a quarrel?

Geltrude. May I ask why you will not accept this fan?

Candida. Because it is not mine; because it was not meant for me. It would not become either you or me were I to accept it.

Geltrude. Signor Evarist, can you answer this?

Evarist. I can if I may.

Candida. Excuse me. [*Turns to leave.*]

Geltrude. Stay here! I command it. [*Candida obeys.*]

Baron. [*To* Count.] What is all this imbroglio?

Count. [*To* Baron.] I know nothing about it all.

Evarist. Susanna, do you know this fan?

Susanna. Yes, sir. It is that you bought from me this morning. I most imprudently concluded you had bought it for Nina. I confess I was wrong, but appearances were against you, for in truth you gave the fan to the girl.

Evarist. Nina, why did I give you that fan?

Nina. That I might give it to Signorina Candida; but when I went to do so, the ladies would not let me speak, and turned me out of the house. I then wanted to give it back to you, and you would not have it, so I gave it to Crispino.

Crispino. And I fell down, and Coronato took it.

Evarist. But where is Coronato? How did it leave Coronato's hands?

Crispino. Don't call him! As he is not there, I will tell the truth. I was annoyed, went into the inn to fetch wine, saw it lying about, and carried it off.

Evarist. And what did you do with it then?

Crispino. I gave it to the Count.

Count. And I gave it to the Baron.

Baron. [*Contemptuously.*] And then took it back again!

Count. Yes, and restored it to Signor Evarist.

Evarist. And I present it to Signorina Candida.

[Candida *accepts it with a deep courtesy, smiling sweetly.*]

Baron. What comedy is all this? what complication have we here? Am I made ridiculous through your fault?

Count. I swear to Heaven, Signor Evarist, I swear to Heaven—

Evarist. Come, come, Count, do not distress yourself. We are friends. Give me a pinch of snuff.

Count. [*Offers him the box.*] Yes, I am like that; if I am treated well, I don't excite myself.

Baron. You may not, but I do.

Geltrude. Baron!

Baron. And you, too, helped to make me ridiculous.

Geltrude. Excuse me; you don't know me, sir. I

have not failed in my engagements. I listened to your proposals, my niece heard and accepted them, and I consented with pleasure.

Count. [*To the* Baron.] You hear? That was because I spoke.

Baron. [*To* Candida.] And you, Signorina Candida, why did you give me hope? why did you deceive me?

Candida. I must ask your forgiveness, sir. I was torn by two conflicting passions. The desire for revenge made me wish to be yours, and love gives me back to Evarist.

Count. I did not know this.

Geltrude. And if you had been a bolder lover and a sincerer friend, you would not have found yourself in this case.

Baron. It is true. I confess my passion, I condemn my weakness; but I despise the friendship and conduct of the Count. [*He salutes and moves off.*]

Count. There, there, it is nothing. Let us be friends. We are joking. Among colleagues these things are understood. Come, let us think of these weddings.

Geltrude. Let us go into the house, and I hope all will be arranged to universal satisfaction.

[Candida *fans herself.*]

Geltrude. Are you contented to have that much-desired fan in your hands?

Candida. I cannot express the measure of my content.

Geltrude. A great fan! It has turned all our heads, from the highest to the lowest.

Candida. [*To* Susanna.] Is it from Paris, this fan?

Susanna. Yes, from Paris; I guarantee it.

Geltrude. Come, I invite you all to supper, and we will drink to this fan which did all the harm and brought about all the good.

THE SPENDTHRIFT MISER

(AVARICE AND OSTENTATION)

A COMEDY IN FIVE ACTS

DRAMATIS PERSONÆ.

Count Casteldoro.
Marquis Del Bosco.
Chevalier Del Bosco.
Giacinto.
Frontino.
Fiorillo.
Tailor.
Jeweller.
Araminta.
Eleonora.
Dorimene.

Visitors and a Notary who do not speak.

Scene—Paris.

THE SPENDTHRIFT MISER.

ACT I.

Scene I.—Count.

Count. At last I am determined to marry. How! I marry! I, who have always avoided expense! I, who have detested all intercourse with ladies! Well, in this case, I am hurried away in my own despite. Ambition has induced me to obtain a title; therefore, should I die without children, my money is lost! and children themselves will but bring trouble! [*Calls.*] Frontino!

Scene II.—*Enter* Frontino.

Front. Here, sir!
Count. Hark ye!
Front. I have found a tailor, sir, as you ordered me; and a tailor of the first notoriety.
Count. Will he come directly?
Front. Very soon. He was obliged first to wait on a duke. I was lucky enough to find him at home when he was about to step into his coach.
Count. His coach?
Front. Yes, sir.
Count. His own coach? His own horses?
Front. Beyond all doubt. A superb carriage, and excellent nags

Count. O Lord! He's too rich. Is he in repute?

Front. In the greatest. He works for the first families in Paris.

Count. But his honesty?

Front. On that subject I have nothing to say. But why, Signor Count, did you not employ your own tailor?

Count. Fie! My own tailor on such an occasion! I have need of several suits; and, as they must be grand, magnificent, and made to perfection, shall I, if any one should ask who is my tailor, shall I answer, "Signor Taccone," whose name nobody knows?

Front. Then, sir, from what I hear, you are soon to be married?

Count. So soon, that this very day, and in this very house, I am to sign the contract: I have therefore called you to give the necessary orders. On this occasion, I shall have a large company to dine with me, and must have such a dinner—in short, brilliant! grand! splendid! Not that I would satiate the indiscreet, or gorge my guests; but I would surprise, by an air of grandeur— you know what I mean?

Front. Yes, sir, tolerably well; but to do all this will not be quite so easy. I must inquire whether the cook—

Count. No, no, Frontino; I would not have you dependent on the caprice of a cook. Take the direction of everything upon yourself. I know your talents, the readiness of your wit, and your zeal for your master's interest. There is not in the whole world a man like Frontino! You can work miracles; and on such an occasion will surpass yourself.

Front. [*Aside.*] Ha! his usual mode. Coaxing me when he wants me; but afterwards—

Count. Here is a list of the guests whom I have

invited. My sister lives in this house, and my future spouse and her mother have the adjoining apartments. Here is a note of the other guests. We shall be thirty at table. Hasten to them all, and get a positive answer from each, that, in case of refusals, other persons may be invited.

Front. Thirty guests! Do you know, sir, how much a dinner for thirty will—

Count. Perfectly; and will employ your discretion to combine economy and magnificence.

Front. For example, you gave a supper a few nights ago to three gentlemen, and—

Count. Ay, that was a trifle; at present I would be talked of.

Front. But this trifling supper you thought so dear that—

Count. Lose no time in useless words.

Front. You threw the account in my face, and have not yet

Count. Here is my sister. Begone!

Front. [*Aside.*] O Lord! what will become of me? This time, friend Frontino, by way of recompense, prepare yourself to be kicked out of doors. [*Exit.*

Scene III.—*Enter* Dorimene.

Count. Good morning, dear sister; how do you do?

Dor. Perfectly well. How are you?

Count. Never better. Fortunate and happy man! I am to possess a bride of high birth and merit.

Dor. Then you are determined in favour of Eleonora?

Count. Ay, sweet sister! She is your relation; you proposed her to me, and I therefore have reason to give her the preference.

Dor. [*Ironically.*] Her and her portion of one hundred thousand crowns, with as much more perhaps at the death of her mother.

Count. You will allow, sister, that such conditions are not to be despised.

Dor. True; but you, who are so—

Count. I understand you. A man like me, having sacrificed a considerable sum to obtain a title, should have endeavoured to marry into an illustrious family. I have thought much, and combated long this reigning inclination, but I know the prejudices of the old nobility; I must have paid dearly for the pompous honour of such an alliance.

Dor. That is not what I wish to say.

Count. I am determined to marry the charming Eleonora.

Dor. But if the charming Eleonora should feel no love for you?

Count. My dear sister, I do not think myself a person to be despised.

Dor. But inclinations are capricious.

Count. Has Eleonora told you she cannot love me?

Dor. She has not precisely told me, but I have great reason to doubt it.

Count. [*To himself, vexed.*] This is a little strange.

Dor. Why are you angry? If you take in ill part—

Count. No, no; you mistake me. Speak freely and sincerely.

Dor. You know the confidence you have placed in me. Having discoursed together concerning this family, I wrote to Madame Araminta, inviting her and her daughter to pass a few days at Paris.

Count. And they have been a fortnight with you. This I know must give trouble, and bring expense;

and as you have done it for my sake—I—my duty—my obligations are eternal.

Dor. By no means, brother. The expense is trifling, and the inconvenience small. I love this family, and, beside being related to my husband, am greatly interested in its behalf. Eleonora is the best girl on earth, and her mother is no less respectable. A good heart, economical, and to the most exact economy she unites prudence and regularity of conduct.

Count. Excellent; and so has been the education of her daughter. But now tell me—

Dor. Sincerely, brother, in my opinion, Eleonora loves you neither much nor little.

Count. On what do you found this strange suspicion?

Dor. I will tell you. When your name is mentioned, she looks down and gives no answer.

Count. Bashfulness.

Dor. When she hears or sees you coming, she is in a tremor, and wishes to hide herself.

Count. At her age that is not extraordinary.

Dor. When this marriage is mentioned, the tears are in her eyes.

Count. The tears of a child? Can anything be more equivocal?

Dor. And though so equivocal and so full of doubt, will you dare to marry her?

Count. Certainly, without the least difficulty.

Dor. It seems you love her to distraction.

Count. I love—I do not know how much.

Dor. You have scarcely seen her twice.

Count. Is not that enough to a feeling heart like mine?

Dor. Ah, brother, I know you.

Count. Your penetration is a little too quick.

Dor. I do not wish that you should hereafter have to reproach me.

Count. Yonder is Frontino.

Dor. If you have business—

Count. [*With affected kindness.*] Will you go?

Dor. We shall meet again soon. I only wish you to think a little on what I have said, and before you marry—

Count. Fear nothing, dear sister. Do me the pleasure to dine with me to-day. I will send to invite Madame Araminta and her daughter. We shall have many guests. The notary will be here after dinner, and the contract will be signed.

Dor. To-day?

Count. No doubt: Madame Araminta has pledged her word.

Dor. [*Ironically.*] I give you joy.—[*Aside.*] I will never suffer Eleonora to sacrifice herself for my sake. If I could but truly understand her heart—I will try.

[*Exit.*

SCENE IV.—*The* Count, *and then* Frontino.

Count. Poor girl! A little too diffident of me. Does not think me capable of subduing a tender and inexperienced heart! Besides, she carries her delicacy rather too far: in marriages of convenience, not the heart, but family interest is consulted. Well, Frontino, what have you to say?

Front. The tailor is come, sir.

Count. Where is he?

Front. At the door, sending away his coach, and giving orders to his servants.

Count. His servants?

Front. Yes, sir.

Count. Apropos: that reminds me that you must

write immediately to my country steward, that he may send me six handsome youths, tall, well made, the best he can find on the estate, that the tailor may take their measure for liveries.

Front. Six clowns in liveries!

Count. Yes, to honour my wedding. Tell the steward that all the time they stay here, their country wages shall be continued, besides having their board. You know this sort of people take care not to overload their plates.

Front. Never fear, sir, they will not die of indigestion.

Count. Hold. Take the key of the closet where the plate is kept; let it be displayed, and all brought on the table.

Front. But, sir, your plate is so antique, and so black —it will be necessary at least to have it new polished.

Count. Oh, silver is always silver. Here comes the tailor, I suppose.

Front. Yes, sir. Enter, Signor, enter.

SCENE V.—*To them the* Tailor.

Tail. I am the most humble servant of your most illustrious lordship.

Count. Come near, sir. I was impatient to see you. I want four suits for myself, and twelve liveries for my servants.

Tail. It will do me honour to serve you, and have no doubt but it shall please you.

Front. My master pays well.

Tail. I have the honour of knowing him. Who is it that does not know the illustrious Count Casteldoro?

Count. The occasion requires all possible display of splendour.

Tail. I will show you stuffs of gold and silver.

Count. No, no; I do not wish to look as if caparisoned in gilded leather. The dresses must be noble and rich, but nothing with a shining ground.

Tail. You prefer embroidery?

Count. I do; four embroidered suits, but in the best possible taste, the patterns rich and delicate.

Front. [*Aside.*] Hey-day! I do not know my master.

Tail. Rich, but light embroidery?

Count. No, sir: Spanish point—ample, massive, and of the best workmanship; well designed, splendid, but nothing that shines.

Tail. Everything that you can desire. Shall I take your measure?

Count. Yes—on one condition.

Tail. What is it?

Front. [*Aside.*] Ay, let us hear the condition.

Count. You must tack on the embroidery slightly, that it may not be spoiled. I would have no buttons of false diamonds. I shall wear my four suits each of them twice during the first eight days of my nuptials, so that your embroidery will still be new, and may again be sold as such. You must now tell me what you will charge for the cloth, the making, and the use of your ornaments.

Front. [*Aside.*] Yes, yes, he is still himself.

Count. But first concerning the liveries.

Tail. With your permission, I wish to have the honour of speaking to you in private.

Front. [*Angrily to the* Tailor.] If I must not stay, I can go.

Count. By no means. Frontino is part of the family: you may speak before him.

Front. [*To the* Tailor.] You see, sir! Hem!

Tail. No, friend; I did not mean you, but—look to see if we have no listeners. [*Slily gives* Frontino *a crown.*]

Front. [*Aside.*] A crown! It is long since I had so much.

Tail. Sir, I comprehend the nature of your project. You are not naturally inclined to pomp; but, sagacious and prudent as you are, you willingly sacrifice to appearance and convenience. I esteem myself most fortunate in having the honour to serve you. I admire gentlemen who think like you, and laugh at those who ruin themselves, while I give them every aid in my power, that they may be ruined in style. In me you have discovered the only man fit for your purpose: set your heart at rest; I have the means to satisfy you.

Count. [*Aside.*] If I do not mistake, this is a most smooth-tongued, artful— [*Aloud.*] Well, then, you will make my four suits!

Tail. Pardon me, sir, your idea is not practicable. I could not avoid paying extremely dear for the embroidery; and my delicate conscience would never permit me to sell it again as new.

Count. [*Aside.*] His delicate conscience! Why did he come to me?

Tail. I will confide a secret to you which I have treasured jealously; for, were it known, I cannot tell you how much it would prejudice my character and credit. I, who am the court-tailor, tailor to the principal nobility of Paris, I secretly, and under a borrowed name, carry on a flourishing trade in old clothes.

Count. An old clothesman keep his coach?

Tail. Which is maintained by that very means.

Front. [*To the* Count.] You see, sir, I have found you a man of sincerity; a man whose heart is as open as his face; a man who merits all your confidence.

Count. [*Aside.*] I perceive.—[*Aloud.*] Should I find this to be to my interest?

Tail. I will show you two dozen of most magnificent

suits, all new, that never were worn but once or twice at the most.

Count. Will they be known again?

Tail. No danger of that; everything that enters my magazine assumes a new face. I export the most splendid samples that France produces, and I import the spoils and riches of the principal cities in Europe. You shall see suits the most superb, and stuffs of the greatest rarity. It is a pity you will have neither gold nor silver.

Count. Nay, should it be anything of uncommon beauty and taste, gold and silver would not offend me.

Front. To be sure, if the streets were to be paved with gold, we must walk.

Count. But the price.

Tail. See, admire, and select; act just as you please.—[*Aside.*] I have found the very man I wished for.—I will soon be back, dear sir.—[*Aside.*] Paris is the place; everything a man wants is there to be found.

Front. Have you by chance anything that will sit genteel, and make me look like a gentleman's gentleman?

Tail. [*Aside.*] I will clothe you from head to foot, only be my friend.

Front. Your friend! On such conditions, who could refuse?

END OF THE FIRST ACT.

ACT II.

SCENE I.—Dorimene *and* Eleonora.

Dor. Come here, my dear Eleonora; I wish to speak to you alone. My brother, I believe, is gone out. [*Looks out.*] He is not in his cabinet.

Eleon. [*Aside.*] What can she have to say? She has a friendship for me, but I believe her interest is more for her brother. I can expect no consolation.

Dor. We are alone, and may speak freely. Permit me first to observe that within these few days you have had a serious, melancholy air, which seems but little to suit your expectations.

Eleon. It is natural to me, Madame; more or less, I am always so.

Dor. Excuse me; but on your arrival at Paris you had no such gloomy expression. You are entirely changed, and certainly not without cause.

Eleon. But really there is no such change.

Dor. My good young friend, you conceal the truth, and want confidence in me. Be a little more just, and rest assured that, though I proposed a marriage between you and my brother, no foolish ambition makes me wish it should succeed at the expense of your heart. Tell me openly what are your wishes; speak freely, and you shall see whether I am your friend.

Eleon. [*Aside.*] If I durst, but— No, no.

Dor. Have you any dislike to my brother?

Eleon. I have not long had the honour of his acquaintance, Madame.

Dor. His age, for example, may seem a little too great when compared with your own.

Eleon. The age of a man does not appear to me a thing of great importance.

Dor. You perhaps think that my brother is rather too economical.

Eleon. You know, Madame, I have been educated in economy.

Dor. If so, my dear Eleonora, to my great satisfaction, I have been entirely mistaken, and you will be perfectly happy with my brother.

Eleon. I!—Do you think so?

Dor. No doubt; it cannot be otherwise. I have questioned you with the best intentions, and you have answered—sincerely, as I must believe.

Eleon. Oh, certainly.

Dor. Then be at peace; your heart tells me you will be happy.

Eleon. [*Affected.*] My heart, Madame!

Dor. Your heart.

Eleon. Ah! I do not understand my own heart.

Dor. Why are you so much moved?

Eleon. [*Looking off the stage.*] Did not some one call me?

Dor. Called? Where? By whom?

Eleon. [*Going.*] Perhaps my mother—perhaps somebody—

Dor. No, no; pray stay. Your mother knows you are with me, and therefore cannot be in fear. I have something more to say to you.

Eleon. [*Aside.*] How difficult to disguise my feelings!

Dor. Remember, your heart has told me—

Eleon. [*Timorously.*] What, Madame?

Dor. You are in love with another.

Eleon. [*Confused.*] I, Madame!

Dor. You; your blushes confirm it.

Eleon. [*Aside.*] Heavens! have I betrayed myself?— [*Aloud.*] You will not tell this to my mother? I shall be lost!

Dor. No, no; fear nothing. Though you have discovered that you cannot confide in me, I love you tenderly, and am incapable of giving you needless pain. Here your mother comes; let us consider between ourselves.

Eleon. Ah, Madame! [*Embracing.*]

Scene II.—*Enter* Araminta.

Aram. Well, child; I fear you are troublesome.
Eleon. Pardon me, but—
Dor. We are friends, and I entreated her to keep me company.
Aram. You are kinder to her than she deserves. I cannot understand her; she is become so melancholy and dull.
Dor. The air of Paris may not agree with her.
Aram. Do you think so? Since she left the place of her education, she is no longer the same. Nothing pleases, nothing diverts her. Music, reading, and drawing are all forsaken. I have spared no expense, and have taken no little delight in perceiving her progress; while, at present, I am equally surprised to see her thus negligent. I willingly incur expense for any good purpose; but no one can be more angry than I am at squandering money.
Eleon. [*Aside.*] It is very true. I no longer know myself.
Dor. Nay, Madame.
Aram. If she wishes to return to her retirement, why not say so?
Dor. Oh, no, Madame; she has no such wish.
Aram. But why, then, child, are you so gloomy, so indolent? You are soon to be married, and to direct a family; this requires activity, attention, and order, as you may see by my example. I am busy from morning to evening, here and there, going, coming, helping, commanding, and sometimes obliged to find fault; but, by these means, all goes well.
Eleon. [*Aside.*] I hoped to do the same, but all my hopes are flown!

Dor. Oh, Madame, when your daughter's heart shall be at ease—

Aram. At ease! What does she want? Is not the marriage contract to be signed to-day?

Dor. Here comes my brother! He can best inform you—

Eleon. [*Aside.*] How miserable am I!

Scene III.—*Enter the* Count *and a* Jeweller.

Count. I am happy, ladies, to find you together. I came purposely to ask your advice.

Aram. On what subject? Ladies are sometimes excellent advisers.

Count. [*To the* Jeweller.] Show your case of jewels.

Aram. [*Aside.*] Jewels! He may well ask advice in such articles; it is easy to be cheated.

Jew. [*Presenting the case to* Dorimene.] Please examine if there can be purer and more perfect diamonds.

Count. Pray give me your opinion.

Dor. I think them admirable! What say you, Eleonora?

Eleon. [*With indifference.*] I do not understand such things.

Aram. I do—show them to me. Though I never wore any diamonds, trade has made me well acquainted with them. [*Taking the case.*] These are fine, indeed! Perfectly assorted, and of a beautiful water. What is their price?

Count. Oh, that is a secret between ourselves. [*To the* Jeweller.] Is it not?

Jew. My lord—I have nothing to say.

Aram. [*Aside.*] So much the worse; the Count will be the more easily imposed upon. He comes to ask advice, and then refuses to hear it.

Count. [*Apart, to the* Jeweller.] My good friend, will you trust your diamonds with me three or four days?

Jew. [*To the* Count.] If the ladies think them good, and well chosen, I should prefer—

Count. Nay, friend; jewels of this value must not be purchased without reflection. Knowing me, you cannot be afraid.

Jew. By no means! They are at your service.

Count. Be pleased to return at the end of the week. I know the price, and you shall then have the money or the diamonds.

Jew. I am much obliged to you, Signor. [*Exit.*

Scene IV.

Count. [*Aside.*] Excellent! just as I wished!—[*To* Eleonora.] Will you do me the favour, Madame, to wear the jewels I have the honour to present you, at least for to-day.

Dor. To-day?

Count. It is the day on which we are to sign the contract, and we shall have thirty persons at table.

Aram. Thirty!

Count. At least, Madame.

Aram. [*Aside.*] He will ruin himself! But I will hear more.

Count. [*Presenting the case to* Dorimene.] Dear sister, let me request you to take this case, and to kindly be present at the toilet of this lady, to assist in arranging the diamonds. Will you do me the pleasure, charming Eleonora, to accept my sister's aid?

Eleon. [*Coldly.*] My mamma never wears diamonds.

Aram. Do not be silly, child. I did not wear diamonds, because my husband was too prudent to indulge in such expenses; but, if the Count think differently, complaisance requires your acquiescence.

Eleon. But, you know, mamma—

Aram. Oh, I know—I know, child! You do not know good breeding. Accept them gratefully.

Eleon. [*Aside.*] Unhappy me!—[*To the* Count.] Signor—I am greatly obliged.

Dor. [*Apart to the* Count.] Are you satisfied with such a cold manner?

Count. Perfectly.

Dor. Have you no dissatisfaction; no fears?

Count. Not the least.

Dor. [*Aside.*] What a singular man is my brother?

Scene V.—*Enter* Frontino.

Front. Here is a letter, sir.

Count. With your permission, ladies.

Aram. By all means. [*To* Dorimene.] Let us examine the jewels a little.

Count. [*To himself, having read the letter.*] The marquis comes at an ill time! After a dinner of thirty guests, I must give him a supper! He asks it with so little ceremony too! How can it be managed?

Dor. What is the matter, brother?

Count. [*Affecting cheerfulness.*] Nothing, nothing. I have just received news which gives me pleasure. The Marquis del Bosco is arrived, and coming to sup with me this evening.

Eleon. [*Agitated.*] What do I hear?

Aram. I know the Marquis; his county seat is not three miles distant from mine.

Count. You will see him this evening, with the Marchioness his daughter, and the Chevalier his son.

Eleon. [*Still more agitated.*] The Chevalier! O Heaven!

Count. I hope they will be in time to be present, when we sign the contract.

Eleon. [*Still aside.*] Fatal trial! How shall I support it?

Aram. What is the matter, daughter?

Eleon. Nothing—not much—a sudden giddiness.

Count. [*To* Araminta.] For Heaven's sake, take care of— [*To* Frontino.] Don't go.

Aram. The open air will revive her.

Dor. Let us walk into the garden.

Aram. By all means.

Dor. Is the door open, brother?

Count. No; but here is the key.

Dor. [*Aside.*] He will trust it to nobody, but has it always in his pocket.—Come, Eleonora.—[*Aside.*] This may be a proper opportunity. [*Retiring with* Eleonora.]

Count. [*To* Araminta.] I hope, Madame, this attack is trifling; but the young lady should not be exposed to the least danger. If you think proper, we will defer the dinner of to-day, and have a supper instead.

Aram. Just as you please—but your dinners and suppers—I have much to say to you on such subjects. My daughter may want me; I will return presently.

Scene VI.

Count. [*Earnestly.*] Hark ye, Frontino! send messengers immediately, to inform the guests I have invited that, instead of dinner, I entreat them to honour me with their company at supper.

Front. So, so! But it will be difficult to find them all, so late in the day.

Count. No matter. Those who may come to dinner

must be told of the change. They will return to supper, or not, as they please.

Front. Yes, Signor.—[*Aside.*] Admirable! quite in character! [*Exit.*

Count. This visit comes at a lucky time! Nothing could be more fortunate.

Scene VII.—*Enter* Araminta

Count. Well, dear Madame? Eleonora?

Aram. All, I hope, will be well.

Count. Then I shall be happy; for health should be our first care. I have sent round to the guests, with an invitation to supper this evening.

Aram. Thirty persons at supper!

Count. I hope so, Madame.

Aram. Permit me to speak openly, and tell you all I think.

Count. You cannot give me greater pleasure.

Aram. Is it not extreme folly to assemble thirty persons, twenty of whom, at least, will make a jest of you?

Count. A *jest* of *me?*

Aram. Beyond all doubt. Do not think I am avaricious; thank heaven, that is not my defect; but I cannot endure to see money squandered.

Count. But, on such a day, and under such circumstances.

Aram. Are they your relations, whom you have invited?

Count. By no means. A select company; the nobility! the literati! the magistracy! all persons of distinction.

Aram. Worse and worse! Vanity, ostentation, folly! My good friend, you do not know the value of money.

THE SPENDTHRIFT MISER.   249

Count. [*Smiles.*] I do not know the value of money!

Aram. Alas, you do not! Your sister made me believe you were economical; had I known the truth, I should never have married my daughter to a spendthrift.

Count. So you think me a spendthrift!

Aram. I first perceived it by the considerable sum you threw away in the purchase of a title; which sacrifice to vanity has no beneficial end.

Count. How! Are you not aware the rank I have acquired will impress a character of respect on myself, your daughter, and our descendants?

Aram. Quite the reverse. I would have rather given my daughter to you, as Signor Anselmo Colombani, a well-known merchant, than to the Count of Casteldoro, a newly-made nobleman.

Count. But, Madame—

Aram. Your ancestors have saved what you will scatter.

Count. Scatter! I! You are mistaken, Madame. You do not know me.

Aram. Oh yes, yes. I saw the manner in which, without any knowledge of diamonds, or asking the least advice, you were led away by the jeweller.

Count. Oh, with respect to the diamonds—

Aram. Ah, ay! I know your answer. They are to decorate the Countess of Casteldoro. And who is the Countess of Casteldoro? My daughter, Signor, has been well educated, but with no such expectations. Everything has been done in abundance, that could contribute to convenience, decency, and information; but nothing to pomp and vanity. The ornaments of my daughter ever will be modesty, obedience, and that self-respect which she could not but acquire from such an education.

Count. [*A little moved.*] But, Madame—

Aram. [*Very warmly.*] But, Signor—[*softening*]—I ask your pardon—Perhaps you may think me too warm; but I see you hurried into a gulf of expense that makes me tremble. My daughter's happiness is concerned: I give her a hundred thousand crowns in marriage.

Count. [*Somewhat haughtily.*] Am I not able to settle an equal sum upon her?

Aram. Yes, at present. But wealth will diminish; and especially when we have the vanity to be profuse, grand, and magnificent.

Count. I once more assure you, Madame, you do not know me.

Aram. Signor, had you been a different person, I had conceived an excellent plan. My annual income is five-and-twenty thousand livres: I might have lived with you and my daughter, and the two families might have become one; but, at present, Heaven preserve me from taking such a step!

Count. [*Aside.*] She will drive me mad!—[*To Araminta.*] Pray hear me. [*Whispering and cunningly.*] You mistake my character. Few people indeed understand economy so well as I do, as you will soon be convinced. I willingly close with your proposal, and—

Aram. By no means! You try in vain to persuade me against conviction. Respecting my daughter—I have promised—we shall see—but for myself it is different. Not all the gold on earth should induce me to make such an arrangement, with a man who does not know the use of money, but lets it slip through his fingers faster than flour through a sieve. [*Exit.*

Count. This is admirable! I never imagined I should pass for a prodigal. [*Exit.*

END OF THE SECOND ACT.

ACT III.

Scene I.—*The* Count *and* Frontino.

Count. Frontino.

Front. Signor?

Count. Go and inquire how Eleonora is.

Front. One of your guests is without, and desires to speak with you.

Count. Who is he?

Front. The young gentleman who lately read you a comedy written by himself.

Count. Oh! Signor Giacinto. Bid him enter.

Front. Please to come in, Signor. [*Exit.*

Scene II.—*Enter* Giacinto.

Count. Good morning, Signor Giacinto. I am very sorry that the messenger, sent by me, did not find you at home; he came to inform you that an accident has caused me to put off the dinner, but that I hoped to see you at supper.

Giac. It is just the same to me, Signor. Meanwhile, permit me the honour to—

Count. I hope to see you without fail this evening.

Giac. I am infinitely obliged to you; but, having now the good fortune to find you alone, and at leisure, I wish to lay before you certain alterations made in the dedicatory epistle; as I have nothing so much at heart as your satisfaction.

Count. Well, Signor Giacinto, since you are absolutely resolved to dedicate your comedy to me, I have thought—it would be best to inform you—of certain particulars respecting myself. Not from vanity—oh no! Heaven preserve me from that!—but solely to give an opportunity to your eloquence, and lustre to your work.

Giac. You see, Signor, I have made a good use of the materials which you have so kindly furnished; but I have done something more.

Count. Have you mentioned my pictures?

Giac. Oh yes.

Count. And my library?

Giac. Certainly.

Count. Including the books which I told you I intend to purchase?

Giac. But — Signor — a catalogue of books in a dedication —

Count. Where is the difficulty? You may say, in a note at the bottom of the page, the Count of Casteldoro possesses a superb library, of not less than ten thousand volumes. A man of wit, like you, knows how to take advantage of everything. The supper of this evening, for example, may furnish some new ideas—something animated, witty, poetical.

Giac. That may be possible; but I have been employed on a subject more essential: I have written your genealogy.

Count. [*Coldly.*] My genealogy? No, no, friend. I have no taste for that science. You might, I grant, say things that should happen to do me honour; but I am an enemy to vanity, and would prefer reticence, especially on the question of genealogy.

Giac. As you please; but I have made discoveries that have cost me much time and study, of which I thought you might wish to be informed.

Count. [*With curiosity.*] Discoveries that relate to me?

Giac. That relate to you, Signor.

Count. My dear Signor Giacinto, let me hear.

Giac. Your true family name is not Colombani.

Count. I grant it may have been changed.

Giac. Do me the favour to listen. The great Columbus, who discovered America, and who was ennobled by the king of Spain, had two brothers, and various relations. Now, in looking through authors to discover annotations for my Life of Petrarch, I found that one of the relations of Christopher Columbus went from Genoa, his native place, to the city of Avignon, in France. By corruption of the termination, I find the name of Colombo or Columbus, has been changed to Colombani; and I demonstrate, beyond all doubt, that you are a descendant of that ancient, illustrious family.

Count. [*Much pleased.*] You have demonstrated it?

Giac. Here are my proofs. [*Presenting papers.*]

Count. [*Receiving them.*] From the little I can now recollect, I believe you are right. Ay, ay; it might be. I do not love ostentation, as you perceive, but I shall be highly pleased if your discovery can do yourself honour; I therefore have not the courage to forbid the publication. Have you presented your comedy to the comedians?

Giac. Yes, Signor.

Count. And they certainly received it with approbation?

Giac. On the contrary, Signor, it has been peremptorily refused.

Count. Refused!

Giac. You have heard it read: does it deserve such a reward?

Count. If the comedy be good, why is it refused? Their interest should oblige them to accept it, with thanks.

Giac. What can be expected from such ignorant

judges? But I will have my revenge! It shall be printed! The public shall decide!

Count. Bravo! You are right; have it printed. It might not be greatly successful on the stage, but in the closet it will delight. Your sale will be prodigious.

Giac. Since you approve and encourage me, Signor, would you but have the goodness to pass your word for the expense of printing, and—

Count. [*With a determined tone.*] There is no need of that. Apply to a good bookseller; let him have his profits, and he will answer for the whole.

Giac. To speak the truth, Signor, I have in vain applied to more than one. At last, a bookseller has agreed that, if the Count of Casteldoro will make himself responsible, he will undertake to publish it on my account.

Count. How! Have you mentioned my name?

Giac. I could not avoid it.

Count. You have done very ill. Should it be known that I take an interest in the comedy, it would be said I did so because of the dedication; and I should then appear ridiculous. Drop all thoughts of the press at present; a more favourable opportunity may occur.

Giac. But, Signor—

Scene III.—*Enter* Frontino.

Count. Well, Frontino, what answer?

Front. The young lady is rather better, Signor.

Count. Rather better! But is she well enough to— I will go and inquire myself.—[*To* Giacinto.] You see, Signor, a young lady is ill in my house, and the supper must be deferred. Another time. [*Going.*]

Giac. Then if the manuscript be useless, Signor—

Count. True; it shall be returned. [*Going.*]

Giac. I beg you to recollect the time and trouble it has cost me.

Count. [*Returning the manuscript.*] Very right! You are fond of your own works: I am glad they give you satisfaction, and cannot but thank you for any labour taken on my account. Whenever I can serve you, pray command me.

Giac. Infinitely obliged to the generosity of Signor Count Casteldoro.—[*Aside.*] What ingratitude! Sordid fellow! He shall pay for this, or I am mistaken. [*Exit.*

Count. One guest the less. But I must inquire after Eleonora. [*Going.*]

Fior. [*Without.*] Ho, there! Is nobody to be found?

Front. This is Fiorillo, the servant of the Marquis.

SCENE IV.—*Enter* Fiorillo, *in a travelling dress.*

Fior. [*Bows.*] Signor Count, my master, the Marquis del Bosco, is coming. I rode before, as you perceive, to inform you that his carriage will soon arrive.

Count. [*Coldly.*] Arrive! What, here? And in his coach? Does he come to make any stay?

Fior. No, Signor. To-morrow morning he must be gone to Versailles; for he has affairs at court.

Count. [*Aside.*] I am glad of it!—[*Aloud, pompously.*] I hope the Marquis will do me the honour to remain with me to-night, in company with his son, the Chevalier. With respect to the Marchioness—I'll speak to my sister, and hope she may also be accommodated, as becomes her rank.

Fior. The Marchioness del Bosco does not come with her father; she is with the Countess d'Orimon, her aunt, and is to remain at her house.

Count. [*Aside.*] So much the better.—[*Aloud.*] That is unfortunate. I hope, however, I shall have the pleasure of seeing her. [*Exit.*

SCENE V.—Frontino *and* Fiorillo.

Fior. Your master, like your kitchen, smells well!

Front. We are to have a magnificent supper to-night; no less than thirty guests.

Fior. Indeed! Your master is superb. A rare service! Much to eat, and little to do! Then, as to wages, you will make your fortune, Frontino!

Front. Fortune! I can't say—perhaps!

Fior. You have been long with this master.

Front. Very true; I have an attachment to him.

Fior. And so have I to mine, but without the hope of saving a farthing in his service. If it were not for the profits of the card-tables, I should certainly leave him.

Front. Then you have much play?

Fior. A great deal.

Front. And no less profit?

Fior. Hum—tolerable; but not equal to you.

Front. I! Shall I speak plain to a fellow-servant? I have little wages, and no tips.

Fior. Then you are foolish, Frontino. In Paris, so clever a fellow as yourself may find a hundred services, in which he might profit in a hundred different ways.

Front. Do you know any *one*?

Fior. Certainly; but you are attached to your master?

Front. To part with him would not break my heart.

Fior. If he pays so ill, he does not like you.

Front. That's a mistake; I am his prime minister and favourite.

THE SPENDTHRIFT MISER.

Fior. What do you mean? Were he miserly, so be it; but a generous—

Front. Generous! You little know my master.

Fior. How so? A supper for thirty guests—

Front. Ah, did you know what it will cost me!

Fior. You! Cost you!

Front. Me. Grumbled at, cross-questioned, put to the torture, almost afraid of my life, when I give in my bill. I tremble but to think of it!

Fior. So, so! Very different with us; our master is easily satisfied, and always gay and good-humoured. He has an odd manner of speaking, indeed, and never tells you more than half what he means. He has favourite words, which, right or wrong, he always uses. Everybody laughs at *him*, and he laughs at himself.

Front. I wish I had such a master!

Fior. The worst of it is, he is poor, and seldom has any money.

Front. Yet you say he plays?

Fior. Very true; he always finds money for that. I hear a coach.

Front. Which way does he—

Fior. [*At the window.*] Be quiet! Yes, they are here.

Front. I want to hear more.

Fior. Run and tell your master.

Front. [*Aside.*] I shall hear it all; he can't hold his tongue. [*Exit.*

Fior. Frontino is a good fellow, but he talks too much; that's his fault.

SCENE VI.—*Enter the* Marquis.

Marq. Where is he? Where is the Count?

Fior. His servant is gone to tell him you are here.

Marq. Go, go; see — Good, good, excellent!—His servant?

Fior. Will soon be back.

Marq. Meanwhile — My horses—Nothing to eat—Poor devils—They have done—Good, good, excellent! You might go and see—

Fior. Yes, at once.—[*Aside and going.*] I defy all the servants in the world to understand him as I do. [*Exit.*

Scene VII.—*Enter the* Chevalier.

Chev. My dear father! How can I thank you for all your kindness?

Marq. Say no more—father to be sure—But with you, in truth—You are strange sometimes.

Chev. Most true! Had you not discovered my passion, I scarcely should have dared to own it.

Marq. Keen eyes—Why not, dear boy? Why not? and then I know that Eleonora—Do you know her mother?

Chev. I am slightly acquainted with her, but not enough to speak on such a subject.

Marq. A lady that—Are you at least sure of the daughter?

Chev. Perfectly. I have met her at her cousins, and —we have corresponded.

Marq. Good, good, excellent! We shall want—The Count is my friend.

Chev. And I am acquainted with his sister, Madame Dorimene. I will beg her to entreat for me. Here comes the Count.

Scene VIII.— *Enter the* Count.

Count. Pardon me, Marquis, but—

Marq. Ah, Count! Good day—Good day — Your health — Mine — you see — splendidly well, at your service.

Count. Still the same! Always courteous!

Marq. Oh, I . . . Good, good; excellent!

Count. And you, Chevalier?

Chev. Always your humble servant.

Count. Is the Marchioness with you?

Marq. My daughter? She has come with—You know her aunt?

Count. Yes, I have the pleasure of knowing her, and will call and pay the ladies my respects — I hope to have the honour of their company at supper.

Marq. Always obliging — Good, good, excellent!— Ought to apologise—Come suddenly—No ceremony, I beg.

Count. None on earth. I shall only give you my ordinary supper.

Marq. Good, good, excellent! Family meals— friendly.

Count. Your apartments are here, on the right. They tell me you go to Versailles to-morrow.

Marq. Yes—because—

Count. I am sorry to lose you so soon: but, as I was saying, these apartments shall be yours.

Chev. Permit me, Signor Count, to pay my respects to your sister.

Count. You will do me an honour, and give her pleasure.

Chev. [*To his father.*] Have I your leave, sir?

Marq. Certainly.—[*Aside.*] Poor fellow! He is—but when I was like him—yes, I did as he does.

Count. We may all go together, if you please.

Marq. Ha!—[*Aside.*] No; must not spoil sport.—[*Aloud.*] Go by himself.

Chev. [*Going.*] I know my way.

Count. You will meet a young lady there, with whom perhaps you are acquainted.

Chev. [*Eager to go.*] Indeed? So much the better!

Count. I have something to tell you concerning her, which perhaps you do not know—

Chev. [*Aside.*] Too well! I am on the rack!

Count. But which you will be glad to hear.

Chev. [*Aside.*] Heavens! Perhaps Eleonora may have discovered our passion to her mother—I rush to see. [*Exit.*

Scene IX.—Count *and the* Marquis.

Marq. [*Looking round.*] Now we are alone— Have you time?

Count. I am at your disposal.

Marq. You are my friend.

Count. The title does me honour.

Marq. Good, good, excellent!

Count. [*Aside.*] He is sometimes very ridiculous.

Marq. I should like to beg you — but—a friend, unceremoniously, freely.

Count. [*Aside.*] I bet he wants to borrow money.

Marq. You know my family—

Count. Perfectly.

Marq. I have two children, and must think — a daughter too—Good, good, excellent!—The Chevalier is at an age—you understand me?

Count. I believe I do. You are seriously thinking of establishing your family, which is highly commendable. And, talking of establishments, I think it but right in me to inform you of my approaching marriage.

Marq. Oh, oh!—that way inclined—you too—Good, good, excellent!

Count. I am this day to sign the contract, and think myself fortunate that you, Signor Marquis, will be present, and—

Marq. Very happy—but, at the same time, if you would be so kind—

Count. You well know, Signor Marquis, the various expenses of these occasions; they are endless. To own the truth, I find my pocket empty.

Marq. Good, good, excellent!

Count. Good! I find it exceedingly ill.

Marq. Listen—You are the friend of Madame Araminta.

Count. True; and she, for example, is remarkably rich; she might be of service to your house.

Marq. Precisely so—my very thought—would you but speak to her, but without—What is her daughter's name?

Count. Eleonora.

Marq. True—bad memory—Eleonora.

Count. [*Aside.*] If I had not a great deal of penetration, I could never guess what he means.—[*Aloud.*] I will speak privately to Madame Araminta.

Marq. Ay, but—in a particular manner—so that—you understand me?

Count. I will speak with all possible caution, and hope she will comply—provided she has good security.

Marq. By Jove! If she gives me—I have not—I am not—but—my estates—

Count. What sum do you wish?

Marq. I heard that—ay—a hundred thousand crowns—quite satisfied!—would not wish for more!

Count. [*Aside.*] A hundred thousand crowns! the loan is too great! She will scarcely consent to that.

Marq. When will you speak? Because when I have a project—no sooner said than done—it is in my nature.

Count. I will inform her to-day.

Marq. And you hope she—Good, good, excellent!

Count. I think Madame Araminta will comply, if possible; first out of regard to yourself, and next to me, who am on the point of becoming her son-in-law.

Marq. Ha!—what?—you?—

Count. I am to marry her daughter.

Marq. Marry!—when?—that true?—that possible?

Count. Why so excessively surprised, Signor Marquis? Do you see any reason to the contrary?

Marq. I—no—[*Aside.*] My son!—Fine affair!—Stupid folly!

Count. Madame Araminta intends indeed to give a hundred thousand crowns with her daughter, but do you think she will therefore not have so large a sum to lend you?

Marq. Lend me!—Zounds!—Lend me!

SCENE X.

The Chevalier, *making signs of disappointment and silence to the* Marquis, *enters and goes off without being seen by the* Count.

Count. But, if you please, I will speak to her.

Marq. [*To the* Chevalier.] Yes, yes, I understand.

Count. [*Supposing the answer was to himself.*] And will tell her—

Marq. By no means—don't think—no, no.

Count. Yes and no ! I do not understand you, Signor.

Marq. Lend me !—to me ?—I am—it is true—but then I am not—Good, good, excellent !—I am not—

Count. If you will excuse me, I have business. Those are your apartments.—[*Aside.*] I never met such a ridiculous man. [*Exit.*

Marq. The devil take him—he doesn't know what he is talking of. [*Exit.*

END OF THE THIRD ACT.

ACT IV.

Scene I.—*The* Chevalier *and* Fiorillo.

Chev. While my father rests, I will visit my sister; tell him this, when he wakes.

Fior. Yes, Signor.

Chev. Do you know whether the Count is at home ?

Fior. Yes ; I saw him just now going to speak with Madame Dorimene.

Chev. [*Aside.*] Surely he is not a rival to be feared. At least, I am secure of the heart of Eleonora, and will not yet despair of gaining her mother. [*Exit.*

Fior. So, young gentleman ! I see how it is with you. I pretty well guess your intentions, and how they are thwarted. Ay, ay, I shall have enough to satisfy the curiosity of Frontino. [*Sits down near the door of his master's rooms.*]

Scene II.—*Enter* Count.

Count. [*Not seeing* Fiorillo.] I am tired, bored ! Nothing but indifference ; and, instead of perfect satisfaction, something like contempt. A man like me, who had but to choose! so advantageous a marriage! [*Seeing* Fiorillo.] Is the Marquis at home?

Fior. Yes, Signor; being rather fatigued with travelling, he is taking a nap.

Count. [*Aside.*] How amiable is his daughter! How charming! I felt affected and confused at the courtesy and kindness with which she and her aunt received me. The visit made me cheerful, happy, and reconciled to myself. What difference between the politeness of these ladies and the common and trivial manner of Araminta and her daughter; who neither understand civility nor good breeding. Ah! were the young Marchioness but as rich as she is handsome and engaging—who knows? I have a thought—should her father but be reasonable and easy to manage— Here he comes.

SCENE III.—*Enter the* Marquis.

Marq. [*Rubbing his eyes and calling.*] Fiorillo!
Fior. Signor?
Marq. My son?
Fior. He is gone out.
Marq. Why did not he—where is he gone?
Fior. To visit the Marchioness, his sister.
Marq. I too wish—my coach!
Fior. The horses, Signor—
Marq. [*Angry.*] Good, good, excellent! My coach!
Fior. I will go and see. [*Exit.*

SCENE IV.—*The* Count *and the* Marquis.

Count. Do you wish to go out, Signor Marquis?
Marq. See my daughter—much to say—tell her— Good, good, excellent!

Count. I have just had that honour. It was long since I had seen her. She fully answers the charming promise of her childhood; her sweetness has increased with her years, and the progress of her talents is wonderful. Permit me to congratulate you on possessing such a treasure.

Marq. Oh, Count—ay, ay; a good girl. She has not, let us confess it—but—character, manners—good, good, excellent!

Count. With such talents, so much merit, and blooming eighteen, you should think of a husband for her.

Marq. No doubt. For my part, I—*apropos:* what has just passed—what did you mean to say when—Did you not say *lend me?*

Count. It appears to me that you suddenly changed your opinion.

Marq. I tell you, no—it was not so. You have not—And yet I spoke plainly.

Count. In any case, Signor Marquis, I shall be happy to serve you. I have not spoken to Madame Araminta; for, to own the truth, I am not quite pleased with her daughter. I begin to feel a certain dislike.

Marq. Oh, oh!—That means—Well, why not?

Count. I have done everything to gain their esteem and friendship. A house so richly furnished, carriages and horses the most rare, diamonds worth a hundred thousand livres—

Marq. Is it possible?

Count. 'Tis true; they were shown. Madame Araminta was amazed.

Marq. Grand!—Superb!—Good, good, excellent!

Count. Injustice and ingratitude have been my reward.

Marq. Good, good, excellent!

Count. [*Aside.*] Curse the phrase!

Marq. [*Aside.*] In that case—if Eleonora—if my son—[*Aloud.*] If so, Signor Count—candour—frankly and freely tell them—You understand me? Cut matters short.

Count. Had I paid these attentions to a lady of rank and merit, I should have acted much more wisely.

Marq. Ay, ay—if—certainly.

Count. Do you think a man of rank and fashion, a man like yourself for example, would refuse me the hand of his daughter?

Marq. On the contrary. A person of worth—a person that—oh, what do you mean? Certainly not.

Count. Signor Marquis, you encourage me.

Marq. Oh, I—If so—I'll go this moment!

Count. Where, signor?

Marq. To my daughter. [*Calls.*] Fiorillo!

Count. And may I hope?

Marq. [*Calls louder.*] Fiorillo!

Scene V.—*Enter* Fiorillo

Marq. My coach.

Fior. The coachman is not here, Signor.

Marq. How so? [*To the* Count.] Can you lend me—? Soon return.

Count. It is not a hundred yards; you can easily walk.

Marq. Walk!—Hundred yards!—Enough—Adieu—Soon be back. [*Going.*] Diamonds! A hundred thousand livres! [*Exit with* Fiorillo.

Scene VI.—*The* Count, *then* Frontino.

Count. Courage! The Marquis is enraptured; the daughter's won. All goes well. But I must not lose sight of— [*Calls.*] Frontino! No, no; she must not get possession of the jewels. Frontino! I say!

Front. [*Entering.*] I was busy in planning the dessert.

Count. Go immediately, and tell my sister I beg her to come here; I have something interesting to communicate. And add, but in a whisper, that I request she will bring me the jewels which I committed to her care.

Front. But the supper, signor? I must be everywhere, and look to all!

Count. True. Is everything prepared?

Front. According to your wishes; two essentials excepted.

Count. Which are ——?

Front. Coffee and liqueurs

Count. Liqueurs inflame the blood.

Front. But coffee?

Count. Blockhead! Coffee at night! It prevents sleep.

Front. Surely, Signor!—Not give coffee! Forfeit your character as a liberal host, for such a trifling expense?

Count. Go, Mr. Liberality; do what I bid you.

Front. [*Aside.*] No coffee! I would rather pay for it out of my own pocket. Yet no; he would even swear I had filched the money from other articles. [*Exit.*

Scene VII.—Count *alone.*

Count. Dreadful! Luxury is come to such a height! Thank Heaven, I have not spent one farthing from whim or caprice. I always pay money with prudence and circumspection. I do not yet know the character of the Marchioness; but, being once the Countess of Casteldoro, I will teach her my method; which is to esteem myself, and to despise and laugh at other people.

Scene VIII.—*Enter* Dorimene.

Dor. I am told you want me, brother.

Count. Pardon this liberty. Where are the diamonds?

Dor. Here. Do you want them back?

Count. [*Taking them.*] Yes, yes; you shall know why.

Dor. You need not take the trouble to tell me, for it is not possible to persuade Eleonora to accept them.

Count. So much the worse for her; she will repent. I have a secret to tell you.

Dor. You know how greatly I am interested in your happiness.

Count. I have seen the Marchioness del Bosco, and have great reason to believe that, whenever I please, I may obtain her hand.

Dor. Indeed! What will the Marquis say?

Count. Oh, he will say, "Good, good, excellent!" I am sure of him.

Dor. You know the disorder of his affairs. Will you marry her without a portion?

Count. Oh, no. Thank Heaven, I have not lost my wits.

Dor. What will you do, then?

Count. Listen and learn. First, let me tell you, I am neither blind nor foolish. I perceive the affections of Eleonora are given to another, and I do not think I am greatly mistaken when I suppose the Chevalier her favourite. Omitting to notice the impertinence of father and son, in visiting me under the mask of friendship, I must tell you it may contribute to aid my project, which is this. Let you and me persuade Madame Araminta to give her daughter, with a hundred thousand crowns, to the Chevalier, on condition that his father receive the money, and that he redeem all his mortgages. I will request the Marchioness, his daughter, from him; with these said lands, and, by this means, the son and daughter will both be gratified, and the Marquis will not disburse a guinea. What say you, sister; is not the plan a good one?

Dor. Well imagined, but difficult to execute.

Count. Do not fear; all will be right. The Marquis is gone purposely in search of his daughter. I will join them, and I have no doubt all will be concluded this very day. These jewels—may be of—Sister, you shall see wonders. [*Exit.*

Dor. What does he mean? But, if every one be made happy, I shall be the same.

SCENE IX.—*Enter* Eleonora.

Eleon. [*At the door, timidly.*] Are you alone, Signora?

Dor. I am, my dear; come in.

Eleon. My mother is busy, writing—

Dor. Have you anything to tell me?

Eleon. Forgive my curiosity; have you taken away the jewels.

Dor. Yes; the Count asked for them. Are you vexed?

Eleon. On the contrary, delighted.

Dor. Then you are averse to diamonds?

Eleon. Not at all; but— You know my secret.

Dor. There are things in expectation, my dear—

Eleon. What, what? Ease my heart, if possible.

Dor. My brother feels you do not love him.

Eleon. That I can easily believe.

Dor. And suspects the Chevalier.

Eleon. Heavens! He will tell my mother!

Dor. Your mother, my dear, must and ought to know it; and you ought to conquer your inclinations.

Eleon. Conquer! Oh, it is not possible!
Dor. I love you, as you know, but cannot—
Eleon. [*Suddenly, and looking off.*] Ha! I must go.
Dor. What is the matter?
Eleon. [*Going.*] Don't you see the Chevalier?
Dor. Yes, yes; you are right. Begone!
Eleon. [*Aside, and slowly going.*] I die to stay.

SCENE X.—*Enter the* Chevalier.

Chev. Signora— [*Discovering* Eleonora.] Heavens! does Eleonora see me, and yet go? [*His eyes fixed on* Eleonora.]

Dor. Your pleasure, Signor? [*Turns and sees Eleonora not gone.*] Young lady, your mother expects you.

Eleon. [*Timidly.*] Pardon me, I would speak one word.

Dor. Well, speak. Make haste!

Eleon. [*Gradually approaching.*] The jewels will not be returned?

Dor. I do not fear the return of the jewels.

Chev. Ladies, if I incommode you, I'll be gone.

Dor. [*A little angry.*] As you please, Signor.

Chev. [*Going slowly aside.*] This treatment is severe.

Dor. [*Ironically.*] Well, Mademoiselle, have you anything more to say?

Eleon. No, Signora; but— What offence has the Chevalier committed?

Dor. Really, my dear, you make me smile.

Eleon. I—I cannot smile.

Chev. [*Returning after looking into his father's apartment.*] My father is not there.

Dor. You will find him at your aunt's.

Chev. I just came from there; my aunt and sister are gone out.

Dor. [*More angry.*] Young lady!

Eleon. [*Mortified and curtseying; her eyes fixed on the* Chevalier.] Pardon me.

Dor. [*Ironically.*] Excellent, upon my word!

SCENE XI.—*Enter* Araminta

Aram. [*Surprised, aside.*] Ah, ha!—[*Aloud.*] The milliner is waiting, daughter: go and look at what she has brought. [*Exit* Eleonora, *mortified.*

Aram. Pray stay, Chevalier: I would speak with you.

Dor. Ay, pray do; it is right I should justify myself before you. I see, Madame, that you know something of what is going on; but I assure you I am no party concerned, and that, although this meeting was accidental, I am sorry it should have occurred.

Aram. [*Kindly taking her hand.*] I know you, Madame.

Chev. I am sorry, ladies, if my presence—

Aram. [*Softly to* Dorimene.] Be so kind as to follow my daughter. Poor child! I vex her sometimes, but I love her dearly! Try to console her.

Dor. Most willingly, madam. [*Exit.*

SCENE XII.—Araminta *and the* Chevalier.

Chev. I did not think, Signora, that my conduct—

Aram. Let us speak plainly, Signor. What are your pretensions to my daughter?

Chev. Oh, could I but hope to merit her hand—

Aram. Nothing could be desired better than you: your birth, character, and conduct are all in your favour: and I should think it an honour to call you my son. Permit me only to say that the affairs of your family—

Chev. I own it. My father is the best of men, but has been greatly misled.

Aram. Then, being sensible of this truth, you, better than any person, should be aware of the confusion and distress which might be brought on a young woman, of a good family, and with no contemptible fortune. Would you willingly expose this fortune to the evident danger of being ill managed, and soon dissipated?

Chev. Hear me but a moment; I will speak frankly. I have spent some years in the army, which I have been obliged to quit, because I could not properly support my birth and military rank. Returning home, I have lived privately, without complaint, and concealing my situation. A family friend, interesting himself in my behalf, suggested that a proper marriage might enable me to appear again at my post, and thus excited me to mix with the world, and declare my purpose. I heard of you, Madame, of your daughter's merit, and of the fortune which she was to have. I saw her, and was so enraptured by her charms and mental qualities, that every interested motive instantly ceased, and love alone took possession of my heart. I then, indeed, wished I were rich, and deeply felt the distress of my family. My friends saw my distress, pitied me, would not forsake me, spoke of your goodness, and encouraged me respectfully to declare myself and my hopes. I listened to their advice, or rather to love; and hoped that gratitude and respect would, some time, acquire for me a daughter's love, and a kind mother's consent.

Aram. I approve your candour; yet, do not hope I can give you my daughter, though I am greatly affected by your situation, and disposed to favour you, as far as prudence will permit.

Chev. Your goodness consoles me; but, O heavens! do you refuse me that precious gift, your daughter?

Aram. You must not hope to have her, Signor. It may be ten years before you are in a state to marry. Live in freedom, and leave my daughter to her destiny. If you approve it, thus much I offer. I will lend you the sum necessary to purchase military rank, and even a regiment; depending for repayment upon circumstances, and your word of honour.

Chev. I may die, Madame.

Aram. And I may lose my money; but not the recollection of having done justice to merit, and a worthy gentleman.

Chev. Noble generosity! Yet—your daughter—

Aram. I speak absolutely—you must not think of her.

Chev. Surely it is possible that love and constancy—

Aram. Let us see, what sum will you want? You have friends?

Chev. A few.

Aram. I may increase the number. Let us retire where we can speak more freely.

Chev. Wherever you please. [*Calls.*] Fiorillo!

Aram. Poor youth! The victim of his father's imbecility. [*Exit.*

Scene XIII.—*Enter* Fiorillo.

Chev. Listen, Fiorillo! Tell my father—Here he comes. I have not time to speak to him. Say I am with Madame Dorimene. [*Exit.*

Fior. With the ladies! He is unusually gay. Perhaps his affairs have taken a lucky turn.

Scene XIV.—*Enter the* Marquis.

Marq. Well, the coachman—A rascal!—Returned yet?

Fior. The coachman is not to blame, Signor.

Marq. How so? I am—Good, good, excellent!—Had they gone out?

Fior. Who, Signor?

Marq. My daughter, and—What did the dog say?—Yes, at once—To the devil!

Fior. You should not be angry, Signor. I met him loaded like a porter: his horses were hungry and restive, he went to buy corn.

Marq. How? Very fine—The Count—The stables—

Fior. Ah, yes, none can be finer; but without a single oat, nor dares the coachman buy any, without an express order from his master. Oh, the miser!

Marq. Who? Who? Good, good, excellent! A miser!

Fior. There is not such another on earth.

Marq. Who, I say? Blockhead! Fool! The Count—a man!—Go, go, numskull!

Fior. Everybody I have spoken with, in the house and out of the house, servants, tradesmen, or neighbours, all say the same. Nay, Frontino, his chief favourite, can stay with him no longer.

Marq. How! Could it be?—He refused me his coach?

Fior. From avarice. He walks, for fear of tiring his horses.

Marq. But—a hundred thousand livres in diamonds!

Fior. Do you mean the jewels he has showed to his bride—

Marq. Well?

Fior. And which he will never pay for. Frontino told me they were not bought, but borrowed.

Marq. Borrowed! Damn! Good, good, excellent! —an underhand miser—hypocrite! Damn, damn! A fellow—odious—despicable—My daughter?—Oaf! Sup with him?—Great feast—No oats for the horses—Go and see the poor beasts.

Fior. Not that way, Signor. The stables are in the other court.

Marq. Double court—No corn—Great palace—No oats for his horses! [*Exeunt.*

ACT V.

SCENE I.—*The* Count *and* Frontino.

Count. Make haste! Place and light those candles, that there may be a splendid illumination!

Front. But I want help, Signor.

Count. Pshaw! Thy activity and talents, Frontino, are quite sufficient.

Front. [*Aside.*] So much for compliments.

Count. I am vexed at again not finding the Marchioness and her aunt at home. Surely they will come to supper. See how the candles waste; shut the doors and windows.

Front. The evening is so warm!

Count. No matter; do as I bid you.

Front. [*Aside.*] He has odd modes of saving.

Count. I feel myself quite animated. The supper grand! The illumination grand! The—Some of my guests, and those not mean ones, will acknowledge and do justice to my dessert. I grant the expense is great;

but expense, if it is properly incurred, can be borne once in a while.—[*To* Frontino.] Should any one ask for me, I am here with the Marquis.—[*To himself*.] Let me but finish affairs with him, and the difficulty with his daughter will be but little.

SCENE II.—Frontino, *and then* Fiorillo.

Front. [*Calls.*] Fiorillo!
Fior. [*Entering.*] Here am I. What do you want?
Front. [*Giving him a light.*] Help me to light the candles.
Fior. Willingly. [*Both lighting and chatting at the same time.*]
Front. Gently! gently! Mind how you turn that chandelier; the candles are only short bits fastened on coloured sticks.
Fior. Do not fear. I hope we shall sup together?
Front. Should anything be left. The dishes are large; the contents small.
Fior. We shall have a bottle at least?
Front. Zounds! if we have, I must pay for it.
Fior. Among so many, how can one be missed?
Front. I will tell you. The Count has a certain number of coloured pellets in his pocket. He draws them out one by one as the bottles are emptied.
Fior. Oh, the devil!
Front. [*Seeing the* Count *return.*] Hush!

SCENE III.—*Enter the* Count.

Count. [*Angry and aside.*] Could such a thing be expected? A man of my rank and riches? Rudeness so great! Contempt so visible! Tell me his daughter is not for me! Will not come to supper, and then to sneer and laugh at me! He too!— so weak and foolish! Talk of nothing but oats; a reiteration of oats, oats!— [*To* Fiorillo *haughtily*.] Your master wants you. Go!

Fior. I have had the honour of helping my comrade, Signor.

Count. Have the complaisance now to help yourself, and be gone. [*Exit* Fiorillo.

Scene IV.—*The* Count *and* Frontino.

Front. [*Aside.*] We shall have bad weather; there is something new in the wind.

Count. [*To himself.*] What a blockhead was I! Absurd design! Is not money worth more than ruined antiquity? Oh yes! I will marry the captious beauty; marry her in despite of her and of myself. No more attentions; no more respectfulness; no more complaisance for any one.—[*To* Frontino.] Put out the lights.

Front. Put them out, Signor?

Count. Do as you are bid! Make haste!

Front. Very pretty! [*Begins to extinguish.*]

Count. [*Aside.*] Deceive me! Laugh at me! Once more for Madame Araminta.—[*To* Frontino.] Will you never have done? [*Puts out some candles with his hat.*]

Front. But the supper? Everything ready.

Count. How many dishes?

Front. I have brought out all the silver, as you ordered; and large and small, though most of the last, there will be forty.

Count. [*Putting out a candle.*] They will last forty days.

Front. But, Signor—

Count. Silence babbler! [*Puts out the last, and they are in the dark.*]
Front. So, here we are, and here we may stay.
Count. Why did you put out the last candle?
Front. I do not think it was I, Signor.
Count. Go for a light.
Front. Nay, but how to find the door.
Count. Stop! stop! I hear somebody.

Scene V.—*The stage dark. Enter* Fiorillo.

Fior. What can this mean? All in total darkness! Perhaps there will be no supper?
Front. [*Aside to the* Count.] I think it is Fiorillo.
Count. [*Softly, and holding* Frontino *by the arm.*] Stay where you are, and speak as if I were gone.— [*Aside.*] I may make some discovery.
Fior. [*Stumbling on* Frontino.] Who is there?
Front. 'Tis I.
Fior. Frontino! Why have you put out the lights?
Front. Because—because it was too early.
Fior. 'Sblood! Your master is a miser indeed.
Front. How? Jackanapes! My master a miser!
Fior. Why, you told me so yourself.
Count. Ah, rascal! [*Shaking* Frontino.]
Front. Oh, the liar! I capable of—
Fior. Hold your tongue, and listen patiently. I have thought of a way by which you may crib a bottle of wine, in spite of the pellets.
Front. Vile cheat! What are you talking about?
Fior. Really, my dear Frontino, you are no longer the same. Change thus in a minute! You speak as if your master were here.
Front. I speak as I have always spoken. I love my

master, obey my master, respect my master, and—and —he's a gentleman.

Count. [*Shaking him with great anger.*] Scoundrel!

Fior. And all you have said of his avarice is false?

Count. Villain! [*Shaking* Frontino *till he falls.*]

Fior. What now? Where are you? What has fallen? [*Exit the* Count, *feeling till he finds the door.*]

SCENE VI.—*Frontino and* Fiorillo, *then the* Count.

Front. [*Aside.*] The devil take you!—[*Feeling about.*] Where are you, Signor?

Fior. Who are you talking to?

Front. Signor, where are you?

Fior. Hey-day! You have taken a cup already, my friend.

Front. Ah! ah! Here he comes. God help my poor back.

Count. [*Entering with a candle, speaks softly.*] Traitor! Dog!—[*Aloud.*] Hark you, Frontino!

Front. [*Afraid.*] Ye—ye—yes!

Count. [*Aside.*] If we were alone!—[*Aloud.*] Go and tell Madame Araminta I wish to speak to her, either in her room or my own.

Front. Yes, Signor.—[*Aside.*]—I will not trust his looks.—[*To the* Count.] Do not think—

Count. [*Disdainfully.*] Deliver your message.

Front. [*Aside.*] I see how it is. You must pack off, my friend Frontino. [*Exit.*

SCENE VII.—*The* Count *and* Fiorillo.

Fior. You have a faithful servant there, Signor.

Count. You do not know him, friend. An ungrateful

fellow, to whom I have been kind and generous in vain. A professed liar! I discovered him, gave him warning; and, to revenge himself, the rascal speaks ill of me. [*Going with the light he brought.*]

Fior. Excuse me; this room is dark: permit me to light another candle

Count. Certainly. I can't tell why they were all put out.

Fior. Frontino is a good servant, and knows how to manage.

Count. [*Aside.*] The hound! I would send him to the devil if I could find a servant for as little wages. [*Exit.*

SCENE VIII.—Fiorillo *and the* Marquis.

Fior. If I had not got this light, here I might have stayed.

Marq. [*Entering.*] I should like to know—? [*To Fiorillo.*] Did you not say—? Tell him to come here.

Fior. Who, Signor?

Marq. My son.

Fior. Yes.—[*Aside.*] He is not always to be understood.—[*Aloud.*] First suffer me to light a candle.

Marq. Another—I love—Good, good, excellent! See clear. [*Lights a third himself.*]

Fior. Some one may come to put them out.

Marq. Out! Who?

Fior. [*Laughing.*] The illustrious Count! [*Exit.*

Marq. True! Without a grain of oats!

SCENE IX.—*Enter* Araminta.

Aram. [*Speaking as she enters.*] He is in his room. Marquis, your obedient—

Marq. Humble servant.—All well? All well?

Aram. At your service.

Marq. Good, good, excellent! I wished to—My son will tell you.

Aram. Your son, my daughter, and Dorimene, have so stunned and tormented me that I can hear no more.

Marq. If so, Madame—But—you know me—I have not—Very true; but — my property — my estates—Forest, lordship, seven springs — High lands, low—Pasture, arable—A barony. Good, good, excellent! Two millions, Madame!

Aram. What matter your millions? My husband made a fortune from nothing; you, with millions, are ruined! He took care of his own affairs; I managed the house. But permit me to say, Signor Marquis, in your family all has been disorder.

Marq. The Marchioness, heaven bless her! was a little too fond—Poor woman! Always lost. For my part—the chase—good hounds—fine horses—Then—my son—Good, good, excellent! Oh, a brave boy!—Who, some day or other—our estates—our lands—

Aram. Had I the management of them, they would soon free themselves.

Marq. Good, good, excellent! Take—act—give 'em up—Oh, with all my heart!

Aram. Surely you do not imagine, Signor Marquis, that it becomes me to be an agent?

Marq. No; I did not say that. You are still—I am not old—Understand me.

Aram. You are jesting.

Marq. Jest when I—? Good, good, excellent!

Aram. I have no intention to marry; and, if I had, it would not be vain titles, but happiness that I should seek.

Marq. Right—if you—no one interfere—mistress of everything—carte blanche. Good, good, excellent!

Aram. Carte blanche?

Marq. Without restriction.

Scene X.—*Enter the* Chevalier.

Chev. My father sent for me.

Marq. You see, Madame! only son—good youth.

Aram. I know it, and know his merit.

Chev. Ah, Madame!—[*To the* Marquis.] Did you, sir, know the kindness, the liberality, with which this lady overwhelmed me, how you would be surprised!

Marq. All is concluded? Eleonora—thine? [*Overjoyed.*]

Aram. Not too fast, Signor Marquis; I have told you how tenderly I love her, and that I will not risk either her happiness or her fortune.

Marq. But—speak, boy—our affairs—Good, good, excellent! Speak the truth; this lady may—as for me—here I am—my heart, my hand, carte blanche.

Chev. To which, dear father, I willingly subscribe. I leave everything to your discretion. [*Flying to the side scene.*] Approach, dear Eleonora; conquer your fears; join your prayers to ours, and move the heart of a mother, who doubts only through delicacy.

Enter Eleonora *and* Dorimene, *who remains in the background.*

Eleon. [*Falling at her mother's feet.*] Oh, my mother! you know my heart, and how religiously I have always obeyed your commands. You would unite me to a man whom I can never love; virtuous affection has taken possession of my soul. I ought to have told you, but fear and respect forbade me; yet my feelings, however ardent, I was determined should be sacrificed to obedience to that affection which I have ever felt for you, and that tender attachment in which I have been educated. Ah, do not force me to a marriage I detest! and which will render me the most disconsolate and wretched woman on earth.

Aram. [*Aside.*] Poor child! Did she know my heart!

Marq. [*Wiping his eyes.*] Now — if — Good, good, excellent!

Aram. Be it so on one condition. The carte blanche—

Marq. [*Presenting his hand.*] Sign it—pray accept—

Aram. Your hand?

Eleon. My dear mother, your superintending prudence and goodness will secure our felicity.

Chev. Oh yes. Your orders shall be respected; your example the rule for our conduct; your advice our guide.

Aram. [*Aside.*] My child! my child!

Marq. [*Still tenderly presenting his hand.*] Madame!

Aram. [*Cheerfully.*] Signor Marquis—I am yours.

Marq. And I—Good, good, excellent!

Dor. [*Coming forward.*] Permit me, ladies and gentlemen, to say I have thus far been silent, being desirous to promote this young lady's happiness; but I think you will remember my brother ought to be, in some degree, consulted in this affair.

Eleon. Heavens! what say you, Madame?

Aram. My daughter should have been his, had he been less of a spendthrift.

Marq. I would have given him mine if he had not been a miser.

Eleon. [*Sees the* Count *coming.*] Oh, my mother!

Marq. Fear nothing—I'll speak—Yes, I—quite clearly —Good, good, excellent!

Scene XI.—*Enter the* Count, *and afterwards* Frontino.

Count. [*Aside.*] She is here; now is the time to oblige her to determine.—[*To* Araminta.] I sent a request, Madame—

Aram. I was coming, but was stopped by the Marquis.

Marq. Yes, Signor Count, I have to inform you—

Count. Pardon me, Signor; I have business with this lady.—[*To* Araminta.] The notary will soon be here, and we must sign the contract.

Aram. And do you still persist in claiming my daughter? Have you not renounced her?

Count. No, Signora. My design, of which my sister may have informed you, was to propose conditions honourable to all parties; but these the Marquis disapproves.

Marq. Hear me speak. You asked me—yes—I would have — why not? But — be so kind — Good, good, excellent! No anger — a hundred thousand livres, diamonds, and not a grain of oats!

Count. Why do you thus reiterate oats? I cannot understand; can you, ladies?

Dor. [*To the* Count.] Your coachman, brother, may have refused—

Count. [*To the* Marquis.] How! have your horses not been fed? If so, am I responsible for my coachman's error? Must I be thought a miser—I!—[*Aside.*] My servants have babbled, and I shall lose my reputation.

Front. [*Entering to the* Count.] Persons without are asking for you, signor.

Count. [*Aside.*] My supper guests perhaps; the moment is favourable to the support of my honour.—[*Aloud.*] Is the notary among them?

Front. Yes, Signor.

Count. Bid him come in. Show the other persons into the card-room. Let the house be illuminated and the supper served. [*Exit* Frontino.

Marq. Good, good, excellent!

SCENE.—*The last.*

Enter the Notary, *the* Jeweller, Giacinto, *and others.*

Count. [*To the* Notary.] Signor, please to read the contract, that it may be signed. So, Signor Giacinto, you have discovered that my bride is better, and that the supper will take place.

Giac. No, Signor, I have made no such discovery. But I have discovered some literary gentlemen, who, since I am not enabled to print my comedy and your genealogy, will publish the genealogy at their own expense, with all necessary and some remarkable annotations.

Count. [*Enraged.*] I understand the insult. [*Dissembling.*] Have you the genealogy in your pocket?

Giac. Here it is, Signor.

Count. [*Receiving and concealing the MS.*] Signor— I have a proper esteem for talents—they have ever been encouraged and recompensed by me.—[*Aside.*] A mercenary scoundrel!—[*Whispers* Giacinto.] Accept these five-and-twenty louis, and let me hear no more.— [*Tears the paper.*] [*Exit* Giacinto.

Aram. [*Aside.*] What a man! He would quickly have scattered my daughter's fortune.

Count. [*To the* Notary.] Once more, the contract.

Jew. [*Advancing with a bow.*] Signor Count.

Count. How now! What do *you* want?

Jew. Permission to speak.

Count. [*Softly to the* Jeweller.] I desired you to come in a week.

Jew. 'Tis true. But hearing you are this evening to be affianced, permit me to observe that, after my jewels have been seen—

Count. Ay, ay.—[*Vexed and aside.*] The rascal knows what he is about.—[*Privately returns the jewels and angrily whispers,*] Here, take your diamonds, and trouble me no more. [*Exit* Jeweller.

Front. [*Entering.*] The supper is ready; must it be served?

Count. Wait till I call you. Once more, the contract; with your leave, madam, we will read it, that it may be signed.

Aram. Signor, while I was a widow the power was my own, but now I am once more married.

Count. Married! Who is your husband, Madame!

Marq. Good, good, excellent! Yes, signor, 'tis I.

Count. [*Aside.*] Here is a blow! Oh, all hopes are gone!—[*Aloud.*] Then Eleonora—

Aram. I love my daughter too much to willingly part with her; once to-day you have refused her hand, which I shall now give to—

Marq. Good, good, excellent!—To my son.

Count. [*To* Dorimene *indignantly.*] I am derided, sister, disdained.

Dor. I warned you, brother, yet you would persist. Be prudent; you are in the presence of many people; do not risk your reputation.

Count. [*Aside.*] Very true. Come what will, I must dissemble.—[*Aloud.*] You're happily come, ladies and gentlemen, to witness the signing of a contract between —the—Chevalier del Bosco and this young lady.— [*Aside.*] My tongue is parched; I have not the power to proceed.—[*Aloud.*] The honour of contributing to this—ceremony—is mine.—[*Aside.*] Oh that the house were on fire!—[*Aloud.*] Let us walk into the library till the supper is ready.

Aram. Long live the spendthrift!

Marq. And down with the miser! [*Exeunt omnes.*

THE END OF "THE SPENDTHRIFT MISER."